4470569700

CONVEYANCING 2020

D1634588

WITHDRAWN from STIRLING UNIVERSITY LIBRARY

JED
6.4
REI

CONVEYANCING 2020

Kenneth G C Reid WS

Professor Emeritus of Scots Law in the University of Edinburgh

and

George L Gretton WS

Lord President Reid Professor of Law Emeritus in the University of Edinburgh

24 Hours

with a contribution by Alan Barr of the University of Edinburgh
and Brodies LLP

UNIVERSITY OF STIRLING

2 1 DEC 2022

LIBRARY

Library
University of Stirling
STIRLING   FK9 4LA

Edinburgh Legal Education Trust
2021

Pol - 2000
04/22

Published by
Edinburgh Legal Education Trust
School of Law
University of Edinburgh
Old College
South Bridge
Edinburgh EH8 9YL

First published 2021

© Kenneth G C Reid and George L Gretton 2021

The authors assert their moral rights.

ISBN 978-1-9996118-7-3

British Library Cataloguing in Publication Data
A catalogue record for this book is available from the British Library.

All rights reserved. No part of this publication may be reproduced, stored in a retrieval system, or transmitted in any form or by any means, electronic, mechanical, photocopying, recording or otherwise, without the written permission of the copyright owner. Applications for the copyright owner's permission to reproduce any part of this publication should be addressed to the publisher.

Typeset by Waverley Typesetters, Warham, Norfolk
Printed and bound by Bell & Bain Ltd, Glasgow

CONTENTS

PREFACE

This is the twenty-second annual update of new developments in the law of conveyancing. As in previous years, it is divided into five parts. There is, first, a brief description of all cases which have been reported, or appeared on the websites of the Scottish Courts (www.scotcourts.gov.uk) or of the Lands Tribunal for Scotland (www.lands-tribunal-scotland.org.uk/), or have otherwise come to our attention since *Conveyancing 2019*.

The next two parts summarise, respectively, statutory developments during 2020 and other material of interest to conveyancers. The fourth part is a detailed commentary on selected issues arising from the first three parts. Finally, in part V, there are two tables. A table of decisions on the variation or discharge of title conditions covers all decisions since 2019; an earlier, cumulative table of all cases from 2004 to 2018 can be found at the end of *Conveyancing 2018*. This is followed by a cumulative table of appeals, designed to facilitate moving from one annual volume to the next.

We do not seek to cover agricultural holdings, crofting, public-sector tenancies, compulsory purchase or planning law. Otherwise our coverage is intended to be complete.

We gratefully acknowledge help received from Alan Barr, Douglas Ballantyne, Ian Bowie, Malcolm Combe, Lynne Johnstone, Chris Kerr, Roddy Paisley, Andrew Steven and Scott Wortley.

Kenneth G C Reid
George L Gretton
14 March 2021

TABLE OF STATUTES

TABLE OF ORDERS

TABLE OF CASES

PART I

CASES

CASES

MISSIVES OF SALE

(1) Ramoyle Developments Ltd v Scottish Borders Council
[2020] CSIH 9, 2020 SC 290, 2020 SLT 537

Scottish Borders Council owned property at Burgh Yard, Galashiels, Selkirkshire. It entered into missives to sell it to Ramoyle Developments Ltd, the price being £1,053,000. The missives had the following provision (clause 2.5.2):

> The Purchasers shall lodge the application for planning consent … as soon as reasonably practicable following the date of purification or waiver of the suspensive condition contained within Clause 2.2.4 and no later than the date falling 6 months after the said date of purification or waiver … In the event that the Purchasers have failed to submit the said application for planning permission with the local authority by the expiry of the said 6 month period then either party shall be entitled to rescind the Missives …

The buyer, Ramoyle Developments Ltd, submitted an online planning application within the six-month deadline, but it did not pay the application fee until after the deadline. The seller rescinded the missives, on the basis that the six-month time limit had not been met. The buyer responded with the present action, seeking declarator that the application for planning permission had been timeously submitted and that accordingly the seller was not entitled to rescind. Regulation 14(1) of the Town and Country Planning (Development Management Procedure) (Scotland) Regulations 2013, SSI 2013/155, says: 'An application … is to be taken to have been made on the date on which the last of the items … required to be contained in or accompany the application in accordance with regulations 9, 10, 11 or 12 respectively is received by the planning authority.' These requirements include payment of the fee. Accordingly the seller's position was strong.

Nevertheless the Outer House found in favour of the buyer: [2019] CSOH 1, 2019 SLT 284, *Conveyancing 2019* Case (1). The seller reclaimed. The Inner House has now affirmed the decision of the Outer House. It said (para 14):

> Condition 2.5.2 uses ordinary, non-technical words which anyone would readily understand. Until the requisite fee is paid, a planning authority is under no obligation to process an application, but this does not mean that a planning application cannot be lodged or submitted before the fee is paid. If the council had wished to require full compliance with the 2013 Regulations, in the sense of provision of a validated

application as per reg. 14 within the six months period, that could have been specified in the missives.

(2) Shine Properties Ltd v Biggar Museum Trust
[2020] SAC (Civ) 4, 2020 GWD 25-329

Shine Properties Ltd concluded missives to buy property in Biggar, Lanarkshire, from Biggar Museum Trust. One term of the missives was that the seller should provide, before settlement, a title insurance policy in respect of access issues concerning part of the subjects of sale. (No details of the access question are given in the case, nor are the terms of the clause in the missives quoted.) The insurer wished to know whether the buyer intended to build on the area. But requests for this information were ignored. (Seemingly the requests went from the seller's agents to the buyer's agents, but the latter could not obtain this information from their client.)

After the date of entry had passed the seller rescinded the missives. The buyer argued that the rescission was unwarranted and raised the present action for damages for breach of contract. Its argument was simple: the missives had stipulated that the title policy should be available before settlement. It was not available before settlement. Therefore the seller had been in breach. This argument did not persuade the sheriff, and the buyer appealed. The Sheriff Appeal Court rejected the appeal, saying at para 24:

> The provision of the policy was wholly dependent upon the appellant providing certain information to the respondent as to the appellant's intention as to the property. The appellant knew the date … for settlement but it did nothing in response to the request for information. The appellant did not ask for further time or provide any explanation as to why there might be a delay. Had the information been provided timeously the transaction could have settled. The appellant cannot rely upon the apparent failure on the part of the respondent to provide the policy when it failed to give the respondent the information it required to satisfy its obligation.

(3) Syred v Liddell-Grainger's Exrs
[2020] CSOH 65, 2020 GWD 23-301

Ayton Castle in Berwickshire is a large and imposing edifice. Its core is medieval, with later additions. In 2014 Mr Syred concluded missives to buy it from the executors of David Ian Liddell-Grainger, and the transaction settled. In this action the buyer claimed that fireplaces and wall lights had been removed by the sellers in breach of the missives, and also that the water supply failed to meet the standard required by the missives. The defenders pled to the relevancy of the pursuer's averments. Proof before answer was ordered.

(4) New Ingliston Ltd v Edinburgh Airport Ltd
[2020] CSOH 64, 2020 SLT 1281

The pursuer had in its land bank about 88 hectares of greenbelt land on the western outskirts of Edinburgh, adjacent to the airport. In 2001 it sold to

Edinburgh Airport Ltd an option to buy about 8 hectares of this land. The option period expired on 29 October 2016. On 26 October 2016 Edinburgh Airport Ltd served a notice exercising the option. In response the pursuer raised the present action, seeking declarator that the option had not been validly exercised.

The option agreement had certain suspensive conditions (called by the English term 'conditions precedent'):

> The conditions precedent to the service of an Option Notice … are that … the whole or the majority of the Subjects is zoned for a use which is consistent with the Main Agreement in accordance with the Key Objectives.

The 'Main Agreement' was a contract between the pursuer and the defender and BAA plc, an earlier owner of the airport, and the 'Key Objectives' were as set out in a schedule to that contract. The dispute was about whether this suspensive condition had been purified. After hearing evidence the Lord Ordinary (Lord Ericht) concluded (para 129): 'In my opinion, as at the date of service of the Option Notice the whole or the majority of the Subjects was zoned for a use which was consistent with the Main Agreement in accordance with the Key Objectives. The Option Notice was valid and of legal effect.'

TENEMENTS, DEVELOPMENTS AND FACTORS

(5) Lacey v McConville
[2020] SC EDIN 35, 2020 SLT (Sh Ct) 237, 2020 Hous LR 108

The pursuer owned the upper flat in a two-flat tenement in Edinburgh dating from the 1930s; the defenders owned the lower flat. The tenement was made of brick, finished off with rendering. The external walls of the building were common property of the two flat-owners.

The rendering was in poor condition, but the parties were unable to agree whether to replace the rendering in it its entirety or just to patch it up. In this action the pursuer sought (i) declarator that she was entitled to replace the rendering in its entirety, and also (ii) to recover half the cost from the defenders. She founded on s 8 of the Tenements (Scotland) Act 2004, which, in respect of parts of a tenement owned in common, allows an individual co-owner to carry out repairs provided the repairs are necessary for the provision of support or shelter to the tenement.

Following a proof, in which expert evidence was led for both sides, the sheriff (N A Ross) pronounced absolvitor. The pursuer had failed to prove that the rendering contributed to the sheltering of the tenement from rain; and in any event the ambitious programme of new rendering went beyond what was 'necessary' to repair the walls. See **Commentary** p 216.

(6) **Proven Properties Scotland Ltd v Upper Tribunal for Scotland**
[2020] CSIH 22, 2020 SC 455, 2020 SLT 566, 2020 Hous LR 32

Proven Properties provided management services in respect of a block of flats in Helensburgh, most of which they owned and rented out. They did not charge for the service. Were they 'property factors' within the Property Factors (Scotland) Act 2011, and hence subject to a requirement to register as well as to the Property Factors Code of Conduct. The definition of 'property factor' in s 2 of the 2011 Act is limited to persons who manage common parts 'in the course of that person's business'. Held: that although Proven Properties operated a property-letting business, it was not a 'property factor' because its management services were not provided as part of a business as property managers. See **Commentary** p 222.

(7) Zukowski v Charles White Ltd
[2020] UT 26, 2020 GWD 30-386

Not all factors have been validly appointed as such. This case provides a striking example. The deed of conditions governing a development at Newmains, Kirkliston, West Lothian, known as The Steadings provided for a factor to be appointed by the developers and thereafter by the owners' association. The attractively-named Safehands Ltd were appointed as factor under this provision and continued to act until 2003 when they 'transferred their management interests' to Charles White Ltd. The homeowners were informed but not, it seems, consulted. With the exception of Mr and Mrs Zukowski, however, they appear to have been content with the new arrangements. The Zukowskis, though, were not, and in the present application they challenged the right of Charles White Ltd to act as factor.

The First-tier Tribunal held that (i) while not validly appointed under the deed of conditions, nonetheless (ii) Charles White Ltd was entitled to act as factor on the basis of custom and practice. The idea seems to have been that a contract of some sort could be inferred between Charles White Ltd and the homeowners on the basis of the long period during which Charles White had factored the property. The Zukowskis appealed. Charles White Ltd, as respondent, accepted that it had not been appointed under the deed of conditions, but maintained that, as the First-tier Tribunal had held, it had been appointed on the basis of custom and practice.

The Upper Tribunal rejected that argument and quashed the decision of the First-tier Tribunal. The latter had neither heard evidence nor explored the legal conditions necessary to establish a contract by custom and practice. The decision could not therefore stand. In the course of its Opinion, the Upper Tribunal made a preliminary and incomplete survey of the legal and factual issues which might arise in cases such as this. See **Commentary** p 224.

COMMON PROPERTY

(8) Accountant in Bankruptcy v Brooks
[2020] SAC (Civ) 15, 2020 GWD 38-488

This is the latest case on s 113 of the Bankruptcy (Scotland) Act 2016. Mr Brooks was sequestrated. His only significant asset was the family home in Falkirk which he shared with his wife and 46-year-old son. His wife was co-owner of the house. In order to realise the house for the benefit of creditors, the trustee in sequestration raised an action of division and sale. Mrs Brooks pled s 113 which gives the court discretion to delay or refuse division and sale of a family home 'having regard to all the circumstances of the case'. Five non-exhaustive circumstances are listed in s 113(2) four of which, as the Sheriff Appeal Court pointed out, concern the debtor's spouse and family (eg 'the needs and financial resources of the debtor's spouse').

It is for the person seeking to invoke the s 113 defence to aver the 'circumstances of the case' on which the court might be persuaded to exercise its discretion. At first instance, the sheriff held that there were insufficient averments on behalf of Mrs Brooks for a case on s 113 to go to proof. On appeal, this judgment was affirmed by the Sheriff Appeal Court. Giving the Opinion of the court, Sheriff William Holligan explained that (para 22):

> [T]he defenders' averments are very limited ... The defenders aver issues as to the amount owing by the first defender; a rather unusual admission as to how long the defenders have resided in the subjects (a fact one would have thought would have been a matter of express averment on the part of the defenders); and the prospect of homelessness for them and for their adult son. There is a vague averment as to debts without any adequate specification as to the significance thereof or the correct quantification ... Proving those bald averments would not make it unreasonable for the family home to be sold. Nothing else is averred. Given what we have said as to the correct approach to section 113, on no view could these averments amount to a relevant case for the defenders. They are irrelevant both because on their own they do not go far enough and because they give no fair notice to the pursuer of what case he would have to meet.

REAL BURDENS

(9) Duffus v Malcolm Allan Housebuilders Ltd
2020 GWD 16-236, Lands Tribunal

The amenity ground in an Aberdeen housing estate (Kingswells) had been retained by the developers with the idea, not in the event realised, that it would be taken over for maintenance by the local authority. This was what is sometimes referred to as the 'land-owning' model for amenity ground: see eg *Conveyancing 2019* p 127. After 27 years of factoring and maintaining the amenity ground without charge, the developers invoked a provision in the deed of conditions which permitted a new factor to be chosen by the homeowners. At the same time the question arose as to future liability for maintenance of the amenity area. A clause in the deed of conditions purported to impose liability on the homeowners. In this application to the Lands Tribunal, the validity of that clause as a real burden was challenged by one of the homeowners. The challenge was successful, the Tribunal holding that the burden was void for uncertainty in respect that (i) the area to be maintained was not properly identified, and (ii) the standard of maintenance was not adequately specified. See **Commentary** p 201.

(10) Triplerose Ltd v Beattie
[2020] UKUT 180 (LC), [2020] HLR 37, [2021] 1 P & CR 4

In this English case, Mr and Mrs Beattie employed an agent to let their flat in Newcastle on Airbnb and Booking.com. Typically, this involved weekend lets. The flat was held on a 125-year lease, one of the conditions of which was that the flat was not to be 'used for any purpose other than as a private dwelling house for occupation by one family at any one time'. In an application to the Upper Tribunal at the instance of the landlord, it was held that short-term letting was a breach of this condition. See **Commentary** p 197.

PRE-EMPTION

(11) West Lothian Council v Clark's Exrs
[2020] SC LIV 30, 2020 SLT (Sh Ct) 269

The defenders' property, at West Calder, West Lothian, was subject to a pre-emption. Originally constituted as a feudal real burden, the pre-emption now bound the defenders only as a matter of contract. The pre-emption holder was West Lothian Council, the statutory successors of the original superiors (Lothian Regional Council).

A dispute arose as to whether, in the particular circumstances that arose, the pre-emption was still alive. The defenders had notified the Council of their intention to sell part of the subjects, a notification to which the Council had failed to reply with an offer to purchase within the 21 days prescribed in the clause of pre-emption. The Council argued that the defenders' notification was flawed in the respect that it did not properly identify the part of the subjects that was to be sold. Hence the pre-emption remained alive, and the defenders were bound to offer the property back to the Council. Following a proof, this argument was accepted by the court.

The court also remarked that, had the notification been valid, it would have been treated as an offer-back under s 84 of the Title Conditions (Scotland) Act 2003. Normally, the Council's failure to accept such an offer would have extinguished its right to buy. In the present case, however, the Council's queries as to the extent of the property mentioned in the notification would be viewed as an objection to the reasonableness of its terms under s 84(5), with the result that the Council's right to buy would have remained in place.

For discussion, see **Commentary** p 190. The decision has been upheld by the Sheriff Appeal Court: [2021] SAC (Civ) 11 (see next year's volume).

(12) Toomey v Smith
2020 GWD 10-146, Lands Tribunal

In this application for discharge of real burdens, one of the burdens was a pre-emption contained in a disposition of 1995, of property at Mid Calder, West Lothian. The first sale after 1995 had taken place in 2006. According to the applicants, who had been the purchasers in 2006, the property was not offered back to the pre-emption holder at that time. This breached the pre-emption. Accepting this evidence the Tribunal found that the pre-emption had been extinguished by negative prescription, in terms of s 18(2) of the Title Conditions (Scotland) Act 2003, five years after the breach took place. See **Commentary** p 189.

[Another aspect of this case is digested as Case (25) below.]

SERVITUDES

(13) McCabe v Patterson
[2020] SC GLA 14, 2020 GWD 11-155

This was an action to interdict the defenders from using property (at Gillies Lane, Baillieston, Lanarkshire) said to belong to the pursuers for 'parking, storing and depositing vehicles and storage units' and for 'locking or otherwise securing the gates at the southern boundary'. To this the defenders offered two main defences. In the first place, they said, they owned all or part of the property. In the second place, insofar as they did not own the property, they had a range of servitudes over it. The argument as to ownership is discussed at p 55 below (where the facts of the case are given more fully); here the concern is only with the argument as to servitudes.

The defenders claimed that, by prescription, they had established a range of servitudes over the property, namely servitudes of (i) access; (ii) parking; (iii) use; and (iv) storage. In relation to the servitude of parking they also claimed to have, as an ancillary right, the right to lock a gate which gave access to the property.

Of these various servitudes, the pursuers conceded (i) (although a dispute remained as to the precise area over which access could be taken), and a proof before answer was allowed in respect of (ii). The sheriff (Aisha Y Anwar) rejected (iii) and (iv), largely on the pleadings but also because she thought that the rights claimed were not among the 'known' servitudes recognised by law: see **Commentary** p 129. She also rejected the argument that a right to lock the gate could be ancillary to a servitude of parking, or indeed could be a servitude at all: see **Commentary** p 141.

[Another aspect of this case is digested as Case (64) below.]

(14) Soulsby v Jones
[2020] CSOH 103, 2021 SLT 286

The parties owned adjoining houses in Elie, Fife, both dating from the seventeenth century. Between the houses was a narrow strip of land sufficient for the purposes of carrying out maintenance on each. For some of its distance, the strip was a passageway, owned in common by both parties. For the rest, the strip was on land which belonged solely to the defenders. The present dispute concerned the latter part of the strip. Narrow at the best of times, it had been made narrower still by the erection of an extension to the defenders' house. The pursuer had objected to the extension at the time but the building work had gone ahead anyway. In this action the pursuer sought (i) declarator that he had a servitude right of access over the strip 'for the purposes of inspecting, cleaning, maintaining, repairing and renewing' his house, (ii) declarator that the defenders were not entitled to build on the strip, (iii) declarator that the obstruction of access for repairs constituted a nuisance, and (iv) an order ordaining the defenders to remove the offending structure.

Insofar as the case was based on nuisance, it failed on the evidence and need not be further discussed here. The pursuer's main argument, however, was based on servitude. Such a servitude was said to have been established either (a) by positive prescription, or (b) without possession, by force of necessity. Following a proof, the claim failed on both counts. For a discussion of (b), see **Commentary** p 130. The account here considers only (a).

To establish a servitude for repair by prescription faces, as the Lord Ordinary (Lady Carmichael) pointed out (at para 296), the 'particular challenge' that 'a right of access for repair will be exercised infrequently if at all'. So it proved in this case. On the evidence, Lady Carmichael concluded that 'the only user of regularity and frequency which I am satisfied has occurred is access for the purpose of window cleaning' which took place 'at most ten times per year' (para 320). As for other acts of maintenance, 'there was no suggestion from any witness that the exterior wall itself had been painted at any time between 2005 and the erection of the extension in 2018' (para 322), and the same was true of the gutters (para 325). There was no evidence as to roof repairs (para 330). No doubt the proximity to the sea made a reasonably frequent cycle of maintenance desirable, but the evidence led did not support the view that this had occurred. On a balance of probabilities the strip had been used by the pursuer (or his mother) on up to three occasions each year to inspect the condition of the property. None of this, said Lady Carmichael, was sufficient for the purposes of prescription.

In the course of the judgment the question of onus of proof was discussed quite extensively, and many previous decisions were quoted (paras 304–317). Unluckily, Alasdair Peterson's new book on *Prescriptive Servitudes*, which was published during the summer of 2020, came too late to assist the deliberations of the court. As Dr Peterson explains in chapter 9, the onus is on the pursuer to prove that there has been a sufficient volume of possession to indicate that a servitude is being asserted – and hence to sweep away any idea that the possession was due to tolerance (as opposed to lassitude) on the part of the defender. Only then does the onus switch to the defender to establish, if the defender can, that the possession was explicable by the exercise of some kind of right (whether in private or public law) and hence not, after all, in assertion of a servitude. Only the first of these two stages was at issue in *Soulsby v Jones*, and so the onus was on the pursuer to demonstrate user that was of a sufficient quantity and character to be treated as an assertion of right' (para 317). But, said the court, there was no additional requirement 'positively to prove that the proprietor of the servient tenement was not, subjectively, of the view that he was tolerating the user'; that 'would be entirely unworkable' (para 317).

In the event, the onus on the pursuer was not discharged. The pursuer was not helped by the type of servitude at issue (para 333):

The nature of the claimed servitude in this case is such that use is infrequent. It is in the interests of neighbourly relations to permit access for cleaning and repair, and it is in the interests of the proprietor of the servient tenement that a building at his boundary be kept in sound repair and reasonable cosmetic order. These are factors which are capable of yielding the inference, objectively, that access has been permitted.

A final issue was whether access taken by a tradesperson working for the pursuer counted as possession by the pursuer himself. The answer, thought the court, must be yes, even without evidence of a specific instruction having been given.

If the pursuer had succeeded in establishing the existence of a servitude, he would have won on the remaining points of the case. For the defenders it had been argued: (i) that they were entitled to reduce the width of the maintenance strip by building an extension; (ii) that the pursuer, having allowed the construction of the extension to go ahead, was personally barred from asserting the servitude; and (iii) that even if the extension was found to have breached the servitude, the court should exercise its discretion to refuse to order its removal. All three arguments failed.

On (i), the court found that, with the narrowing of the strip, it was now materially less convenient to carry out inspection and repairs, as well as being more expensive.

On (ii), the court accepted and applied the view, expressed in E C Reid and J W G Blackie, *Personal Bar* (2006) para 6-49, that objection to the building work might not, in itself, be sufficient to block personal bar unless specific reference was made to the breach of servitude. As Reid and Blackie explain:

> If, for example, the benefited proprietor has cited amenity reasons in objecting to the grant of planning permission but has made no reference to the servitude, it is arguable that this is insufficient to prevent acquiescence. In those circumstances the right to oppose the development in terms of the relevant planning legislation has been invoked, but acquiescence relates to a different right, namely to exercise common law remedies in order to prevent obstruction of the servitude.

In the present case, however, the pursuer had indeed invoked the servitude prior to the commencement of the building work. As a result (para 395):

> From the point at which a servitude right was asserted, the defenders were put on notice of it, but chose to continue with the building project. A servitude right of access is one which they were not entitled to obstruct, and they proceeded at their own peril, in the knowledge that the right had been asserted.

This point has not previously been the subject of decision.

As for (iii), the fact that the defenders proceeded with the building work in the knowledge of the servitude, and of the pursuer's objection, put them in bad faith; whereas good faith, it had been held in the leading case of *Anderson v Brattisanni's* 1978 SLT (Notes) 42, was one of the prerequisites for the invocation of the judicial discretion not to order demolition. But even if the defenders had proceeded in good faith, the court would still have ordered demolition (had the servitude been established) to the extent that the extension was built on the maintenance strip. It was true that demolition would be both disruptive and also expensive (£58,000 plus VAT) for the defenders. But that must be set against the malign effect of the extension on the exercise of the servitude. In balancing the interests of the parties in a case like the present, the loss to the encroaching proprietor from demolition must not merely be disproportionate to the gain to the other proprietor but, as the First Division had said in *Anderson*, 'wholly disproportionate'. That exacting standard could not be met on the facts of the present case.

The decision has been reclaimed.

(15) Duncan v Glasa LLP
[2020] CSOH 26, 2020 SCLR 821

A deed of servitude was granted and registered in respect of a joint venture to develop a hydroelectric dam and turbine on the Kildermorie Estate in Ross-shire. Following the failure of the project, the validity of the deed of servitude was challenged on a number of grounds, including (i) the presence of clerical errors; (ii) the omission of a pricing table from the deed; and (iii) non-compliance, in the case of servitude conditions, with the praedial rule. The result was a scoring draw: some aspects of the challenge succeeded, others did not. See **Commentary** p 135.

(16) Ruddiman v Hawthorne
[2020] CSIH 46, 2021 SLT 111

The pursuer (and respondent) was the owner of Bieldside House in Aberdeen (title number ABN7030) and the defenders (and reclaimers) were owners of two contiguous areas of land ('site 1' and 'site 2') which, until 1990, had been part of Bieldside House. The first and second defenders (Mr and Mrs Hawthorne) had previously owned the entire property, but in 1990 they disponed Bieldside House while retaining sites 1 and 2. In 2005 site 2 was conveyed to their children (the third to fifth defenders).

Access to Bieldside House from the public road was by means of a horseshoe-shaped driveway which began and ended with the road. The driveway was owned by the pursuer as part of the policies of Bieldside House. The split-off disposition of 1990 (which conveyed Bieldside House) had reserved a pedestrian and vehicular servitude of way over the driveway for the benefit of site 1 but not of site 2. The failure to include site 2 within the dominant tenement resulted in an action for professional negligence by Mr and Mrs Hawthorne against their solicitors which, in the event, was unsuccessful: see *Hawthorne v Anderson* [2014] CSOH 65, 2014 GWD 13-247 (*Conveyancing 2014* Case (62)).

The defenders built and lived in a house ('Bieldside Lodge') on site 1. For a number of years they have sought to obtain planning permission for site 2. Apart from the awkwardness of the site (a steeply sloping area of scrubland and bushes), there was the problem that the only possible means of access, at least for construction traffic, was over the horseshoe driveway.

In this action the pursuer sought (i) a declarator that the use of the driveway was restricted to access for the benefit of site 1 only, and (ii) interdict against the defenders from using the driveway for access to site 2. The pursuer's action had been initiated as long ago as 2010, but had stopped and started to allow for negotiations. Interim interdict was granted in 2015 but now the pursuer wanted her declarator as well as a permanent interdict. At a Procedure Roll debate the defenders attempted to have the application dismissed but the Lord Ordinary rejected that motion in favour of a proof before answer: see [2019] CSOH 65, 2019 GWD 29-463 (*Conveyancing 2019* Case (18)). The defenders appealed.

In considering the appeal the First Division focused mainly on the assertion by the defenders that, if they received planning permission to build on site 2, it would be within the terms of the servitude for the parking for the development to be on site 1. Having parked their car there, they could then proceed into site 2 on foot. Refusing the appeal, the First Division held that the defenders' proposed course of action was contrary to the rule, set out in cases such as *Irvine Knitters Ltd v North Ayrshire Co-operative Society Ltd* 1978 SC 109, that a servitude could only be used for the benefit of the dominant tenement – in this case, site 1. See **Commentary** p 126; and also Hannah Leslie, 'Time to bin the *Irvine Knitters* principle? Court of Session revisits access rights' (2020) 168 *Greens Property Law Bulletin* 4.

(17) Johnston v Davidson
[2020] SAC (Civ) 22, 2021 SCLR 17

A disposition of property in Carnoustie, Angus, recorded in 1998, granted a 'heritable and irredeemable servitude right of access' over (i) a driveway and (ii) a path. It was held, as a matter of interpretation, that the servitude in respect of the driveway extended to vehicles as well as to pedestrians. See **Commentary** p 138. It was further held that a right to park on the driveway could be implied as a right ancillary to the grant of servitude. See **Commentary** p 140.

ELECTRONIC COMMUNICATIONS CODE

(18) EE Ltd v MacDonald
2020 GWD 14-210, Lands Tribunal

This is the first of a number of decisions of the Lands Tribunal in respect of applications under the Electronic Communications Code, which is set out in sch 3A of the Communications Act 2003. For discussion of the Code, see *Conveyancing 2017* pp 71–73. The Electronic Communications Code replaced the Telecommunications Code, set out in sch 2 of the Telecommunications Act 1984, with effect from 28 December 2017. The first decisions on the new Code are beginning to come through both in Scotland and in England. Only the former can be covered in this series.

The purpose of the Code (as of its predecessor) is to facilitate telecommunications companies ('operators') in the installation and maintenance of appropriate apparatus. There is provision for entering into voluntary arrangements with the owners or occupiers of land for the conferral, against compensation, of the 'Code rights' set out in para 3 of the Code. Such rights, once conferred, are real rights and run with the land. In the event that agreement cannot be reached, an application may be made to the sheriff court or Lands Tribunal for the compulsory conferral of Code rights. This was such an application. The case is noted briefly by Megan Macdonald in (2020) 166 *Greens Property Law Bulletin* 6.

EE Ltd, an 'operator' within the meaning of the Code, proposed to install telecommunications apparatus at a site at Loch Striven, Colintraive, Argyll. Agreement was reached with the owners. The site, however, was landlocked, being reached by a track leading off the B836 Dunoon to Tarbet road. Although negotiations took place, EE was unable to agree access arrangements with Mr MacDonald, the owner of the track. Hence this application, which was for the compulsory conferral of Code rights by virtue of para 20 of the Code.

An application for compulsory conferral is only possible in respect of rights which fall within the definition of Code rights. But, argued Mr MacDonald, there is no provision in para 3 of the Code for rights of access over land other than the land on which the apparatus is actually to be installed. And certainly, and as the Lands Tribunal noted, surprisingly (para 33), there was no such express right. Paragraph 3(d), however, lists among the Code rights a right 'to carry out works on the land for or in connection with the installation of electronic communications on, under or over the land *or elsewhere*'. On a purposive interpretation, said the Lands Tribunal, this could be read as including the right to take access over other property ('elsewhere'); and a purposive interpretation was fully justified as the Code 'should be interpreted in a way which makes it work' for its 'undisputed purpose' of improving electronic communications throughout the country' (para 35). If access rights were found to be excluded from the Code, operators risked being held to ransom by the owners of the land in question. The word 'works' in para 3(d) was admittedly rather awkward, but it would be absurd if operators could only take access through other land on the basis that they did 'works', ie constructed or improved the access. In the present case there was a perfectly adequate track, and no reason why it should not be used.

(19) Cornerstone Telecommunications Infrastructure Ltd v Fothringham 2020 GWD 31-408, Lands Tribunal

Due to the existing site for Cornerstone's telecommunications equipment on the Murthly Estate in Perthshire having been compulsorily acquired for the purposes of dualling the A9, Cornerstone was obliged to negotiate with Mr Fothringham, the owner of the Estate, for a new site. An interim conferral of Code rights having been made (see 2020 GWD 11-166), broad agreement was reached on a 10-year arrangement. A number of matters, however, remained at issue which Cornerstone asked the Lands Tribunal to resolve in terms of para 20 (compulsory conferral of Code rights) of the Electronic Communications Code. A conferral cannot be made under para 20 unless the Tribunal is satisfied as to the two conditions set out in para 21, namely (i) that any prejudice is capable of being adequately compensated by money, and (ii) that the public benefit of making an order outweighs such prejudice. For the purposes of the application Mr Fothringham conceded that both conditions were satisfied.

The main dispute between the parties was as to the level of compensation to be paid. Cornerstone offered £253 per annum; Mr Fothringham suggested £5,600. Expert evidence was led for both parties. It was accepted that the principles to be applied were those set out in a recent Upper Tribunal decision in England, *EE Ltd v Islington LBC* [2019] UKUT 53, [2019] 2 P & CR 13. The starting-point was the market for the site: this was for woodland/countryside use (other than the telecommunication use now being envisaged). Both experts offered comparator figures from previous cases but these were hard to evaluate without more information, and figures produced in respect of the previous Code (ie the Telecommunications Code) were unreliable in respect that the new Code, in para 24(3)(a), required a valuation on the assumption that the transaction did *not* relate to the provision or use of an electronic communications network. In the absence of suitable comparators, the Tribunal focused on the effect of the agreement on the site provider. No doubt the agreement would be a 'not inconsiderable imposition' (para 79); on the other hand, the agreement in relation to the previous site did not seem to have created difficulty. The Tribunal fixed a sum of £1,500 for the first year of the agreement (in acknowledgement of the disruption caused by installation) and £600 for the remaining nine years. 'We do not pretend', the Tribunal added (at para 82), 'that there is either maths or science involved in arriving at these figures ... They are simply set at levels at which we think a willing seller acting prudently would consider it worth taking on the risks and obligations.'

Two others of the matters in dispute may be mentioned. One concerned para 17 of the Code, which allows operators to share their electronic equipment with others – a standard industry practice – subject to two conditions, namely (i) that this has no or only minimal adverse effect on the appearance of the apparatus, and (ii) that it 'imposes no additional burden on the other party to the agreement' (ie Mr Fothringham). Emphasising the public and the commercial importance of sharing (which was not in dispute), Cornerstone argued that the agreement should allow unlimited sharing, ie without the safeguards provided by the two conditions. An initial question, as to which the Tribunal reserved its position, was whether it was competent for the Tribunal (as had been held in England) to confer rights greater than provided by the Code. But even if it was competent, the Tribunal was not disposed to do so. In para 17, Parliament had already sought to strike a balance between the interests of the operators and the public on the one hand and those of the site provider on the other. That balance should not be disturbed except for compelling reasons. None had been produced. Nor were the conditions in para 17 likely to prove troublesome in practice.

The other disputed matter was whether, on the termination of the agreement, Cornerstone should be required to remove not only its own equipment but equipment belonging to third parties. The Tribunal thought it not 'unreasonable that the applicants should take responsibility for clearing the site and yielding it up with vacant possession' (para 30). But the Tribunal accepted that Cornerstone would often lack the legal power to remove equipment that was not theirs. The result was a compromise. The agreement should be amended to oblige Cornerstone to use its best endeavours to procure the removal of the equipment.

(20) Arqiva Ltd v Kingsbeck Ltd
2020 GWD 26-353, Lands Tribunal

Arqiva Ltd, the statutory successor of the Independent Broadcasting Authority, is (with its sister company, Arqiva Services Ltd) the sole national provider of terrestrial television and radio, having some 8,000 telecommunications towers across the UK. The case concerns one of Arqiva's electronic communication masts which was located on Unthank Farm, Coulter, Biggar, Lanarkshire, a property owned by Kingsbeck Ltd. As is permitted under the Electronic Communications Code (and the predecessor Telecommunications Code), the mast was also used by certain mobile network operators (EE, Vodafone, O2, BT and ITS) (as to which see *SSE Telecommunications Ltd v Millar* [2018] SCA (Civ) 14, 2018 SC (SAC) 73 (*Conveyancing 2018* Case (26)). In addition, these operators had other equipment on site, including cabins.

A dispute arose concerning the basis on which Arqiva could continue to use the site, and its right to regulate who else used it. Kingsbeck had served a notice to quit on Arqiva whereupon Arqiva had served a notice under para 5 of the Old Code (ie the Telecommunications Code which was then still in force) requiring Kingsbeck to agree to grant a lease. When the statutory period of 28 days passed without Kingsbeck having responded, Arqiva exercised its right under para 5 to ask the sheriff court to confer the lease. The application was decided substantially in favour of Arqiva by the Sheriff Appeal Court – see [2019] SAC (Civ) 28, 2019 SC (SAC) 95, noted in *Conveyancing 2019* pp 21–22 – but that decision is now the subject of an application for leave to appeal to the Inner House.

The present application to the Lands Tribunal was for the grant of interim Code rights under para 26 of the new Code (ie the Electronic Communications Code, now in force), pending the determination of the main application just described, so as to allow two of the site's sharers (EE and Cornerstone Telecommunications Infrastructure Ltd) to upgrade their equipment. This was resisted by Kingsbeck on a number of grounds, only two of which need be mentioned here.

The first was that it was only competent to apply for interim Code rights, Kingsbeck said, where there was also an application for permanent Code rights. No application for permanent rights was made by Arqiva because these were being settled by the earlier application to the sheriff court. This argument was rejected by the Lands Tribunal, following in this respect a decision of the Court of Appeal in England, *Cornerstone Telecommunications Infrastructure Ltd v University of London* [2019] EWCA Civ 2075, [2020] 1 WLR 2124. The detailed reasoning can be found at paras 55–59 of the Tribunal's Opinion.

The second ground was that the application for interim rights should have been brought, not by Arqiva, but by those who proposed to exercise them, ie EE and Cornerstone Telecommunications Infrastructure Ltd. This gave the Tribunal more trouble but in the end it concluded that the application was competent. Code rights under para 3 required to be rights for the statutory purposes set out in para 4. In this case, the application fell within para 4(b) which, read with para 7, referred to 'the purposes of providing an infrastructure system', including maintaining such a system. The actual work of upgrading was to be done by Arqiva and, at least on a purposive interpretation of the Code, it did not matter that the apparatus was provided by EE and Cornerstone and not by Arqiva.

(21) British Telecommunications plc v Morrison
2020 GWD 30-395, Lands Tribunal

This is another case in which interim Code rights were sought in circumstances where there was not to be an application for permanent rights. Indeed the application was for a one-off event – something which, following a decision of the Court of Appeal in England (*Cornerstone Telecommunications Infrastructure Ltd v University of London* [2019] EWCA Civ 2075, [2020] 1 WLR 2124), was held by the Lands Tribunal to be competent.

The facts were unusual. BT had installed apparatus on land in the Isle of Lewis belonging to the respondent (Mr Morrison) without a written agreement with the respondent. In principle, the respondent wanted the apparatus removed. But when BT attempted to remove one of the items (a cabinet providing a fibre broadband service) which BT accepted should not have been installed in the first place, the respondent denied access to the site. The reason for doing so was that the respondent considered he had a claim in delict for damages for the unlawful encroachment by BT, and the cabinet, he said, was the subject of a lien to secure payment of the damages.

As with permanent Code rights, interim rights can be granted only if the Tribunal is satisfied (i) that any prejudice to the respondent is capable of being adequately compensated by money, and (ii) that the public benefit of making an order outweighs such prejudice: see para 26(3)(b) of the Code, applying para 21. In the present case there was no difficulty as to (ii): the proposal was to re-site the cabinet, thus allowing broadband to be available to a larger number of customers. It was also, thought the Tribunal, hard to see any difficulty with (i). Even if the effect of granting the application was for the respondent to lose his lien in respect of a claim for damages in delict, there was 'no suggestion that the applicants, as an approved code operator, would be unable to meet a claim for damages should the claim succeed' (35). There might in any event be a question as to whether such a common law claim remained competent given the comprehensive nature of the Code, which itself made provision, in para 44(5), for compensation for the wrongful presence of apparatus on land. Furthermore, BT had 'a good arguable case that a lien does not exist at common law in the present circumstances' (39). No case law supported the existence of a delictual lien; and while Andrew J M Steven, *Pledge and Lien* (2008) paras 11–29 to 11–34 offered tentative support for a lien, on analogy with the lien for contractual damages recognised in *Moore's Carving Machine Co v Austin* (1890) 33 SLR 613, the modern case of *Air and General Finance Ltd v RYB Marine Ltd* [2007] CSOH 177 rejected the idea that a lien could secure a claim for damages for breach of a warranty of title in a sale. For critical commentary on this last point, see Andrew Steven, 'Delictual Liens' (www.blogs. law.ed.ac.uk/private-law/).

(22) EE Ltd v Manston Forests LLP
2020 GWD 35-465, Lands Tribunal

This was a more standard case in which an application for interim Code rights was merely a prelude to negotiations (which failing a further application) for permanent rights. The land in question was in Ardochy Forest, Inverness-shire, and EE's intended purpose was to make 4G available on a stretch of the A87.

The interim agreement was designed to last only a few months until permanent rights were fixed. In those circumstances, the Lands Tribunal took the understandable position (para 8) of being 'reluctant to get into potentially complex negotiations and wrangling over terms and conditions in the interim proceedings, only for the whole tortuous business to be repeated a second time in the final proceedings. As far as the interim proceedings with which we are here concerned, where there is a dispute as to the appropriate terms we intend to err on the side of simplicity'.

The parties had agreed a lease in principle but a number of points of disagreement remained which required to be settled by the Tribunal. The only point that need be mentioned here concerned whether EE should be allowed to install a permanent structure (a 20-metre tower on a reinforced concrete base), despite the temporary nature of the rights, or whether, as the respondents argued, EE should have to make do with something more obviously temporary. The Tribunal found for EE (para 14):

> In our opinion the applicants' submissions should be preferred on this point. We think the Code was designed to allow a code operator early access to a site on an interim basis, pending determination of disputes such as the amount of payment. While an interim order could be obtained only for non-invasive survey purposes, as it often is, we see nothing in the Code which restricts the purpose of an interim order to such limited activity. There is no suggestion in the applicants' evidence that the site might not transpire to be suitable for their purposes or that the site search is incomplete. If full rights are ultimately granted, an interim restriction to temporary apparatus will have only served to cause inconvenience to the applicants and potentially also to the respondents by the need to give way for a second installation. On the other hand if the interim agreement expires without full rights having been obtained, the risk of reinstatement is upon the applicants in the light of para 26(8) of the Code and the provisions which parties have agreed. We consider this to be an adequate safeguard for the respondents.

(23) EE Ltd v Duncan
2020 GWD 36-474, Lands Tribunal

The new Code (ie the Electronic Communications Code) replaced the old Code (ie the Telecommunications Code) with effect from 28 December 2017. But agreements made under the old Code remain subject to that Code. From the point of view of operators, that is a disadvantage, because the new Code is more operator-friendly, eg in relation to assignation of rights, or levels of rent. Potentially, the position may change once the existing agreement comes to an end. For once an agreement has expired, or as with a lease continuing by tacit relocation is capable of being brought to an end, paras 33 and 34 of the new Code provide a mechanism for the variation of the agreement or even its complete replacement; in the absence of agreement between the parties, the new terms can be fixed by the court.

This was an application to the Lands Tribunal by operators, in nine conjoined cases, to have the existing agreements, currently continuing by tacit relocation, terminated and replaced by new agreements under the new Code. The main issue, and an important one, was whether the proposed changes required individual and detailed justification (which had not been provided) or whether it was enough for the operators to say, in general terms, that they have a business need to take advantage of the new Code, especially in respect of the freedom given to assign and to share sites, and of the reduced rental payments. The Tribunal was firmly of the former view (paras 59–61):

> There is no doubt that the new code is an attractive option for operators: it was in order to make things easier and cheaper for them (in the public interest) that it was introduced. Given a choice, they would always opt for a new code agreement over an old code one. But did Parliament intend that they would be able to have old code agreements replaced by new code agreements for the asking, which is pretty much the applicants' position in these cases? If it did, why did it not say so? If it did, why did it set the bar as high as 'need'?
>
> We have to bear in mind that the business and technical needs of the operators is only one of the circumstances to which we must have regard: para 34(13) enjoins us to have regard to all the circumstances of the case. These include that the present agreements have been in place for periods varying from 15 to 22 years and there is no suggestion that any change is required in order to give them business or technical efficacy. Furthermore there is no suggestion that consumers of telecommunication services served by the various sites to which the applications relate will be one whit better served by replacement of these agreements than they are at the moment.
>
> In our view more requires to be pled, in the way of particular agreements being unduly onerous or restrictive, in order to justify what Mr Upton [counsel for the respondents] described as 'judicial cancellation of existing contracts'. Obviously, in enacting paras 33(1)(d) and 34(6), Parliament envisaged that there would be some cases where existing agreements would be so unfit for purpose that complete replacement was justified. Frankly, it is hard to envisage what such an agreement would look like but, whatever it might look like, we don't recognise it in any of the subsisting agreements in this case.

It might possibly be competent, said the Tribunal, for operators like the applicants to improve their position by an application for Code rights under para 20. But, be that as it may, they had failed to plead a relevant case under paras 33 and 34.

Along the way, some technical matters were decided by the Tribunal, in particular matters concerning the meaning and scope of para 33(3)(b). Under para 33, an operator seeking to change or replace the existing agreement must serve a notice on the site operator. This must include the date on which the proposed changes are to take place. Not only must that date be more than six months after the giving of the notice, but also, by para 33(b), it must be after (i) the expiry of the agreement or (ii) the time when the agreement could have been brought to an end. In the present application, it was (ii) that was relevant. It was held by the Tribunal: (a) that a lease continuing on tacit relocation was an agreement which could be brought to an end in the sense of (ii); (b) that there was no further requirement that the agreement must also have been terminable by the site provider under para 31(4) (which, for the most part, required breaches of the agreement by the operator); and (c) that the date specified in the notice need not be an anniversary of the ish of the lease.

ROADS

(24) Leafrealm Land Ltd v City of Edinburgh Council
[2020] CSOH 34, 2020 GWD 15-219

A road (with pavement) was edged by a wall that separated it from the adjoining property. The road was listed under s 1 of the Roads (Scotland) Act 1984 as including the wall. Was the wall part of the road? Held: that cases of this type are fact-specific and that in this case the road did include the wall.

[Another aspect of this case is digested as Case (31) below.]

VARIATION ETC OF TITLE CONDITIONS

(25) Toomey v Smith
2020 GWD 10-146, Lands Tribunal

This was an application to discharge the real burdens in a split-off disposition of a field in Mid Calder, Livingston, West Lothian, dating from 1995. The effect of the burdens was to prevent the erection of buildings. Unusually, the applicants did not have a specific project in mind for the field, although it was possible that the planning authorities would allow a housing development in the future.

The nominated benefited property (a house and garden) was built on a slope and, in 1995, looked directly on to the field, which was low-lying. Today, however, the view of the field was largely blocked by other houses. That being the case, it was held by the Lands Tribunal that the new houses were a significant change of circumstances (factor (a) of s 100 of the Title Conditions (Scotland) Act 2003) as a result of which the benefit conferred by the burden was slight (factor (b)). Yet the burden was an obvious impediment to the enjoyment of the burdened property (factor (c)). It would therefore be discharged.

[Another aspect of this case is digested as Case (12) above.]

(26) Christie v Carroll
2020 GWD 31-401, Lands Tribunal

The applicants owned a plot of undeveloped land at the east end of Doune Gardens in Glasgow, immediately adjacent to number 1 Doune Gardens. Ever since the erection of the houses in Doune Gardens in the late nineteenth century the plot had been used as a garden. Owned originally by the proprietors of 167 Wilton Street (which lay immediately to the north, just beyond a lane), it had also been used by the owners of 1 Doune Gardens in terms of an apparent right to do so contained in one of the titles to the plot, namely a disposition of 1882. This provided that the plot was to be 'formed into a pleasure ground for the use only of our said disponee and his foresaids and us and our successors as proprietors of' 1 Doune Gardens. The disposition also imposed as a real burden a prohibition on building.

The applicants sought the discharge of both restrictions. This was needed because they had obtained planning permission to build a house. Given the attractive nature of the area – 'a terrace of fine sandstone townhouses' in the estimation of the Lands Tribunal (para 8) – it comes as no surprise that the original application for planning permission attracted 135 objections. The application to the Tribunal was opposed by the owners of each of the three flats into which 1 Doune Gardens had now been converted.

A preliminary question was the enforceability of the right conferred on the owners of number 1 to make use of the garden. If it was to be binding on successors, it would have to be constituted as a servitude. But the question of whether Scots law allows a servitude of recreation had never been authoritatively determined. Modern English authority was in favour of such a servitude (easement), notably *In re Ellenborough Park* [1956] Ch 131 and *Regency Villas Title Ltd v Diamond Resorts (Europe) Ltd* [2018] UKSC 57, [2019] AC 553. This issue could not, however, be decided by the Tribunal because it was only in respect of real burdens, and not servitudes, that the Tribunal had the jurisdiction to pronounce on validity (as to which see Title Conditions (Scotland) Act 2003 s 90(1)(a)(ii)). On the other hand, the Tribunal did have jurisdiction to vary or discharge 'purported' title conditions (s 90(1)(a)(ii)), and so could entertain the application on the basis that the servitude was, or might be, valid. Its validity would therefore be assumed for the purposes of the application.

The Tribunal refused the application. Given that nothing much had changed in the area since the late nineteenth century (factor (a)), the disposal of the application, as so often, turned on the balance to be struck between factor (b) (the extent to which the conditions conferred benefit on the benefited properties) and factor (c) (the extent to which they impeded enjoyment of the burdened property).

The impediment to use was substantial. Unless the conditions were discharged, the house could not be built. No doubt the plot had some value in its present undeveloped state. There might be a market for a nearby proprietor wishing to own it. 'Nevertheless, although there was no direct evidence, intuitively we would think that the potential value of the subjects as a development opportunity would be substantially more than their value as a shared garden' (para 102).

As against that, the benefit to the owners of 1 Doune Gardens was substantial. If the conditions were to be discharged and the house built, there would be the loss of the right to use what was quite a large and attractive garden. There would also be the loss of the view of the garden, although the proposed house had been carefully designed for the site: it was single-storey, with a flat roof which was to be planted with wild flowers to as to provide the appearance of a meadow. Important trees were to be retained. Finally, there would be a loss of general amenity to the area due to the modern style of the proposed house (para 99):

> At the site itself, being the important interface between Doune Gardens and Belmont Street, there is a palpable uniformity and rhythm – we do not say pure symmetry – of traditional Victorian design. Although the new build proposes materials designed to blend with the materials used in the existing buildings, no other aspect of design was drawn to our attention which could be described as a homage to the existing streetscape. It has to be recognised that the market for property in the West End of Glasgow such as the benefited properties is likely to be inhabited by those attracted to traditional design. The weight of the planning objections tends to infer that at least some of that market would be inherently more likely to find the contrast somewhat discordant.

These considerations, thought the Tribunal, outweighed the development blight which the conditions imposed on the applicants. '[W]e are not persuaded that the subjects do not continue to have a long term future as a shared garden as the title conditions envisage. We regard the continuing integrity of the title conditions as a determining issue and accordingly do not think it would be reasonable to discharge them' (para 104).

Three comments may be made. First, in this case, as quite often, factors (b) and (c) were not only strong but also incommensurable. On what basis, therefore, was the Tribunal to choose between them? In the end the choice seems to have come down to the fact that, more than 100 years later, the conditions were still performing the task for which they had been originally designed.

Secondly, the relative strengths of factors (b) and (c) would have looked different if the applicants had first successfully contested the validity of the recreational servitude in the ordinary courts. Perhaps it would have been tactically astute to have sought to do so.

Thirdly, the time has surely come to give the Lands Tribunal the jurisdiction to pronounce on the enforceability of servitudes, as they already can of real burdens. Not being able to do so caused real awkwardness in the present case, as it did also in the next case, *Savage v Thomson* 2020 GWD 30-389. Back in 2003 it may have seemed a bold step to allow the Tribunal to determine the validity and scope even of real burdens, but since then the Tribunal has acquired wide powers to consider the position of servitudes, and much else besides, in the course of applications made under s 82 of the Land Registration etc (Scotland) Act 2012 (concerning the accuracy or otherwise of the Land Register). The Lands Tribunal has built up an enviable expertise in matters of land law. That expertise should be made available in order to determine the validity and scope of servitudes. On this point, see also p 103 below.

(27) Savage v Thomson
2020 GWD 30-389, Lands Tribunal

Former stables in Elie, Fife, occupying the western and southern sides of a courtyard had been converted into three flats. The applicant owned the courtyard;

the respondent owned one of the flats. In terms of a split-off disposition of 1961 there had been granted in favour of the respondent's flat a:

> right of access to the subjects hereby disponed from the said public road by the gateway in the north boundary wall of said courtyard and by the courtyard itself with right to use the same for the parking of cars in front of the subjects hereby disponed which gateway, north boundary wall and courtyard and the remaining boundary walls thereof so far as not forming the boundary of the small piece of common ground or part of the building of said line of flats and stables are hereby reserved to and shall be maintained in good order and repair by us and our successors in all time coming …

The split-off dispositions of the other flats were in similar terms.

The applicant had now obtained planning permission for the erection of a house on the east side of the courtyard. A condition of the planning consent was that there should be parking to the north of the house. In this application the applicant sought a variation of the servitude so as to restrict the access and parking rights to the western half of the courtyard. This would still allow the flat-owners to park a car outside their flats (there was room for only one); but there would be insufficient space for each to park two cars in the restricted area which was being proposed.

An initial question was the scope of the right of parking. In considering this question the Tribunal was constrained by the fact that its jurisdiction did not extend to determining the proper construction of servitudes (unlike real burdens). Nonetheless, it was impossible for the Tribunal to assess the reasonableness of granting the application without forming a view as to the servitude's scope (para 62). Unsurprisingly, given its terms, the Tribunal concluded that the servitude conferred no more than a right to park a single car in front of the owner's flat. But even if the scope had been wider, the Tribunal would still have allowed the variation. The proposed erection of a house was a change in circumstances (Title Conditions (Scotland) Act 2003 s 100 factor (a)), and planning permission had been granted (factor (g)). And while an untrammelled servitude was certainly of benefit to the respondent (factor (b)), this was decisively outweighed by the manner in which it impeded enjoyment of the burdened property (factor (c)). Apart from anything else, it prevented the building of the proposed house. In all the circumstances, therefore, the application would be granted.

(28) Pallot v Carter
2020 GWD 25-335, Lands Tribunal

The applicants and the respondents each owned a half of a traditional cottage, respectively numbers 1 and 2 Heathery Ha', Carlops Road, West Linton, Peeblesshire. The only means of access to number 2 was by means of a driveway, then a path which ran up the side and then the rear of number 1. This access route was secured by a servitude. Wishing to build a rear porch which would interrupt the path, the applicants, who owned number 1, sought a variation of the servitude so that, at the rear, it would follow a new route some 4.5 metres beyond the current route. The overall effect would be to add 50% to the length of the route (about 9 metres). The application was opposed by the owners of number 2.

In principle, the Tribunal was disposed to grant the application, on the basis that the impediment to reasonable use on the applicants (factor (c)) exceeded the benefit of the current route to the respondents (factor (b)): 'on balance we feel that the reasonable opportunity to refurbish the subjects carries more weight than the marginal inconvenience that a slightly longer new route would involve' (para 30). Nonetheless, the Tribunal was not prepared to grant the application as it stood but offered to continue it for a reasonable period (i) so that planning permission could be obtained for the re-routing, whether as currently proposed or (as the Tribunal suggested) in a slightly different line, and (ii) in order for the applicants to specify the materials to be used for the new access. Both of these were to protect the position of the respondents.

(29) Leslie v National Grid Gas plc
2020 GWD 33-436, Lands Tribunal

In this highly unusual application, the applicant sought to *increase* the burden on his land. The applicant owned Flawcraig Farm in Perthshire. In 1981 a predecessor as owner had granted to the British Gas Corporation a deed of servitude for a pipeline. The servient tenement was a strip of land 80 feet in width and 1,903 yards in length. The deed also imposed (presumably as real burdens) use restrictions in respect of the strip, including a prohibition on building. The application was to increase the width of the affected strip, and hence to extend the ambit of the servitude and real burdens. Why? Due to the presence of the pipeline, the applicant had been prevented by the Health & Safety Executive from using a 3.2-acre site for a development of up to 10 houses. In effect the HSE had imposed a broader safety corridor for the pipeline than the original servitude had envisaged. The purpose of the application was to extend the servitude to the full width of the HSE corridor on the view that, by means which were not properly explained, compensation would then be payable to the applicant by National Grid Gas plc (as the successor to the British Gas Corporation). Compensation had in fact been paid, in terms of a clause in the deed of servitude, at the time of the thwarted development, but this was tied to 1981 values leading to 'a sense of unfairness and grievance' on the part of the applicant (para 8).

The application was refused as being 'fundamentally misconceived'. Although 'variation' was capable of including the imposition of a new obligation, provided that the burdened owner consented (Title Conditions (Scotland) Act 2003 ss 90(5)(a) and 122(1) (definition of 'variation')), that could not be the normal use of Tribunal applications (paras 27):

> Although, linguistically, there is no reason why variation of a servitude should not include making it more burdensome, such variation was never within the contemplation of Parliament. Quite the reverse: the whole purpose of s 90 and its predecessor was to provide a means by which burdens could be discharged or relaxed or limited in some way so as to permit some previously prohibited use of land. Thus the test contained in s 98(a) of the 2003 Act is whether the discharge or variation is

'reasonable' having regard to the factors listed in s 100. Although 'reasonableness' may, of itself, be thought to be a fairly neutral test, none of the s 100 factors, to which we are to have regard in assessing reasonableness, (with the possible exception of (a), which refers to changes in the character of the benefited, as well as of the burdened property) contemplates the need for a burden to be increased.

The same was true when the matter was looked at from the viewpoint of the benefited owner: such owners could not seek a variation in order to extend their rights.

There were other reasons, too, for refusing the application. An application could only be made in relation to the burdened property (s 90(1)(a)(i)) and could not be used to affect other land belonging to the applicant. Furthermore, the variation contemplated would confer no benefit on the benefited proprietor: on the contrary, National Grid Gas was entirely content with the servitude in its current form, and indeed was opposing the application. Finally, the application was unacceptably imprecise. 'We understand very well the core of what the applicant wants: it is to transform the *de facto* building restrictions which presently affect his land into a real burden. But it is not said how this is to be achieved' (para 32).

At a subsequent hearing, expenses were awarded against the applicant but under exclusion of the cost incurred by National Grid Gas in employing senior counsel: see *Leslie v National Grid Gas plc (No 2)* 2020 GWD 33-431. On the latter point the Tribunal said (para 6):

On the matter of sanction for the employment of counsel, however, we are with the applicant. In our opinion this was an application which was so obviously misconceived that a solicitor of ordinary competence could have opposed it successfully. The respondents were, of course, perfectly entitled to arm themselves with the firepower of senior counsel but the applicant should not have to pay for it in a case which, at all events when what the application was seeking became tolerably clear, was of so little complexity. So we have refused sanction for the employment of counsel.

(30) Alexander Devine Children's Cancer Trust v Housing Solutions Ltd
[2020] UKSC 45, [2020] 1 WLR 4783

This is an application under the equivalent provisions in England and Wales for the modification or discharge of restrictive covenants affecting land. It is included here partly because of its intrinsic interest, and partly because it marks the first occasion on which the Supreme Court (or, formerly, House of Lords) has heard an appeal on this topic from any of the UK jurisdictions.

After building 13 houses (near Maidenhead in Berkshire) in knowing disregard of a freehold covenant prohibiting building, the applicant (Housing Solutions Ltd) sought a modification of the covenant so as to allow the houses to remain. The applicant was opposed by the benefited proprietor. At first instance, the Upper Tribunal granted the application, but this was reversed on appeal, first by the Court of Appeal and now (on more restricted grounds) by the Supreme Court.

An appeal court should not, it was accepted, simply substitute its own assessment of the merits for those of a specialist tribunal. The decision could be displaced only where the tribunal had made an error of law (para 51). The crucial question in the present case was the approach to be taken to the 'cynical conduct' involved in knowingly disregarding a covenant. In a judgment given by Lord Burrows, with the concurrence of the other Justices, the Supreme Court toyed with, but ultimately rejected, the idea that the tribunal's decision might be 'contrary to principle' (paras 54 and 55):

> [T]he relevant principle in play here was, as I understand it, that an applicant who has committed a cynical breach of the type committed on these facts should have its application refused. In other words, as a matter of principle, a cynical breach such as that committed in this case outweighs what would otherwise be the public interest in discharging or modifying the restrictive covenant.
>
> I am sorely tempted to agree that there is such a principle. However, I have major concerns as to whether, without discretionary qualifications to cater for exceptions, such a principle would be too rigid and would inappropriately fetter the Upper Tribunal's discretion. And once one lets in discretionary qualifications to temper such a principle, it is hard to see how the Upper Tribunal in this case could be said to have made an error of law.

Instead, the Supreme Court decided the appeal on different grounds, of which the most important is that, if an application would have been refused if it had been made before building work took place, it should not be granted where the building work took place in cynical disregard of the building restriction (para 59):

> As Mr Jourdan [counsel for the benefited proprietor] expressed it, in a submission with which I agree, 'It is not in the public interest that a person who deliberately breaches a restrictive covenant should be able to secure the modification of the covenant in reliance on the state of affairs created by their own deliberate breach'. By going ahead without first applying under section 84 [of the Law of Property Act 1925], Millgate put itself in the position of being able to present to the Upper Tribunal a fait accompli where the provision of affordable housing meant that it could (and did) satisfy the 'contrary to public interest' jurisdictional ground. It is important to deter a cynical breach under section 84 but it is especially important to do so where, because the Upper Tribunal will look at the public interest position as at the date of the hearing, that cynical conduct will directly reward the wrongdoer by transforming its prospects of success.

Although its purpose is much the same, the legislation in England is expressed rather differently from the provisions (in the Title Conditions (Scotland) Act 2003) which apply in Scotland. Nonetheless, it is likely that the decision of the Supreme Court will have some influence on future Scottish decisions.

COMPETITION OF TITLE

(31) Leafrealm Land Ltd v City of Edinburgh Council
[2020] CSOH 34, 2020 GWD 15-219

The case concerned rights in the solum of a former boundary wall which, from 1912 until it fell down in 2014, had separated Comely Bank Road, in Edinburgh's Stockbridge area, from ground to the north. The case raised difficult questions of fact as well as an important legal question: did a 'minute of agreement', which had been recorded in the Register of Sasines, have dispositive effect even though, instead of using the word 'dispone', it said merely that the granters 'give up' the property in question. See **Commentary** p 208.

[Another aspect of this case is digested as Case (24) above.]

LAND REGISTRATION

(32) BAM TCP Atlantic Square Ltd v British Telecommunications plc
[2020] CSOH 57, 2020 GWD 25-334

The title sheets of two adjoining properties in Glasgow, A and B, conflicted. The title sheet of A, the older of the two, showed a certain area of land as common property of A and B. The title sheet of B showed the area as the sole property of B. Both registrations took place under the Land Registration (Scotland) Act 1979. Held: (i) that, in principle, the later of the two title sheets should prevail, but (ii) as the conferral of sole property in the title sheet of B was an inaccuracy which might have been reversed under the transitional provisions in sch 4 of the Land Registration etc (Scotland) Act 2012, and as such reversal depended on whether, immediately before the designated day, the area of land had been possessed by the owner of B, a proof was allowed on the question of possession. See **Commentary** p 153. The decision has been reclaimed.

(33) Wyllie v Wittmann
2020 GWD 29-380, Lands Tribunal

A and B were neighbours at Humbie Lawns, Newton Mearns, Glasgow. Each had a registered title (respectively REN77893 and REN145574). On the cadastral map, the boundaries matched: there was neither overlap nor underlap. But A (it was averred) occupied a boundary strip which fell within B's title. In A's view, this strip should not be part of B's title at all because the split-off deed for that property, a feu disposition from 1958, is (A said) a bounding title from which the strip was excluded. Was A, simply by virtue of possession (assuming possession could be proved), entitled to seek rectification of B's title? More precisely, was A entitled to refer to the Lands Tribunal the question of the accuracy of A's title under s 82 of the Land Registration etc (Scotland) Act 2012? Section 82 requires that a question can be referred only by 'a person with an interest'. Did A have such an interest merely by virtue of A's possession?

Of some significance was the fact that first registration of B's property had taken place under the 2012 Act and not under the Land Registration (Scotland) Act 1979. From this it followed (assuming A's averments to be correct) both (i) that registration did not confer ownership of the strip on B (for there is no Midas touch under the 2012 Act) and, in consequence, (ii) that as B did not own the strip, rectification of the Register to remove the strip from B's title would not change anyone's legal position. Whoever owned the strip now would continue to own it after rectification. As the Lands Tribunal explained (para 39):

At this point we are inclined to agree with the applicants that, unlike the 1979 Act, a registration under s 50 of the 2012 Act while conferring real rights does not itself provide rights of ownership beyond the extent of the validity of the underlying registered deeds. The act of registration by the Keeper does not of itself cure underlying defects in title. This is perhaps an example of why it is sometimes said that under the 1979 Act the Keeper was an umpire, whereas under the 2012 Act she is a scorekeeper. For example, additional rights following a 2012 Act registration – such as those of an acquirer in good faith under Part 9 – only occur where additional statutory conditions are met going beyond the act of registration. A 2012 Act registered title is in effect an endorsement by the Keeper that the underlying deeds provide for what is stated in the land register. But of itself a 2012 Act registration provides no particular status to render the title immune from challenge. Equally, should the register be rectified, this has no legal effect in the sense that all that has occurred is the register is being brought into line with underlying rights of ownership. It is in this context whereby s 82 allows a party with an interest to look behind the registered title.

Did, then, A have sufficient interest to make an application under s 82? With perhaps a little hesitation, the Tribunal thought that the answer was yes. A person in possession, as A was, is able to defend that possession (eg by interdict) against a challenger with no title or one that is in doubt. Here the Tribunal relied on *Watson v Shields* 1996 SCLR 81 and *GCN (Scotland) Ltd v Gillespie* [2019] CSOH 82, 2020 SLT 185. Furthermore, in the event that A wished to proceed with an *a non domino* disposition under s 43 of the 2012 Act, A would (because of s 12(2)) first need to procure the removal of the disputed strip from B's title sheet.

All of this seems eminently reasonable and sensible. It remains to be seen whether A is able to prove the facts that have been averred.

A's real target, in fact, was a more ambitious one. In A's view, the disputed strip was truly part of A's property. It had, said A, been included in the split-off conveyance of that property (a feu disposition of 1993) but, in making up the title sheet on first registration, the Keeper had mistakenly failed to include it within the title plan. So in addition to rectifying B's title, A also sought the rectification of A's title to include the disputed strip. This part of A's case was, however, rejected by the Tribunal on the basis (i) that the split-off feu disposition had been granted in favour of a Mr and Mrs Kerr, (ii) that, while A had acquired the property from the Kerrs, the disposition had (presumably) conveyed no more than the Kerrs' registered title, (iii) that, although A had now received an assignation of Mrs Kerr's interest, there had been no assignation of the interest of the late Mr Kerr, and (iv) that accordingly, it would be a breach of the 'unanimity rule' applicable for common property for proceedings to be brought only by one *pro indiviso* owner.

(34) Holwill v Keeper of the Registers of Scotland
7 November 2018 and 2020 GWD 11-162, Lands Tribunal

These were two appeals, on essentially the same facts, made under s 25(1) of the Land Registration (Scotland) Act 1979. In substance, they were claims for compensation of £200,000 from the Keeper on the basis of s 12(1)(b) of the Act.

The first appeal was dismissed on the merits, the second as *res judicata*. A little more may be said about the first appeal.

The appeal concerned two adjoining properties in Broxburn, West Lothian, known respectively as 'Craigbeg' and 'North Lodge'. The appellants owned Craigbeg. In order to resolve uncertainty as to the common boundary, the appellants entered into a Minute of Agreement and Mutual Disposition ('MAMD') with the then owners of North Lodge, a Mr and Mrs Clair. That was in or around 2000. The 'mutual disposition' part of the deed was an excambion of such land as was needed to produce the agreed boundary; but because the Sasine titles were unclear, the description of the land being conveyed was itself rather vague. So far as North Lodge was concerned, the deed provided as follows:

> The second party [the appellants] hereby dispones to and in favour of the first party [Mr and Mrs Clair] equally between them and to the survivor of them and to the executors and assignees whomsoever of the survivor heritably and irredeemably ALL and WHOLE (FIRST) ALL and WHOLE any area of ground presently in the ownership of the second party and falling within and forming a part and portion of the second subjects lying to the north west of the red line running between the points marked 'O' and 'P' on the plan and (SECOND) ALL and WHOLE any area of ground presently in the ownership of the second party and falling within and forming a part and portion of the second subjects lying to the north east of the red line running between the points marked 'P' and 'Z' on the plan; TOGETHER WITH the second party's whole right, title and interest present and future therein and thereto ...

No attempt was made to register this deed.

Later, in or around 2006, Mr and Mrs Clair sold North Lodge to a Mr and Mrs Glendinning. The transaction induced first registration. The Keeper, however, was troubled by the Glendinnings' title and could not, at first, be persuaded to register it. The MAMD was said to be unsuitable for registration because (i) it was a personal agreement between the appellants and Mr and Mrs Clair (only) and so could not be used by Mr and Mrs Glendinning, and (ii) the property conveyed was not identifiable. In fact, however, the deed was, at worst, a general conveyance which could be used as a midcouple for the purposes of the disposition from the Clairs to the Glendinnings. Eventually persuaded that this was so, although not until 2010, the Keeper accepted the application for registration and issued a title sheet showing the boundary as agreed in the MAMD.

On (eventually) discovering this, the appellants were aggrieved, not least because, back in 2006, the Keeper had undertaken to the appellants not to issue a title sheet for North Lodge without some form of remedial action or court order. That undertaking was not kept. The appellants were not legally represented, and it is not easy to follow the precise basis of their claim for compensation. But, probably, it was based on the view (i) that the MAMD could not competently found registration of the Glendinnings' title; (ii) that the effect of such registration was to deprive the appellants of two areas of ground on the common boundary; (iii) that, as the Glendinnings were in possession, the inaccuracy could not be rectified, due to s 9(3)(a) of the Land Registration (Scotland) Act 1979, and (iv) that accordingly, the appellants were entitled to compensation of £200,000, being the value of the land (which had now been built on).

The Lands Tribunal rejected point (i), and with that the whole case for the appellants fell.

SEARCHES

(35) Commodity Solution Services Ltd v First Scottish Searching Services Ltd
[2020] SC DUN 29, 2020 GWD 22-293

What happens if an owner is inhibited and then sells a property that he owns, and the legal report fails to disclose the inhibition? Someone is likely to suffer loss, and to do so unfairly. Either (i) the buyer suffers because the inhibition strikes at the title, yet the buyer knew nothing of it; or (ii) the inhibiting creditor suffers because the buyer is protected by good faith, so that the effect of the inhibition is lost. Whichever is the result, can the party that suffers claim against the firm of searchers on the basis that the legal report was wrong?

These issues came up in *Commodity Solution Services Ltd v First Scottish Searching Services Ltd* which has been grinding its way through the judicial process for some time. It was first heard in the sheriff court on questions of relevancy: 2018 SLT (Sh Ct) 117 (*Conveyancing 2018* Case (53)). That decision was appealed to the Sheriff Appeal Court: [2019] SAC (Civ) 4, 2019 SC (SAC) 41, 2019 SLT (Sh Ct) 63 (*Conveyancing 2019* (Case (51)). For commentary, see *Conveyancing 2019* pp 181–86. The present, third, phase of the case was the proof.

Mr and Mrs Gardner co-owned a property at 6 Arbirlot Place, Arbroath, Angus. In 2012 they sold it to Paul Gardner, their son, and Louise Jones. 'The parties agreed that missives should be dispensed with to save expense. Otherwise the sale and purchase transaction proceeded in the usual manner.' (Findings-in-fact 17 by the sheriff, Pino Di Emidio.) In the event, the absence of missives made no difference. The price was £120,000, and the transaction settled on 25 July 2012. The two secured lenders were paid off, namely Halifax plc (£30,303.26) and GE Money Home Finance Ltd (£27,187.80). After that, and after deduction of outlays and fees, there remained £60,007.14, this being paid equally to the two sellers, ie £30,003.57 each. The disposition was duly registered in the Land Register with no exclusion of indemnity.

The legal report was supplied by First Scottish Searching Services Ltd, and it showed the Register of Inhibitions to be clear. But in fact in December 2011 Commodity Solution Services Ltd had obtained decree against Mr Gardner senior in the sum of £50,000, and in February 2012 it had registered an inhibition against him. How it came about that the searchers missed the inhibition is unknown, but miss it they did.

In 2014 Mr Gardner senior was sequestrated. What, if anything, the inhibitor, Commodity Solution Services Ltd, was paid by way of dividend is not known, but inferentially it must have been small or perhaps nothing at all. What was the inhibitor to do? Could the company raise an action of reduction of the buyers' title, *ex capite inhibitionis*? It did not seek to do so, for a simple reason. In the wake of *Atlas Appointments v Tinsley Ltd* 1997 SC 200, there was concern that a buyer's title might be reducible on account of an inhibition not disclosed in the legal report. The eventual response was s 159 of the Bankruptcy and Diligence etc (Scotland) Act 2007 which says that:

(1) An inhibition ceases to have effect ... in relation to property if a person acquires the property (or a right in the property) in good faith and for adequate consideration ...

    ...

(4) A person is presumed to have acted in good faith if the person –
    (a) is unaware of the inhibition; and
    (b) has taken all reasonable steps to discover the existence of an inhibition affecting the property.

Since the inhibitor was unable to recover its money from the inhibitee, and given that, in the light of s 159 of the 2007 Act, a challenge to the buyers' title would be unlikely to succeed, it decided to sue the search firm. Given that it had no contractual relationship with the firm, this was a delictual action, the inhibitor arguing that in carrying out the search the firm owed a duty of care to those, such as itself, whose rights might be prejudiced by the production of an inaccurate legal report.

An important distinction between the facts of the present case and the well-known line of authority beginning with *Hedley Byrne & Co Ltd v Heller & Partners Ltd* [1964] AC 465 was that in those other cases the duty of care was said to be owed to the person (the 'representee') who had reasonably relied on an erroneous statement. But in this case the pursuer was not a representee: the pursuer had not relied on the erroneous legal report. There had indeed been reliance on it, but that reliance had been on the part of the buyers, and the buyers were not suing. So the pursuer did not have an easy task in satisfying the court that there existed, as between it, as inhibitor, and the search firm, a duty of care. That was the core issue in the first two stages of this litigation, and the pursuer was successful, both at first instance and in the Sheriff Appeal Court.

So there was a duty of care. Was there breach of that duty – negligence? The defender seems not to have attempted to argue this point, so it seems that the failure to disclose was a simple error. There can be cases where a searcher's task of identifying a potentially relevant inhibition can be difficult, for instance where the inhibition specifies a person's business address but the search has been instructed in relation to the residential address. But if there were problems of that general type in this case, nothing was said about them. So simple error seems to be the most likely explanation.

The defender put up a rather thin argument that, notwithstanding s 159 of the 2007 Act, the company could still have attacked the buyer's title. This argument unsurprisingly failed.

Given that there was a duty of care, and given that there was negligence, and given that the negligent breach had had the effect of invalidating the inhibition, the question was one of damages. Here the court had to carry out a 'what if' exercise: what would have happened if the legal report had in fact disclosed the inhibition? If the buyers had known of the inhibition, there were in theory three possibilities. (i) They might have gone ahead regardless, without obtaining a discharge, thus leaving their title vulnerable to attack. (ii) They might have walked away from the transaction. (iii) The third possibility is that the buyers might have gone ahead with the purchase but conditionally on the discharge of the inhibition. In that event the inhibitor would have been paid the whole of the net share of Mr Gardner senior, ie £30,003.57. By contrast, in the first two possibilities the inhibitor would have been paid nothing.

The sheriff concluded, not surprisingly, that the third possibility was the most likely. He commented (para 29) that 'there is nothing in the evidence to suggest that the disclosure of the inhibition would have led to the transaction being cancelled. There is no basis in the evidence to think that the purchasers would have declined to continue with the acquisition. There was no effect on the price they paid'. Since the sheriff preferred the third possibility, he granted decree for Mr Gardner senior's share of the price (£30,003.57).

LEASES

(36) Granton Central Developments Ltd v Len Lothian Ltd
[2020] SC EDIN 6, 2020 SLT (Sh Ct) 71

Granton Central Developments Ltd (despite its name, a Jersey entity) owns land in Granton, Edinburgh, seemingly acquired from the Forth Ports Authority (now Forth Ports Ltd). It has been an active litigant in the Court of Session, with five cases being reported in 2020 alone, three of which we cover here. (One of the others, *Granton Central Developments Ltd v Edinburgh City Council* [2020] CSOH 73, 2020 SLT 1002, is a planning case, and planning law is outwith the scope of this series. The fifth is *Ashtead Plant Hire Co Ltd v Granton Central Developments Ltd* [2020] CSIH 2, 2020 SC 244, 2020 SLT 575, which we were able to include in *Conveyancing 2019* (Case (55)).)

In this and the next case, Granton Central Developments Ltd claimed that it was entitled to cut off the water supply to premises (a warehouse with offices) of which it was the landlord. In the present case it was the landlord who was the pursuer, seeking declarator that the tenant had no right to water. The lease had no specific provision on the point. The tenant pled (i) that there is an implied right to water, part of the more general implied right that the property be tenantable, or reasonably fit for purpose, citing *Tennent's Trustees v Maxwell* (1880) 17 SLR 463, and (ii) that the terms of the lease itself implied a right to a water supply. The first of these is classifiable as an implied-in-law term whereas the latter is classifiable as an implied-in-fact term.

The sheriff (T Welsh QC) agreed with the latter argument, saying at para 21:

[I]f men of commerce insert into the commercial lease of a warehouse and associated premises ... specific clauses that impose on the lessee the obligation to (1) maintain, repair and replace 'all drains, soil and other pipes, sewer, sanitary and water apparatus' in the subjects let … and (2) relieve the lessor of 'all rates, taxes and assessments, and all charges for water, heating, lighting, power and other services exigible in respect of the subjects during the currency of this lease' … then, *a fortiori*, they must necessarily have intended that the lessee receives a supply of water to use and pay for, a factor which was so obvious given the terms of the lease, that it goes without saying …

As to the first argument, namely that the right to water is an implied-in-law term of a lease, it was not necessary to make a decision, but at para 18 the sheriff said:

While I readily understand that a commercial warehouse can function without access to a water supply, depending on the circumstances, I would find it difficult but not impossible to conclude that in the 21st century, the let of an office which serves a commercial warehouse can do so, for obvious reasons of basic sanitation, health and comfort of the warehouse operatives, if there be any. Much would depend on the facts of the case, the kind of warehouse and office in question and the purpose and use made of the office. Were it not for the conclusion I have reached in relation to the meaning and construction of the lease itself and certain necessary implications flowing therefrom, I would have allowed a proof before answer, with some reluctance …

Thus, there is no *automatic* implied-in-law right to water, the point depending on the facts and circumstances. Yet the sheriff strongly hints that in a case such as the present there would be such an implied right. On 26 January 2021 this decision was reversed: [2021] SAC (Civ) 7, 2021 GWD 6-84 (see next year's volume).

(37) Royal Forth Yacht Club v Granton Central Developments Ltd [2020] SC EDIN 10, 2020 SLT (Sh Ct) 77

The essential facts in this case were like those of the preceding case, though here it was the tenant who was the pursuer, seeking declarator that there was a right to water, rather than the other way round. No doubt the reason that the initiative was taken by the tenant was that 'on 26 October 2018 the defender's representative entered the subjects and closed and padlocked the water stopcock' (para 2).

Whereas in the preceding case the tenant won on the basis of what the lease said, so that the common law issue did not have to be decided, in the present case it was the other way round. Though the wording of the lease was comparable, the sheriff (N A Ross) took the view that it did not imply a right to a supply of water. But, as in the preceding case, the tenant also pled the common law principle that a landlord is presumed to warrant the property to be reasonably fit for purpose, and, as in the previous case, reliance was placed on *Tennent's Trustees v Maxwell* (1880) 17 SLR 463 and on the statement in Paton and Cameron that 'a landlord is clearly in breach of his obligation … where the drains and water supply are completely inadequate …', a statement that cites the 1880 case as authority: see G C H Paton and J G S Cameron, *The Law of Landlord and Tenant in Scotland* (1967) p 131. A good deal of the present case involved the question of whether the statement in Paton and Cameron is correct: the sheriff concluded that it was. That, however, did not suffice to win the case for the tenant. The sheriff said (para 27): 'Whether or not reasonable fitness for purpose includes a water supply is heavily dependent on the facts.' Accordingly he allowed proof.

In neither of these cases is the background known. Was the landlord seeking to make the tenant flit? Or to pay more? We do not know.

(38) Glasgow Angling Centre Ltd v Granton Central Developments Ltd
[2020] SC EDIN 49, 2020 GWD 39-502

The pursuer was the tenant of property at Granton Harbour, Edinburgh. Who the landlords were is somewhat obscure. In this action the pursuer convened three defenders, namely (i) Granton Central Developments Ltd, (ii) Granton Central Management Ltd, and (iii) PIP Asset Management LLP, yet it seems that none of these was the landlord. The property had indeed once been owned by the first defender, but for only a few days, before being disponed to (we quote from para 1) 'British Overseas Bank Nominees Ltd and others'. One's head spins. But at all events this über-complexity was, thankfully, not relevant to the points at issue.

The pursuer had paid three invoices for service charges, but now considered that the invoices had been issued in error. It sought declarator, reduction of the invoices, and the return of what had been paid. The lease bound the tenant:

> To pay to the Landlords or to such other party as the Landlords may direct on written demand the proportion applicable to the Subjects in terms of the title deeds or by statute, common law or otherwise of the costs and expenses of repairing, maintaining, renewing, rebuilding, lighting and cleansing of all roads, pavements, sewers, drains, pipes, water courses, walls, fences and any other structure or facility owned or used in common by the Subjects and other adjoining, neighbouring or nearby properties.

The tenant's action was based on the terms of the deed of conditions to which the property was subject, and which was referred to by the quoted text in the lease (though the expression 'the title deeds' could have been improved upon). The defenders pled that the pursuer's action was thus irrelevant, for it failed to refer to the lease itself. The sheriff (N A Ross) agreed, and dismissed the action.

(39) Reay v Dumfries and Galloway Housing Partnership
[2020] SC DUM 19, 2020 Hous LR 86

Problems about noise are of course common, and from time to time reach the courts. For two such cases from last year, see *Cummings v Singh* [2019] SAC (Civ) 11, 2019 Hous LR 41 (*Conveyancing 2019* Case (58)), and *Morris v Curran* [2019] SC KIR 77, 2019 GWD 31-496 (*Conveyancing 2019* Case (83)).

In the present case a public-sector tenant at 102 Mount Vernon Road, Stranraer, Wigtownshire, sued his landlord for damages for excessive noise from his downstairs neighbours. By the time of the action the pursuer had moved to a different property, as had the downstairs neighbours. It may be added that the pursuer was not sole tenant, but joint tenant with his wife, but she does not seem to have been involved in this action. The reason for this is not known.

The claim was for 'stress and family disruption' allegedly caused by the alleged excessive noise. The dispute had a long history even before litigation began. The pursuer had made repeated complaints over the years, leading to numerous site visits by the landlord's staff, all of which had resulted in the conclusion that the noise was not excessive. The pursuer had refused to allow noise meter readings to be taken. 'The pursuer behaved in a threatening and intimidating manner in dealing with the defenders' (para 10 of the findings in fact). The legal ground for the action (which was legally aided) was that the defender should have carried out work to improve the sound insulation between the apartments. The property, the pursuer pled, was not 'reasonably fit for human habitation' – an expression used both in the tenancy agreement and in sch 4 to the Housing (Scotland) Act 2001. In the alternative, he founded on the provision in the tenancy agreements that 'we [the landlord] will repair any other defect we find which will significantly affect your use of the common parts, or the house, within a reasonable period'. Proof before answer was ordered and extensive evidence was heard by the sheriff (Brian Mohan).

The building had been constructed in the 1930s. The soundproofing was of a type normal at that time, and, whilst it did not conform to the current building regulations, such regulations have no retrospective force. In a carefully reasoned judgment, Sheriff Mohan concluded that no 'defect' could be said to exist, and that the level of soundproofing did not mean that the property was unfit for human habitation. The possibly substantial cost of new soundproofing work does not seem to have formed part of the *ratio decidendi*.

(40) Dymoke v Best
[2020] UT 18, 2020 Hous LR 56

Ms Best owned Rossie Priory, a mansion house in south-eastern Perthshire. In May 2015 she let it to Mr and Mrs Dymoke at £3,125 per month. A few months later the tenants ceased to pay the rent, and she raised an action for their removal on the basis of non-payment. Their position was that they were lawfully withholding the rent because of the owner's alleged failure to carry out maintenance in accordance with the 'Repairing Standard' (for which see Part 1 of the Housing (Scotland) Act 2006) as modified by the tenancy agreement. The First Tier Tribunal concluded that there had been no ongoing failure by the landlord, and accordingly decree of removal was granted in her favour. The strictly legal aspects of the case are limited but it is of interest as a bitter dispute between landlord and tenant.

(41) Toscaig Ltd v Poundland Ltd
[2020] CSOH 59, 2020 Hous LR 62

A block of commercial property in Glasgow (187–189 Argyle Street (odd numbers), 169–185 Jamaica Street (odd numbers), and 10 and 11 Adam Court Lane) was owned by Toscaig Ltd, the pursuer in this action. The defender had a lease of part of the block, the term being from 18 October 2010 to 17 October

2020. As is usual where different parts of a commercial property are let out to different tenants, the landlord was obliged to maintain the common parts, coupled with the right to recover the costs from the tenant – the so-called service charges. The wording of the landlord's obligation was 'to pay all running and operating costs associated with and keep in good and substantial repair and in a neat and tidy condition and, where necessary to rebuild, reinstate and replace the Common Parts ...'. The landlord raised the present action for declarator that the defender was liable for a proportionate share of the costs of work to the façade, the replacement/repair of windows, and the removal of asbestos.

This initial stage of the litigation was about the relevancy of the pursuer's pleadings. The defender was unhappy chiefly because the lease was about to end. We quote the Lord Ordinary (Lord Doherty) at para 13: the defender's counsel 'suggested that when assessing the work required to put the Common Parts in good and substantial repair ... regard has to be had to the duration of the lease, and to the fact that it will expire on 17 October 2020'.

This is a problematic area in commercial conveyancing. Since the development of the modern commercial leases sector in the 1960s, it has been the norm to transfer repairing obligations from the landlord to the tenant. That can lead to arbitrary results, the most obvious case being, as here, where major repairs are needed soon before the end of a lease. That aspect was held relevant in one first-instance English case, *Scottish Mutual Assurance plc v Jardine Public Relations Ltd* [1999] EG 43. The Lord Ordinary left the issues open and allowed proof before answer.

(42) Arbitration Appeal No 2 of 2019
[2020] CSOH 51, 2020 GWD 20-270

This case (in which the parties and the property were not identified) concerned a rent review. The lease was for 25 years, running from 2006, and there was a review date in 2016 which was to set the rent for the remaining 10 years of the lease. The parties were at odds as to the way that the definition of 'open market rent' in the rent review clause fell to be interpreted, especially the words in brackets:

> Open Market Rent means the annual rent (at the rate following the expiry of such rent free period of occupation as would normally be granted in the market at the time for fitting-out or similar purposes) for which the Premises if vacant might reasonably be expected to be let, without fine or premium, as one entity by a willing landlord to a willing tenant on the open market at and from the Review Date in question for a period of 10 years on the same terms in all respects as those in this Lease.

The parties went to arbitration. The arbitrator's decision was, claimed the tenant, in need of clarification. Under rule 58 of the Scottish Arbitration Rules (see Arbitration (Scotland) Act 2010 sch 1) a request for clarification must be made within 28 days, unless the court extends that time. Several months after the expiry of the 28-day period the tenant made this application to the court for an extension. The Lord Ordinary (Lord Clark) refused the application. His judgment contains valuable discussion of rent review clauses.

(43) Arbitration Appeal No 4 of 2019
[2020] CSOH 46, 2020 GWD 18-253

This case (in which the parties and the properties were not identified) concerned a purchase option as between tenant and landlord, relating to a group of properties. The option did not state a price, but provided that:

> 'The Price' shall be and mean such amount as the Landlord and the Tenant shall agree as representing, or failing such agreement shall be determined by an expert as hereinafter provided, the price which would be likely to be paid by a willing purchaser to a willing vendor in the open market at the Option Date for the Premises as a whole with vacant possession.

Though this was not a rent review clause the issues were similar. One must – perhaps in a trance-like state with pharmacological assistance – enter a hypothetical universe and decide what would happen there, that universe being specified not by the genius of a great creative writer but by a few lines of crabbed and oddly-punctuated legalese. Pausing here just for a moment, we offer our readers a Prize the Amount to be determined by Professors Reid and Gretton always acting Reasonably and without Deduction or Retention which failing to be determined by Arbitration for what the expression 'shall be and mean' is or means whether hypothetically or, *et separatim*, actually as the case may be, unconditionally disregarding always non-business days, other than where inapplicable under Clause 923(b)(Z)(i) (insofar as applied by Appendix VII(2)), and where not otherwise hypothetically implied *mutatis mutandis*.

The issue in the case was whether the fact that the tenant itself would have been in the market looking for properties in that precise locality was relevant. The arbitrator took the view that the tenant 'as a hypothetical bidder forms part of the hypothetical market' (para 28). The tenant appealed against that decision. The Lord Ordinary (Lord Clark) refused the appeal. His judgment contains a valuable review of the authorities.

(44) Fern Trustee 1 Ltd v Scott Wilson Railways Ltd
[2020] SC GLA 45, 2021 SLT (Sh Ct) 7

The pursuers (together with Fern Trustee 2 Ltd, as joint trustees for Buchanan House Unit Trust) owned an office block at Buchanan House, 58 Port Dundas Road, Glasgow, and the defender held a lease of the sixth floor. The landlords raised this action for payment of rent. The defender denied that rent was payable for the period in question, and, in addition, counterclaimed for the return of certain rental payments that had already been made, on the basis of unjustified enrichment. The nub of the dispute was that extensive renovation works had taken place and had (averred the defender) deprived it of the use of the office space. Accordingly, it argued, it was not obliged to pay rent for the period of deprivation. The pursuers argued that there was no right to abate, one reason being that the terms of the lease allegedly excluded abatement. Various other attacks on the defender's pleadings were made. The case went to debate, and the right to abate was in principle upheld. The case now goes to proof, on both parts of the case, ie both the principal action and the counterclaim. See **Commentary** p 150.

(45) 3639 Ltd v Renfrewshire Council
[2020] CSOH 86, 2020 SLT 1271

The defender was the owner of a shopping centre developed in the 1970s. The whole centre was subject to a 125-year lease, the current tenant being the pursuer. There were various sub-tenancies and sub-sub-tenancies. In particular the supermarket in the shopping centre was subject to a sub-lease running for 63 years, the ish being in 2037, at an annual rental of £268,000. (As far as we can see, this sub-lease was not subject to rent review.) In 2016 the supermarket unit was sub-sub-let to RAMH Ltd, a mental health charity, for an annual rent of £1. In 2019 the pursuer and the supermarket company agreed that the sub-lease held by the latter would be renounced, with the pursuer being paid a premium of £4,250,000.

The head lease provided that 16% of the rental income received by the head tenant (described in the lease as 'rack rental income') would be paid over to the owner (ie head landlord). 'The practical effect of the renunciation … was that instead of receiving 16% of an annual rent from the Co-op of £268,000 for the remaining 18 years of the Co-op sub-lease, the defender would receive 16% of an annual rent from the charity of £1' (para 11). The owner (head landlord) sought declarator that 16% of the part of the premium which represented capitalisation of the annual rent should be paid to the owner. The head tenant, by contrast, argued that it was entitled to keep the whole premium. The Lord Ordinary, Lord Ericht, agreed with the owner, saying at para 59:

> The common intention of the parties to the Head Lease is that the defender as landlord shares in the proceeds of the development of the shopping centre by receiving a percentage of the proceeds. The definition of 'rack rental income' must be read in the light of that common intention. The pursuer's construction would defeat that intention. It would permit the pursuer to keep all of the premium, notwithstanding that part of that premium represents future proceeds in which the defender would otherwise be entitled to participate. It would permit the pursuer to strip out a future income stream as capital. It cannot have been in the contemplation of the parties to the Head Lease that their common intention to share in the proceeds could be easily frustrated by the taking of the proceeds in a lump sum rather than periodical payments. In my opinion the reference to 'rents' in the definition of 'rack rental income' includes the element of the surrender premium which is attributable to rents which would have been payable had the renunciation not taken place.

(46) Peninsula Securities Ltd v Dunnes Stores (Bangor) Ltd
[2020] UKSC 36, [2020] 3 WLR 521

This Supreme Court case from Northern Ireland would seem to be equally relevant to Scotland. In 1980–81 a new shopping centre was built in Derry/

Londonderry. The Anchor tenant was Dunnes Stores (Bangor) Ltd, taking a 999-year lease, and, as is so common in such cases, the owner agreed to a covenant to the effect that no competing unit would be allowed in the centre. The current landlord, Peninsula Securities Ltd, a successor to the original owner, wished to be free of the covenant, and raised an action in the High Court of Northern Ireland for declaration (ie declarator in our terms) that the covenant was unenforceable because it was an unreasonable restraint of trade. The Supreme Court held that the 'restraint of trade' doctrine does not apply in such cases and accordingly found in favour of the defendant. This was because this was a standard covenant in circumstances such as this, and so was accepted as part of the structure of a trading society.

(47) Baral v Arif
2020 Hous LR 11, First-tier Tribunal

Eviction without a court order (technically called ejection *brevi manu*) is, in most types of case, unlawful: see *Conveyancing 2019* pp 135–41. Unlawful eviction will normally give rise to a damages claim at common law. In the case of residential tenancies there is an alternative statutory regime in ss 36 and 37 of the Housing (Scotland) Act 1988. The details are complex, but a key provision is s 37(1) which says:

> The basis for the assessment of damages … is the difference in value … between –
> (a) the value of the landlord's interest determined on the assumption that the residential occupier continues to have the same right to occupy the premises as before that time; and
> (b) the value of the landlord's interest determined on the assumption that the residential occupier has ceased to have that right.

This statutory damages claim is without prejudice to any claim at common law: see s 36(4) and (5). Damages based on the common law would be, as usual with damages, based on the loss to the pursuer, ie tenant, whereas the statutory claim is based on the gain to the defender, ie landlord. (The Legal Service Agency has recommended changes to these provision: see www.lsa.org.uk/docs/Unlawful%20evictions%20damages%20law%20reform%20briefing%20-%2011%20August%202020.pdf/.)

Which type of claim will be more beneficial to the ex-tenant depends on a variety of facts, one of which is the type of tenancy. For instance, as noted in the present case by the First-tier Tribunal (Adrian Stalker and Frances Wood) at para 9: 'Given the very limited security of tenure available to short assured tenants, the difference between the figures in s 37(1)(a) and (b) is not great, because any person purchasing the property can make arrangements to gain vacant possession, fairly quickly, by raising proceedings under s 33 of the 1988 Act.' In the present case, however, the tenancy was not a short assured tenancy, so the statutory measure of damages was the one more favourable to the ex-tenant.

In the present case the tenant of Flat 0/2, 28 Elizabeth Street, Glasgow, was Dambaru Baral, aged 61 and unemployed. His landlords were Mohammed and

Khalda Arif, whose agent was Zahad Arif. Mr Baral was in rent arrears. While he was out, Zahid Arif entered the property, removed the contents into the close, and changed the locks. The ex-tenant claimed damages, under ss 36 and 37, for unlawful eviction. The landlords asserted (see para 83) that 'Zahid Arif believed, and had reasonable cause to believe, that the applicant had ceased to reside in the property'. But the First-tier Tribunal concluded (para 84) that 'the evidence … did not support that assertion'. The ex-tenant was awarded statutory damages in the sum of £18,000.

(48) Ali v Serco Ltd

This case, concerning the ejection *brevi manu* of failed asylum seekers, was covered last year: [2019] CSOH 34, 2019 SLT 463 affd [2019] CSIH 54, 2020 SC 182 (*Conveyancing 2019* Case (66)). The pursuer sought leave to appeal to the Supreme Court, but leave has been refused: see govanlawcentre.org/2020/04/06/supreme-court-refuse-appeal-ali-v-serco-group-plc/.

(49) Fieldman v City of Edinburgh Council
[2020] SC EDIN 28, 2020 SLT (Sh Ct) 220, 2020 Hous LR 74

The regime for licensing properties in 'multiple occupation' is contained in Part 5 of the Housing (Scotland) Act 2006. An HMO licence normally lasts for three years (s 134), but of course the owner can seek renewal. In this case the pursuer owned numerous properties with HMO licences. For one of them, a property in a tenement at Flat 3F2, 44 Montpelier Park, Edinburgh, she sought renewal, but without success. There had been complaints from other occupants in the tenement about noise and other problems. The Council refused to renew the HMO licence. The owner appealed. The sheriff (Tom Welsh QC) found the reasons for the Council's committee's decision to be unclear and remitted the case back to the committee for a fresh decision. At para 24 he said:

> I want to make it clear to the pursuer that it remains open to the committee to refuse the application for a new HMO licence on the basis of the material before it relating to noise and nuisance complaints about the occupants and or the failure to have the floor coverings down before the application was heard, notwithstanding the fact that such remedial work may have now been done … Whether it does refuse to grant or not is a matter for the committee. I should also make it clear that this decision does not give the pursuer a right to be heard again before the committee. This remittal sends the case back to the committee to reconsider its decision in the light of the judgment. The net result could be a grant or a refusal of the HMO licence without hearing further from the pursuer but that is a matter for the committee to decide, not me.

The judgment contains valuable discussion of the HMO licensing system.

(50) Affleck v Bronsdon (No 2)
[2020] UT 44, 2020 Hous LR 94

A flat, at 95 Forrest Road, Edinburgh, had four tenants, each paying the landlords £350 per month. Each had a bedroom, while the kitchen, bathroom and living-room were shared. One tenant left and, on 1 January 2018, was replaced by Ms Affleck. There was no written lease. She asked for one, but agreement on its terms could not be reached, the chief sticking point being that the landlords wished her to be liable jointly and severally for the rent of the other tenants, which Ms Affleck would not agree to. Litigation began in the First-tier Tribunal, and was appealed to the Upper Tribunal: see [2019] UT 49, 2019 GWD 30-473 (*Conveyancing 2019 Case* (63)). The First-tier Tribunal decided that Ms Affleck did not hold a private residential tenancy under the Private Housing (Tenancies) (Scotland) Act 2016. The Upper Tribunal agreed, but for different reasons. As we noted in last year's volume, s 2 of the 2016 Act was overlooked: this says that a person in Ms Affleck's position can be the holder of a private residential tenancy under the Act.

There was then a further appeal to the Court of Session, which, seemingly without issuing a judgment, quashed the Upper Tribunal's decision, and remitted the case back to the Upper Tribunal. The Upper Tribunal, now considering the case for a second time (but as if for the first), has overturned the decision of the First-tier Tribunal, and held that Ms Affleck was, after all, a tenant under the 2016 Act. Moreover, s 10 of that Act requires landlords to give to tenants the terms of the tenancy in writing, and, if that is not done, allow an award of a discretionary sum to be made against the landlord in favour of the tenant. The landlord here had been in breach of s 10 and the Upper Tribunal awarded to Ms Affleck two months' rent, ie £700.

STANDARD SECURITIES

(51) Lindsay's Exr v Outlook Finance Ltd
[2020] CSOH 90, 2020 GWD 37-476

The battle between these parties has been going on for some years: for an earlier stage, see *Outlook Finance Ltd v Lindsay's Exr* 2016 Hous LR 75 (see *Conveyancing 2016* Cases (52) and (69)). In this latest phase William Lindsay, as executor of his father Euan McIntyre Lindsay, sought reduction of two loan agreements entered into by his father, and reduction of a standard security over Harperfield Farm, Sandilands, Lanarkshire. He also sought a declarator relative to a property near Gretna, but on the English side of the border. The basis of the pursuer's case was a claim that the agreements and securities had been obtained through facility, circumvention and lesion. The factual background is not known to us. The defender challenged the relevancy of the pursuer's averments, but the Lord Ordinary (Lady Wolffe) held the pursuer's averments to be relevant and ordered a proof.

(52) Skye Loans Ltd v McEwan
2020 Hous LR 39, Sh Ct

This was an action to enforce a standard security over residential property at 7 Barlanark Drive, Glasgow. The debtors did not deny that they were in default. Their defence to the action was that the creditor had not correctly complied with the statutory pre-action requirements.

The Applications by Creditors (Pre-Action Requirements) (Scotland) Order 2010, SSI 2010/317, art 2(4) says that 'the information required to be provided to the debtor ... must be provided as soon as is reasonably practicable upon the debtor entering into default'. In this case the creditor sent the debtors the required information shortly after the expiry of the calling-up notice, but instead of giving detail about charges the letter referred to a previous letter sent a few weeks earlier, which had set out the charges in full. The defenders argued that the creditor should have sent full detail of the charges a second time, ie after the expiry of the calling-up period. The sheriff (Iain M Fleming) disagreed, holding that the reference to the previous letter was sufficient compliance: 'The pre-action requirement requires the provision of information. In my view that requirement is not breached if the defenders are directed to a source of information which had been previously provided rather than being physically given documentation with all of the information after the default' (para 23).

The word 'default' in the legislation has different meanings according to context. In this case it seems to have been taken for granted that default in this particular context meant the expiry of the calling-up notice.

These technical defences against enforcement of standard securities, even when successful (unlike here), are of limited value, because the debt still exists and the security still exists. When the defence succeeds, the debtor gains some time, but nothing more, and time may not even be helpful – sometimes even the reverse, with the debtor merely sinking deeper into the financial bog.

FAMILY PROPERTY

(53) Pert v McCaffrey
[2020] CSIH 5, 2020 SC 259, 2020 SLT 225, 2020 Fam LR 28

If cohabitants break up, s 28 of the Family Law (Scotland) Act 2006 allows one party to claim compensation from the other, according to certain criteria set out in the section. Any action to enforce such a claim has to be raised within the period of 12 months of the separation. Prior to the 2006 Act cohabitants sometimes made claims based on the common law of unjustified enrichment, the breakthrough decision here being *Shilliday v Smith* 1998 SC 725. Does the existence of a statutory claim mean that an enrichment claim is no longer possible? In *Courtney's Exrs v Campbell* [2016] CSOH 136, 2017 SCLR 387 it was held that that is indeed the case. So: miss the deadline under s 28, and that is the end. By contrast, prior to the 2006 Act, enrichment claims had no deadline, apart, of course, from the general law of negative prescription. In the present case *Courtney's Exrs* was challenged, and overruled. See **Commentary** p 184.

(54) Brenchley v Whyte
[2020] SC FOR 08, 2020 GWD 5-74

Joan Brenchley and Douglas Whyte were in a relationship and in 1999 they had a child. The relationship broke down about 10 years later, following which Mr

Whyte bought a house in Montrose for his former cohabitant and their child to occupy. Some years later Ms Brenchley claimed that Mr Whyte had agreed to transfer the property to her, without payment. She raised the present action to compel him to dispone to her.

There was nothing in writing. Naturally, Ms Brenchley argued that 'statutory personal bar' was applicable, so as to get round the problem of absence of writing, but that was merely her backstop argument. Her first argument was that the alleged agreement to dispone did not need to be in writing anyway, and she cited *McFarlane v McFarlane* [2007] CSOH 75 and *DWS v RMS* [2016] SC GRE 47, 2016 GWD 22-402 to support that position. Sheriff S G Collins QC rejected those authorities. He allowed proof on the question of whether the facts of the case met the requirements of statutory personal bar. See **Commentary** p 200.

(55) Malak v Inglis
[2019] SC HAM 100, 2020 Fam LR 47

Wissam Malak and Dawn Inglis were married, and they co-owned, in equal shares, the matrimonial home in Ladywell Road, Motherwell, Lanarkshire. In 2016 they separated. Ms Inglis remained living in the matrimonial home. Mr Malak moved to London. In 2019 they were divorced. (In Wales. Why Wales? We do not know.) No financial claims were made in the divorce action. Thereafter Mr Malak raised the present action for division and sale of the house in Motherwell.

That he was entitled to insist on sale was not disputed: the point at issue was whether the division of the net proceeds should be equal or not. Mr Malak asserted that it should be equal. Ms Inglis asserted that, despite the equal title, 100% of the net proceeds of sale should be paid to her. Her argument was that Mr Malak had contributed nothing to the purchase of the property. The property had been bought from her father at a price of £75,000 when it was worth £190,000, so that her father had contributed £115,000 as a gift, which, she claimed, was a gift to her alone. She had, she said, also paid the mortgage.

Mr Malak argued (see para 4) that 'since the defender failed to resolve any financial claims by seeking a remedy in the divorce proceedings, she is now barred from relying upon unjustified enrichment'.

The sheriff (Daniel Kelly), allowed the case to proceed to proof. See **Commentary** p 182.

(56) Peberdy v Peberdy
2020 SC GLA 4, 2020 Fam LR 59

The parties married in 2006 and parted in 2012. There were no children. They co-owned a house, and when they parted Mrs Peberdy continued to live in it while Mr Peberdy continued to pay the mortgage, which he did until two years after their separation. When he stopped paying, the bank began enforcement proceedings, and at that point Mrs Peberdy began to pay. At about the same time Mr Peberdy raised an action for divorce. They both executed an agreement whereby the house would be sold, and the proceeds divided equally (after deduction of expenses, the secured loan, council tax arrears, and utilities arrears). Mrs Peberdy then decided not to co-operate in the sale. The court ordered sale in terms of the agreement and appointed a selling agent. When the non-co-operation continued the agent withdrew from acting. The court appointed a new selling agent, at which point Mrs Peberdy began to co-operate, and the property was marketed, and missives concluded. She then decided she would remain in the property and the sale fell through. (Whether the buyer sought damages is not known.)

In the present phase of the divorce action Mr Peberdy sought orders, under the Family Law (Scotland) Act 1985, for implement of the agreement, including re-marketing of the property and removal of his wife from the property. It is to be noted that he sought these orders in the context of the divorce action, not by way of an action for division and sale.

The sheriff (Aisha Y Anwar) held in his favour, and the legal interest in the case consists in the sheriff's interpretation of the scope of orders that can be made under the 1985 Act. The whole facts and circumstances of the case – which can be appreciated only from the full judgment itself – will also be of interest to those concerned with property transactions. Expenses were awarded against Mrs Peberdy, which, given the long history of her resistance to implementing the agreement, would, one suspects, be significant.

(57) Campbell's Exx v Campbell's Exrs
[2020] CSIH 4, 2020 SCLR 394

This is possibly the strangest case of 2020. As was said at para 5 of the opinion of the Inner House, given by the Lord President, Lord Carloway, 'the pursuer's pleadings are of extreme length ... Her averments are, in substantial part, repetitive, irrelevant, discursive, argumentative and occasionally contradictory'.

Mrs Campbell died in 2016. She and her husband, who survived her, had two daughters and a son. Daughter X was her executor. She raised the present action against her father about the matrimonial home. In 2018 he followed his wife to the grave, and his executors, Y and Z, who were the son and the other daughter, were sisted as the defenders, in place of the late father. Thus the action, begun as a battle between daughter and father, became a battle between siblings.

Mr Campbell had bought the matrimonial home, in Carnoustie, in 1981, from a Ms McLean. The title was in his sole name. Therefore when Mrs Campbell died in 2016, she was not a co-owner, and when he died two years later the whole property was part of his estate.

Mrs Campbell, and thereafter her executor, took the view that when the property had been acquired it ought to have been acquired in joint names. But finding any legal clothing for that 'ought to have been' was the problem. In the pleadings, the conclusions were the following (see para 2):

> The conclusions are, first, for a declarator that the disposition of the subjects by Annie McLean to Mr Campbell is 'void' (there is no conclusion for reduction). Secondly, and in the alternative, the pursuer seeks 'to ordain' the defenders to convey the subjects to the pursuer's daughter [ie the granddaughter of the deceased Mrs Campbell].

Thirdly, as an alternative to both the first and second conclusions, the pursuer seeks payment from the defenders of £200,000; that sum representing one-half of the value of the subjects.

This is all obviously odd, but we will begin with just two exegetical comments. The first is that the second conclusion should, one suspects, have been that the defenders were to convey not the whole subjects, but a one-half share of the subjects. The second comment is: in the third conclusion, to whom was payment sought? One guesses that it was to the pursuer's daughter, for only that would fit in with the second conclusion.

Why the pursuer's daughter anyway? The basis may have been that 'Mrs Campbell had told the pursuer that she had left her estate equally between the pursuer and her (the pursuer's) daughter' (para 15). The relevance of this is, however, hard to discern. Did Mrs Campbell bequeath her estate to them? Or did she not? What Mrs Campbell may have 'told the pursuer' is surely neither here nor there. And since the pursuer was Mrs Campbell's executrix, she must have known perfectly well what Mrs Campbell's will said. In any event, if she did bequeath her estate equally to them, then the logic would be that the granddaughter would receive one half, not all, of the half share of the house that the pursuer was claiming.

Now back to the real substance of the dispute. Clearly there had been something unusual about the conveyancing when the property was bought. The standard security had been granted not by Mr Campbell on his own, but by both Mr and Mrs Campbell. When that deed was drafted and executed, therefore, the expectations of those involved were, seemingly, that the spouses were to be co-owners. What was going on? We suspect that what was going on was muddle. What did the missives say? They were not produced to the court, and quite possibly no longer existed, but no attempt was made to claim that Mrs Campbell was a party to the missives. In other words it was accepted that in disponing to Mr Campbell alone Ms McLean was simply doing what the missives said (cf para 39). The transaction settled in December 1981, but the disposition was not recorded until 1983. This delay of more than a year was, however, not discussed in the case, and whether it was linked to the muddle is impossible to say.

In 1984 there was some discussion about putting the title into joint names, but that was not done, seemingly on the basis of expense (see para 8). It was supposed that not only would there be the expense of the transfer but also the expense of a new standard security. That, however, is a puzzle: the existing standard security would have remained good.

The pursuer's claim that Mrs Campbell had thought that she was co-owner, and had not realised the contrary until shortly before her death, seems by no means impossible. But, as already indicated, the problem was to convert that belief (if there was such a belief) into a legally valid claim, and in that she failed, both in the Outer House and (unanimously) in the Inner House.

The first conclusion, that the disposition to Mr Campbell was void, was unstateable, and at the Inner House hearing was abandoned. If sound, it would have been of no benefit to the pursuer anyway, because it would have meant that Ms McLean was undivested owner, and the pursuer or her daughter would have been no further forward – indeed less so. As the Inner House observed, the claim was incompetent anyway since Ms McLean had not been convened in the action (see paras 32 and 39). In this connection it should be noted that, if the disposition was void, Ms McLean would now be liable for repayment of the price, plus interest since 1981. In any event (though this point is not made by the court) the very furthest that the pursuer's case could conceivably have gone would have been that the disposition would have been voidable.

The second and third conclusions were for conveyance of a half share in the house to the pursuer's daughter, which failing payment to her of the value of the half share. As was observed by the court, this conclusion was clearly incompetent in an action to which the pursuer's daughter was not a party. In any event the case was lacking in specification as to whether it was based on 'agreement' or 'enrichment' (see eg paras 41 and 42). Finally, even if the pursuer had had any claim, it would have been cut off by negative prescription (para 44).

Being decided on relevancy and specification, the case never went to proof. Accordingly, some of the factual background is murky. Indeed, since the conveyancing happened nearly 40 years ago, and given that the two central figures are both deceased, it may be that a proof would have run into serious evidential difficulties. The question of whether any criticism could be made of the solicitor who acted was not explored.

Something should be said about the loss that the pursuer said her mother had suffered. It is rather elusive. For countless marriages, the location of title does not much matter. Mr and Mrs Campbell lived in the Carnoustie property from 1981 until the 58-year marriage ended through her death in 2016. In practical terms, how was she worse off than if title had been in joint names? Would she have been in reality better off if title had been in her sole name? In substance any 'loss' (though no loss could in fact be established) was suffered not by her but by the side of the family that inherited from her.

In this connection, a self-destructive aspect of the pursuer's case was that 'she had believed that the title was in joint names *and their survivor*' (para 10). Had that been the case, the whole property would, on her death, which was the first death, have vested in her husband anyway.

So (i) no loss could be established; (ii) had there been loss, it was more nominal than real, except for other family members; and (iii) even if there had been any loss, the fact that Mrs Campbell predeceased her husband would have extinguished that loss, because, as she pled, the title should have been in joint names with a survivorship destination.

In many legal systems, property acquired by either spouse is (subject to various ifs and buts) considered to be co-owned, regardless of what the property registration system may say (though subject always to rules protecting third parties transacting *in bona fide*). If Scotland had such a system of matrimonial property law, Mrs Campbell would have had a half share of the property. Whatever view may be taken as to what the policy should be for spousal property, Scots law does not go down the 'community property' road. As s 24 of the Family Law (Scotland) Act 1985 says, 'subject to the provisions of any enactment ...

marriage … shall not of itself affect the respective rights of the parties to the marriage … in relation to their property'. See **Commentary** p 179.

SOLICITORS

(58) Ford v W & A S Bruce
[2020] SC KIR 9, 2020 Rep LR 56

Mr Ford was the sole owner of a house. He became engaged, and in 2000 he gratuitously disponed a half share in the house to his fiancée, soon to be his wife. In 2013 his wife died. Her will bequeathed her half share in liferent to Mr Ford and in fee to her children from a previous relationship. Mr Ford was unhappy. He sued the law firm that had done the original conveyancing for having failed to discuss with him the possibility of having a special destination. The substantive issues were never determined because the defenders' plea of prescription was upheld. See **Commentary** p 147.

(59) Soofi v Dykes
[2020] CSIH 10, 2020 GWD 10-152

In 2008 a company called Bonafied Enterprises International Ltd ('BEI') bought a petrol station (with car wash and shop) in Alexander Street, Airdrie, Lanarkshire, the seller being a Ms Young. The price was £450,000 for the heritable property, £385,000 for the goodwill, and £15,000 for fixtures and fittings. The business did not do as well as the buyer had hoped. BEI went into administration in 2010 and was later dissolved. In the present action the pursuer, as assignee of BEI, claimed damages for professional negligence against the solicitor who had acted in the purchase.

The case has had two stages. The first was about whether the pursuer's case had been relevantly pled. It was held, both in the Outer House and thereafter in the Inner House, that it had been: [2017] CSOH 2, 2017 GWD 2-14 affd [2017] CSIH 40, 2017 GWD 21-332 (*Conveyancing 2017* Case (61)). The second stage has been a proof. Like the first stage, it has been fought in both the Outer House and the Inner House. The Outer House case was covered in last year's volume: [2019] CSOH 59, 2019 GWD 27-442 (*Conveyancing 2019* Case (74)). The pursuers then reclaimed. In the first stage there was a single pursuer, Sajjad Soofi. In the second stage there were two, Sajjad Soofi and Rumella Soofi. We do not know the reason for the change. It may be added that in the first stage the pursuer was legally represented, but in the second stage the pursuers were party litigants. It seems that the first pursuer was the director and main shareholder of BEI (see para 1).

The Inner House adhered to the decision of the Lord Ordinary: since an appellate court will not normally overturn findings in fact made by the lower court, questions of evidence being essentially a matter for the trial court, the failure of the present appeal is unsurprising.

The Outer House decision is of interest to conveyancers in that there was close scrutiny of the duties of a solicitor acting in the purchase of retail property.

(60) Grondona v Stoffel & Co
[2020] UKSC 42, [2020] 3 WLR 1156

This is a decision of the Supreme Court in an English appeal. Maria Grondona bought a leasehold of a property at 73b Beulah Road, Thornton Heath, Surrey, from Cephas Mitchell. She borrowed most of the price from a lender. A law firm, Stoffel & Co, acted for all three parties. The firm failed to carry out a discharge of Mitchell's existing mortgage. It failed to register the Mitchell/ Grondona transfer. It also failed to register the new mortgage for the loan that Ms Grondona obtained. When Mr Mitchell became insolvent, and later died, Ms Grondona claimed damages from the firm. It was not disputed that the firm's failures were negligent.

There was, however, a twist. It emerged that the Mitchell/Grondona transaction was not what it seemed. The underlying, secret, deal had been that Ms Grondona would hold the property as Mr Mitchell's nominee and that the proceeds of her mortgage would be given to him, on the footing that he would pick up all expenses, that is to say, the expenses of servicing her mortgage, the cost of redeeming it and all the costs relating to the property itself. The reason for this rigmarole was that his credit rating was poor, whereas hers was good, so that she could borrow on terms not available to him. She was to receive a sweetener for lending him her name. The true nature of the transaction was concealed from the lender. The present case concerned the particular property mentioned above, but in fact several other properties were also involved in the Mitchell/Grondona shenanigans.

The law firm, while not denying negligence, argued that *ex turpi causa non oritur actio* and accordingly the claim fell to be rejected. Her fraudulent conduct, it argued, barred Ms Grondona from claiming damages. In the terminology of English law, they asserted the 'illegality defence'. This defence failed at first instance, and also in the Court of Appeal. The case has now failed in the Supreme Court, which again upheld the first-instance decision.

In *Patel v Mirza* [2016] UKSC 42, [2017] AC 467 (a case not involving property, but insider dealing) the Supreme Court had set out a new approach, very much policy-based, to the illegality defence, and the present case accepted *Patel* and applied it to very different facts. To what extent these recent developments in England may influence the law in Scotland remains to be seen.

(61) Law Society of Scotland v Bowie
4 October 2019, Scottish Solicitors Discipline Tribunal

Edwin McLaren (also known as David Johnston) and his wife Lorraine McLaren are convicted property fraudsters. (Their trial, which ended in 2017, has been described as the longest criminal trial in UK history: see eg www.theguardian.com/uk-news/2017/jun/13/couple-jailed-for-16m-after-preying-on-vulnerable-people/.) The present case involved Mr McLaren in some way, though precisely how is unclear, and we do not know whether it involved one of the transactions in respect of which he was prosecuted.

Mr McLaren had contacted Mr Bowie, the respondent, telling him that Ms X wished to sell her house, and requesting the respondent to act for Ms X. Thus began a transaction whose ending was that the respondent was struck off the roll of solicitors.

As we say, many of the details are unclear, but it seems that Mr McLaren had told Ms X, who, it seems, was in financial difficulties, that he (or perhaps an associate or nominee) would buy her house, at below market value, and would pay off the mortgage and other debts, and that she would be able to continue living there. (A deal of this sort can, of course be *bona fide*, being a type of so-called 'equity release'.)

The findings of the Discipline Tribunal, which led to its decision, were as follows. (i) The respondent began the conveyancing transaction without instructions from Ms X. (ii) He failed to discuss with her the terms of the missives, or on what basis she could remain in the property following the sale (the missives provided for vacant possession). Nor did he discuss with her the oddity that the buyer was, in the course of the transaction, represented by three different law firms. And (iii) an affidavit by Ms X (as to solvency) which the respondent notarised had not in fact been sworn by her.

JUDICIAL RECTIFICATION

(62) PHG Developments Scot Ltd (in liquidation) v Lothian Amusements Ltd
[2020] CSOH 58, 2020 SLT 988

This was a petition under s 8 of the Law Reform (Miscellaneous Provisions) (Scotland) Act 1985 for the rectification of a deed of conditions in relation to a block of 55 flats on the waterfront at Edinburgh's Portobello. The developer (and petitioner in this application) was PHG Developments Scot Ltd ('PHG') The deed of conditions had been granted by PHG and registered in the Land Register in 2015 under title number MID51821. In the usual way the deed was then incorporated, both for pertinents and for burdens, in the split-off dispositions of each of the 55 flats. So far as pertinents were concerned, each disposition conveyed the flat in question together with 'the whole rights, common, mutual and exclusive (if any) and others more particularly described in the Deed of Conditions aftermentioned'.

Among the pertinents in the deed of conditions was a right to park in the basement car-park. Although there were only 55 flats, the car-park had 73 spaces. The additional 18 spaces had been intended for an adjacent development to be carried out by a different developer, Lothian Amusements Ltd ('LEL'), and missives had been entered into with LEL for the sale of the spaces. In the event, that development did not proceed. In a subsequent action for damages by LEL for breach of the missives, it was held that PHG's deed of conditions had granted to each of the 55 flats in the main development a servitude of parking over the entire car-park (ie including the additional 18 spaces) and that, furthermore, the wall through which access would have been taken to the adjacent development was, under the deed of conditions, the common property of the 55 flat-owners. See *Lothian Amusements Ltd v The Kiln's Development Ltd* [2019] CSOH 51, 2019 GWD 23-354 (*Conveyancing 2019* pp 12–13). The upshot was that the missives with LEL could no longer be implemented, leaving the seller in breach.

The purpose of the present petition was to put PHG in a position to implement the missives to LEL. To that end PHG sought rectification of the deed of conditions to the effect of (i) removing the 18 car-parking spaces from the servitude of parking, and (ii) excluding the access wall from the development common parts. The application was made under para (b) of s 8(1) of the 1985 Act and not, as is usually the case, under para (a). A preliminary issue concerned the difference between the two. Section 8(1) of the 1985 Act provides that:

> Subject to section 9 of this Act, where the court is satisfied, on an application made to it, that –
>
> (a) a document intended to express or to give effect to an agreement fails to express accurately the common intention of the parties to the agreement at the date when it was made; or
>
> (b) a document intended to create, transfer, vary or renounce a right, not being a document falling within paragraph (a) above, fails to express accurately the intention of the grantor of the document at the date when it was executed,
>
> it may order the document to be rectified in any manner that it may specify in order to give effect to that intention.

Paragraph (b) can only apply where para (a) does not. But when it does apply it carries the advantage, from the petitioner's point of view, that only the intention of the grantor of the deed is at issue and not, as with para (a), the intention of both parties. In this case the application was brought, correctly, under para (b). The Lord Ordinary (Lord Tyre) explained the difference between the paragraphs in this way (para 28):

> Section 8(1)(b) of the 1985 Act differs from s 8(1)(a) in that it is concerned with the unilateral intention of the grantor of a document, whereas s 8(1)(a) is concerned with documents which either express an agreement or give effect to an agreement already reached between two or more persons. As Gretton and Reid point out (*Conveyancing* (5th edn, 2018), at para 21-05), it is now accepted that the boundary between deeds falling within subpara (a) on the one hand and subpara (b) on the other is not delineated by whether the deed is unilateral in form: as the authors note, most conveyancing deeds are unilateral in form. The relevant distinction is whether or not the deed gives effect to an earlier agreement; if so, it will fall within subpara (a).

'A deed of conditions', Lord Tyre continued, 'may, depending upon the circumstances, fall into either category.' In the present case there was no prior agreement to which the deed of conditions was giving effect. Hence the application was properly brought under para (b).

The main issue was different, and difficult. Rectifying the deed of conditions would be of no help to PHG unless the 55 split-off dispositions were also altered (to use a neutral term). And the obvious way to achieve such alteration was to seek rectification of the dispositions as well. This is allowed under s 8(3):

where one deed is rectified, it is possible to procure the rectification of other deeds which are 'defectively expressed by reason of the defect in the original document'. So for example where a disposition is rectified and the disponee had gone on to grant a standard security, the standard security too can be rectified under s 8(3). But there was a problem for PHG with using s 8(3): s 8(3A) provides that a document which is registered in the Land Register in favour of a person acting in good faith cannot be rectified under s 8(3) unless the person consents. So, if s 8(3) was to be used, it would be necessary to obtain the consent of each of the 55 disponees to a rectification that would deprive them of common property as well as restrict their servitude of parking. It was improbable that such consent would be forthcoming. As it happened, none of the 55 had chosen to oppose the current application but, as Lord Tyre made clear (at para 34), this failure to oppose could not be taken as consent for the purposes of s 8(3A).

If, therefore, the dispositions could not, as a practical matter, be rectified under s 8(3), how then were they to be altered? The argument advanced by PHG was this. (i) Rectification of the deed of conditions, if allowed, was retrospective in effect: s 8(4) (except in relation to its 'real effect' as to which see s 8A). (ii) The 55 dispositions incorporated the pertinents set out in the deed of conditions. (iii) If the pertinents in the deed of conditions were changed by rectification, then the same change would occur, automatically, to the pertinents in the 55 dispositions. (iv) Hence, on registration of the order for rectification in terms of s 8A, the 55 disponees would lose their common property in the wall and also have their parking servitude restricted.

This argument was accepted by the court and a proof before answer allowed on the question of whether, in the respects averred, the deed of conditions failed to reflect PHG's intentions. In Lord Tyre's words (paras 33 and 34):

> Nor, in my opinion, is there any need for PHG to seek an order for rectification of the dispositions in favour of the apartment owners. If an order is granted for rectification of the deed of conditions, the deed will have effect as if it had always been in its rectified terms. The references to the deed of conditions in the dispositions would therefore be deemed retrospectively to be to the deed in its rectified terms. There is nothing in the terms of the dispositions which would require consequential amendment. It is, of course, the case that in terms of s 8A an order for rectification would not have real effect unless and until registered in the Land Register, and that it would therefore be necessary, as the letter from the Scottish Government Legal Directorate pointed out, for an application to be made to register any court order against all of the apartment owners' title sheets. But that is all that would be required in order to give (prospective) real effect to the rectification of the deed. For these reasons an order for rectification could in my opinion be pronounced without the consent of the apartment owners.

The argument which prevailed has a certain logical force. It can also be justified by reference to the statutory provisions (though other readings are also possible). But can it be right as a matter of legal policy? If PHG had used s 8(3), the 55 disponees could have blocked the rectification and hence preserved their rights. If, instead, PHG had made a direct application to rectify the dispositions – an application which would have fallen under para (a) of s 8(1) – the disponees would have had the opportunity to argue that there was no discrepancy between the dispositions and their missives with PHG to which the dispositions gave effect, and hence no basis for rectification. It is true, as Lord Tyre pointed out, that even as matters now stood the disponees were entitled to be heard (para 31):

> The protections afforded by the 1985 Act to the grantee, in addition to the onus incumbent on the applicant, are (a) the right to enter the court process and oppose the application, and (b) the discretion of the court to refuse rectification even if satisfied that the grantor's intention was not accurately expressed.

But any opposition to the application would have to be on PHG's terms, for the main question before the court would be what PHG did or did not intend in drawing up the deed of conditions. In this inquiry the question of what the disponees had agreed to buy from PHG would be irrelevant. The effect of the decision, in other words, is that the disponees could be deprived of their rights even although PHG had bound itself in the missives (if that was the case) to confer those very rights.

If the decision is correct, it suggests that there is a gap in the protective framework provided by the legislation. If the dispositions had been freestanding deeds (like the standard security mentioned earlier), PHG would have been forced to proceed under either s 8(1)(a) or s 8(3). But the dispositions were linked deeds. Some of their content derived from another deed, ie the deed of conditions. And if the deed of conditions is ultimately rectified, following the proof, then, on the basis of this decision, the dispositions too will be altered, and the disponees deprived of rights.

If none of this seems very satisfactory, the question arises as to whether another view could have been reached. Of the possible counter-arguments the following is probably the strongest. (i) The main purpose of a deed of conditions is to save labour. Rather than repeating the same words 55 times in 55 dispositions, the drafter can set the words out once, in the deed of conditions, and then incorporate the relevant parts of the deed by reference in each disposition. (ii) There is thus no difference in principle between (a) a disposition which incorporates clauses from a deed of conditions and (b) one which writes the clauses out in full. The first is just a short-hand version of the second. (iii) Where (a) is used, the deed of conditions is being employed as a static text – as a sort of style bank. The words imported into the dispositions are the words as they were at the time of importation. (iv) Subsequent changes to the deed of conditions are accordingly irrelevant. That is as true of judicial rectification as it would be of a variation of the deed of conditions effected by PHG. (v) Judicial rectification, admittedly, is retrospective; but it is retrospective only for the deed being rectified (ie the deed of conditions) and not for some other deed into which the unrectified words had previously been incorporated. By rectifying one deed you do not alter the others. (vi) Rectification of the deed of conditions, therefore, has no effect on the 55 dispositions.

The decision was upheld by the First Division on 12 February 2021: [2021] CSIH 12, 2021 GWD 7-100 (see next year's volume).

(63) Briggs of Burton plc v Doosan Babcock Ltd
[2020] CSOH 100, 2021 GWD 1-9

On 15 November 2017 A and B entered into heads of agreement in respect of a sublease of premises at Porterfield Road, Renfrew to be granted by A to B. The heads of agreement stipulated that they were 'not intended to form part of any legally binding contract'. Beginning later in the same month, solicitors acting for the parties exchanged drafts of the sublease and of accompanying missives. In principle, these were meant to implement the heads of agreement. However, text prepared by A's solicitors, which ultimately found its way into the sublease, departed from the heads of agreement in two significant respects, one of which was the point at which a break in the sublease could be triggered by B. A's solicitors did not draw express attention to this change; but the change was apparent from the text, and was, at least to some extent, identified by B's solicitors. The negotiations having been completed at the end of March 2018, the sublease, for a period of 24 months, commenced on 4 June.

It was not long before B discovered the changes. In this action B sought rectification of the sublease in order to bring its terms into line with the heads of agreement. B relied on s 8(1)(a) of the Law Reform (Miscellaneous Provisions) (Scotland) Act 1985, which provides that:

> Subject to section 9 of this Act, where the court is satisfied, on an application made to it, that (a) a document intended to express or to give effect to an agreement fails to express accurately the common intention of the parties to the agreement at the date when it was made ... it may order the document to be rectified in any manner that it may specify in order to give effect to that intention.

The sublease, argued B, was intended to express or give effect to the heads of agreement. It failed to do so. Hence rectification should be allowed.

The case turned on how s 8(1)(a) should properly be interpreted. An initial question was the relevant date for the purposes of ascertaining the 'common intention of the parties'. That, said the Lord Ordinary (Lord Tyre) at para 62, 'clearly refers to intention at the time of execution of the document whose rectification is sought' (from which it must follow that the second 'it' in s 8(1)(a) refers to the document which is to be rectified and not the prior agreement which it is intended to express). The question then became: could there be said to be a common intention, when the sublease was executed, that the sublease reflect the terms of the heads of agreement? Only if that could be established would B succeed.

In this connection a distinction fell to be made, said the court, between (i) a document which followed on from an earlier binding agreement and (ii) a document which, as in the present case, did not. In the first case, the common intention of the parties to the document must be taken to be to give effect to what had previously been agreed. Hence rectification was available to the extent that the document strayed from that earlier agreement. In the second case, however, it was open to either or both parties to depart from their previous informal understanding. Lord Tyre explained the difference in this way (para 62):

[I]n the former case the relevant principle is that parties should be required to adhere to their contractual obligations, and accordingly that they should be presumed to intend that the document will reflect the common intention expressed in that contract. In the latter case, however, where the parties have reserved the right to depart from the antecedent agreement, no such assumption should be made, and the starting point is rather that their respective rights should be determined by the contract into which they enter with the intention of being bound by it. That, in my view, is the approach likely to be most productive of certainty.

In the second case there was nothing inherently wrong in taking account of the (subjective) intentions of one of the parties – A in the present case – provided that the change of mind was communicated to the other party. On the contrary, it would be unsatisfactory to make an (objective) attribution of 'a common continuing intention to parties where one of them has, as a matter of undisputed fact, changed his intention during the period since entering into an expressly non-binding agreement' (para 59). That would be to hold 'one of the parties to a contract which he never intended to make and never misled the other party into believing that he intended to make' (para 61). In the present case, A changed its mind in the period between the heads of agreement and the execution of the sublease, and also sufficiently communicated that change to B in the form of proposing the relevant draft terms of the document. In the result, 'there was no continuing common intention' in respect of the matters that were changed. Instead, 'the terms of the formal documents accurately reflected the subjective intention of the defender, communicated to the pursuer, without any intentional or unintentional concealment, by means of the terms of the draft sublease' (para 64). That was fatal to B's application for rectification.

In reaching his decision as to how s 8(1)(a) ought properly to be interpreted, Lord Tyre drew on *Macdonald Estates Ltd v Regenesis (2005) Dunfermline Ltd* [2007] CSOH 123, 2007 SLT 791 and, especially, on *Angus v Bryden* 1992 SLT 884. He also took account of English authority, and in particular of the decision of the Court of Appeal in *FSHC Group Holdings Ltd v GLAS Trust Corporation Ltd* [2019] EWCA Civ 1361, [2020] Ch 365.

This is a case of some importance in the law of judicial rectification. It prevents informal and non-binding understandings from trumping a subsequently negotiated agreement unless that agreement was actually – subjectively – intended by both parties to implement faithfully the previous understanding.

BOUNDARIES AND POSITIVE PRESCRIPTION

(64) McCabe v Patterson
[2020] SC GLA 14, 2020 GWD 11-155

The defenders' property at Gillies Lane, Baillieston, Glasgow ('Property B') was used, and had been used for decades, as a commercial garage. The defenders themselves had acquired the property in 2012, their title being registered under title number LAN211580. The previous owners were, at various times, different members of the Marshall family who had used the property as a depot for their bus company, Marshall Coaches. Currently, Property B was tenanted and occupied by a business called Gearbox and Clutch Xpress.

The pursuers owned, among other property, a narrow strip of land approximately 11.78 feet wide and 248 feet long ('Property A'), their title being registered under title number LAN184963. Property A lay immediately to the east of the Property B. As shown on the Land Register, Properties A and B thus had a common boundary but (naturally) without overlap.

Property A was not used by the pursuers or, it seems, by their predecessors in title. But it was used extensively by the defenders, and had been so used for many years by the Marshalls, their predecessors. In particular: (i) access to Property B was through Property A; (ii) Property A was used for the parking of buses and other vehicles, and for storage; (iii) Property A had been repaired and tarmacked to different extents over the years; and (iv) many years ago, a gate had been installed at the southmost end of Property A; this was now secured by a combination padlock, the number of which the defenders offered to make available to the pursuers.

Why the pursuers should have chosen this moment to assert their ownership of Property A is unclear. But in this action they sought interdict to prevent the defenders using the property for 'parking, storing and depositing vehicles and storage units' and from 'locking or otherwise securing the gates at the southern boundary' of the property. To this the defenders offered two main defences. In the first place, they said, they had acquired ownership of all or part of Property A. In the second place, insofar as they did not own Property A, they had a range of servitudes over it. The argument as to servitudes was discussed at p 9 above; here the concern is only with the argument as to ownership.

The main ground for claiming ownership was positive prescription. There had been ample possession, or so the defenders averred, for much longer than the 10 years needed for prescription. But the position as to title was much more difficult. Until recently, prescription could not run on a Land Register title, except in the unusual case that indemnity had been excluded. The position was changed, with effect from the designated day (8 December 2014), by the Land Registration etc (Scotland) Act 2012, amending the Prescription and Limitation (Scotland) Act 1973. As amended, s 1 of the 1973 Act applies virtually the same rules to the Land Register as apply to the Register of Sasines. The title for prescription is provided by a registered deed – in other words, a foundation writ – and it is the deed which is determinative for the purposes of prescription and not the title sheet. Further details can be found in paras 17.1–17.11 of K G C Reid and G L Gretton, *Land Registration* (2017).

The 10 years of possession must follow and be founded on the registered deed, in the usual way. So the deed must come first, then possession. Hence if first registration took place within the 10-year period, as seems to have happened in respect of the defenders' title, the foundation writ for prescription cannot be the deed inducing first registration but must rather be the first deed outside the 10-year period which was recorded in the Register of Sasines. In the present case, that was a disposition by the trustees for the firm of Marshall's Coaches in favour of three members of the Marshall family, recorded in 2006.

Although the legislation does not say so, it is assumed that prescription is not interrupted by first registration, so that a person (such as the defenders) who holds on a Land Register title can still acquire by prescription on the basis of a deed (the 2006 disposition) which was recorded in the Register of Sasines. That, quite properly, was the view taken by the sheriff (Aisha Y Anwar) in the present case (at para 50).

The new law does not, however, seem to have troubled the defenders. Rather than pleading a case based on the 2006 disposition, they relied mainly on the terms of the defenders' title sheet, as qualified and potentially expanded by the tolerances of scaling. That case failed, as it was bound to, and the averments as to prescription were excluded from probation (paras 62–64). A proof before answer was allowed on other aspects of the case.

In all probability, a case based on the 2006 disposition would not have been easy to make out. The description in that deed was:

> ALL and WHOLE that plot of ground situated at Crosshill, Baillieston in the Parish of Old Monkland and County of Lanark containing One thousand Five hundred and Eleven square yards or thereby Imperial Standard Measure being the subjects described in and delineated on the plan annexed and described as relative to a Feu Disposition by Mrs Agnes Neilson or Nelson or Scott in favour of William Birrell Senior and Henry Birrell dated Ninth December Eighteen hundred and Seventy four and recorded in the Division of the General Register of Sasines applicable for the County of Lanark (Book 145–Folios 27–31) on the Second day of June Eighteen hundred and Seventy five.

The description incorporated from the 1875 feu disposition was a bounding one, with the boundaries being described both in words and by plan. In order for the defenders to succeed, therefore, it would have been necessary for them to show that some or all of Property A, the target property, lay within the boundaries set out in the 1875 deed. As the original deed, and hence the plan, could not be found, the task would have been far from easy. (Before the Conveyancing (Scotland) Act 1924, s 48, deed plans could not appear in the Register of Sasines.) The verbal description of the boundaries, characteristically, was only of limited assistance:

> ALL and WHOLE that plot of ground situated at Crosshill, Baillieston in the Parish of Old Monkland and County of Lanark containing One thousand Five hundred and Eleven square yards or thereby Imperial Standard Measure; Bounded on the North by the property now or formerly of Robert Thomson along which it extends fifty three feet nine inches or thereby measuring along the centre line of a thorn hedge; on the West by the property now or formerly of Robert Ward along which it extends in a straight line Two Hundred and thirty nine feet nine inches or thereby; On the South by the property now or formerly of Mrs John Scott along which it extends Fifty nine feet or thereby measuring along the centre of a thorn hedge and range thereof and along the East by the centre line of a proposed fourteen feet wide street along which it extends Two hundred and fifty feet nine inches or thereby;

In the event, the attempt was not made, and the defence failed insofar as it rested on prescription.

The defenders also made a different argument in respect of ownership. The respective title sheets of pursuers and defenders showed Properties A and B as lying alongside each other with a common boundary. But, taking this to be generally correct, it contained inherent inaccuracy caused by (i) the limitations of scaling (at 1:1250 the relative accuracy was said by the defenders to be +/- 1.1 metres) and (ii) the thickness of the Keeper's red line separating the properties. Given the defenders' possession of all of Property A, their title, so they argued, should be interpreted in such a way that all tolerances operated in their favour. The result, so they claimed, would be to award them a significant part of what was, after all, a very narrow strip. This argument, too, was rejected by the sheriff. No doubt there could be cases where prior Sasine titles can usefully be examined in order to delineate a precise boundary. This had been done before; here the sheriff referred to *North Atlantic Salmon Conservation Organisation v Au Bar Pub Ltd* 2009 GWD 14-222 (*Conveyancing 2009* pp 174–77); *Clydesdale Homes Ltd v Quay* [2009] CSOH 126, 2009 GWD 31-518 (*Conveyancing 2009* p 49); and *Welsh v Keeper of the Registers* 2010 GWD 23-443 (*Conveyancing* 2010 pp 158–59). But the case as averred by the defenders was utterly insufficient for this purpose (para 39):

> In my judgment, if a party is to challenge the Land Register titles, and to claim a better title, it is necessary that he or she specify clearly what the nature of the dispute is, make clear reference to descriptions, physical boundaries (historic or present), measurements or plans of prior titles and set out precisely where it is said that a boundary falls to be drawn (not merely where it is capable of being drawn owing to the extremes of scaling inaccuracies or the width of delineated boundary lines) – the averments must in my judgment, 'stake a claim'. Vague averments regarding the tolerances of scaling or the width of the red line used to delineate the boundary will not suffice. Those tolerances and the apparent ambiguity of the width of the red line may be of no consequences at all, or they may operate to reduce or increase an area of ground by any measure up to the fullest extent of a margin of error.

(65) Ardnamurchan Estates Ltd v Macgregor
[2020] SAC (Civ) 2, 2020 SC (SAC) 1, 2020 SLT (Sh Ct) 49, 2020 SCLR 408

This was a dispute about the ownership of about an acre of ground at Glenborrodale, Acharacle, Ardnamurchan, Argyll. The pursuer raised an action to reduce an *a non domino* disposition, recorded in the Register of Sasines in 1994, by the defenders in favour of themselves, while the defenders counterclaimed for declarator that they had a good title. The defenders also claimed that, failing such declarator, they had a servitude of way over the ground in question. The present phase of the case was about whether the 1994 disposition, being in the 'A-to-A' or 'self-granted' form, can constitute a good foundation writ for the purposes of positive prescription. At first instance the sheriff answered that question in the affirmative: see *Conveyancing 2019* Case (76). The pursuer appealed, and the Sheriff Appeal Court has now reversed the decision appealed against, and followed *Board of Management of Aberdeen College v Youngson* [2005] CSOH 31, 2005 1 SC 335. See **Commentary** p 167.

(66) Finlayson v Munro
[2020] SAC (Civ) 18

This boundary dispute involved three small areas of ground at Contin, Ross-shire. Both sides to the dispute held Sasine titles, and the problem was the familiar one that it was difficult to map the titles with any real precision on to the Ordnance Survey. The sheriff found in favour of the pursuers. The defender appealed, and the Sheriff Appeal Court has partially reversed, rejecting the pursuers' claim to two of the areas but accepting it for the third. As to the first two areas, it was held that the defender's title was capable of being interpreted as including them, and there had been possession of them by him for the prescriptive period. There is extensive citation of the case law, and also of the literature. It remains to add that the dispute between the parties seems to have a considerable history: see *Munro v Finlayson* 2015 SLT (Sh Ct) 123 (*Conveyancing 2015* Case (82)).

COMMON GOOD

(67) Guild v Angus Council
[2020] CSIH 50, 2020 SLT 939, 2020 SCLR 685

On part of Forfar Country Park is a leisure centre, the Lochside Leisure Centre, now disused. Angus Council decided to demolish it and restore the site to parkland. Two Forfar residents raised the present action for reduction of that decision and for interdict against demolition. Their case was that 'disposal' and 'change of use' of common good property both require a consultation process (see s 104 of the Community Empowerment (Scotland) Act 2015), and that Angus Council had not conducted such a process.

At first instance the Lord Ordinary (Lady Carmichael) held that demolition would be neither a disposal nor a change of use. It would not be a disposal because no rights were being granted to anyone else: the site was not being disponed or leased. And it would not be a change of use because its use for leisure purposes would continue, albeit in a different form. In addition she held (para 45) that 'the common good property in this case was the land, and not the building' so that what was to be demolished was not itself common good property. Accordingly the petition failed. The petitioners reclaimed. The Inner House, by a majority (the Lord President and Lord Menzies, with Lord Malcolm dissenting) reversed the Lord Ordinary's decision on both points, holding both (i) that the building as well as the ground was common good property, and (ii) that the demolition would amount to both a 'disposal' and a 'change of use'. Hence s 104 was engaged. See **Commentary** p 195.

HIGH HEDGES

(68) Rizza v Scottish Ministers
[2020] CSOH 22, 2020 SLT 388

This appears to be the first reported case on the High Hedges (Scotland) Act 2013. It concerns rather a fundamental question. The Act is about high hedges – but what is a hedge? Mr Rizza was ordered by Highland Council to cut back his trees, in suburban Inverness, because they were too high, but he said that he had no *hedge*: what he had was *woodland*. He appealed to the Scottish Ministers, and a reporter was appointed. She confirmed the Council's decision. Mr Rizza then sought judicial review. Once again he was unsuccessful. See **Commentary** p 170.

INSOLVENCY

(69) O'Boyle's Tr v Brennan
[2020] CSIH 3, 2020 SC 217, 2020 SLT 152, 2020 SCLR 470

Shortly before he was sequestrated, Mr O'Boyle gave his girlfriend, Ms Brennan, £190,960 with which to buy a house, in her name. After his discharge, she sold the house and paid him the net proceeds, £197,462.20. The trustee in sequestration then raised the present action, seeking (i) declarator that the original payment (£190,960) by Mr O'Boyle to Ms Brennan had been a gratuitous alienation, and (ii) decree ordaining her to pay that sum to the pursuer. The pursuer was successful at first instance: see [2018] CSOH 90, 2018 GWD 29-369 (*Conveyancing 2019* Case (83)). The defender reclaimed, and the Inner House has now affirmed the decision. The case is notable for its use of the 'dual patrimony' theory of trust law. See **Commentary** p 205.

TIMESHARES

(70) Club Los Claveles v First National Trustee Co Ltd
[2020] CSIH 33, 2020 SC 504, 2020 SLT 880

This case concerned a timeshare in Tenerife, Spain. The trustee, ie the defender, was an Isle of Man company. (Why a dispute involving Spanish property held by a Manx company was to be heard and determined by the Scottish courts was not revealed in the case.) The pursuers had sought to terminate the defender's trusteeship, and have a new trustee appointed. The chief point at issue was whether the terms of the deed which the defender was to execute should contain certain indemnities. The defender so insisted, but the pursuers disagreed. The pursuers raised this action for declarator that the defender's appointment as trustee had ended, and specific implement ordaining it to execute a deed of resignation, assumption and conveyance in favour of a new trustee. Held: that the defender remained trustee until the execution of the new deed, and that the defender was not entitled to insist on the inclusion of indemnities in the deed. (In this connection, the deed of trust contained certain indemnities.) But some factual matters remained open, and a proof was allowed.

NUISANCE

(71) MacBean v Scottish Water
[2020] CSOH 55, 2020 SLT 707

The pursuer lived in a house in Boat of Garten. The defender constructed a waste water treatment plant near the pursuer's house. The pursuer complained of the smell and eventually raised the present action for declarator, damages and interdict. During the course of the action declarator was granted, but thereafter, with the action still continuing, the defender carried out remedial work. Whether that work was sufficient then became a matter of dispute, the Lord Ordinary (Lord Woolman) finally holding that it was sufficient. The case contains a useful discussion of the law of nuisance especially in the context of works done in the public interest.

PART II

STATUTORY DEVELOPMENTS

STATUTORY DEVELOPMENTS

Non-Domestic Rates (Scotland) Act 2020 (asp 4)

Responsibility for non-domestic (business) rates is fully devolved to Scotland, and the regime continues to diverge from the position in the rest of the UK. A major revision of primary legislation was completed in 2020, with the passage of the Non-Domestic Rates (Scotland) Act 2020. See **Commentary** p 233.

Coronavirus (Scotland) Acts 2020 (asp 7 and asp 10)

The Covid-19 pandemic gave rise to two emergency statutes of the Scottish Parliament: (i) the Coronavirus (Scotland) Act 2020, which received the Royal Assent on 6 April 2020 and came into force the following day ('the first Act'), and (ii) the Coronavirus (Scotland) (No 2) Act 2020, which received the Royal Assent on 26 May 2020 and also came into force the following day ('the second Act'). Both had expiry dates of 30 September 2020, but in both cases the expiry date was extended to 31 March 2021 by the **Coronavirus (Scotland) Acts (Amendment of Expiry Dates) Regulations 2020, SSI 2020/299**. Further extension to 30 September 2021 is possible (s 12(3)(b) of the first Act and s 9(3)(b) of the second), and not unlikely. Both statutes also allow for earlier termination of specific provisions (respectively s 13 and s 10), and indeed these powers have been used although not in relation to the provisions relevant to property law: see **Coronavirus (Scotland) Acts (Early Expiry of Provisions) Regulations 2020, SSI 2020/249**. The account that follows is limited to the provisions on property law.

Eviction in residential tenancies

Both Acts contain temporary measures to make eviction of tenants more difficult. This acknowledges both the financial pressure on those who have been without work because of the pandemic, and also the undesirability, not least from the viewpoint of public health, of making people homeless. Corresponding provisions for England and Wales are contained in sch 29 of the Coronavirus Act 2020 (c 7).

Schedule 1 to the first Act, as amended by the **Coronavirus (Scotland) Act 2020 (Eviction from Dwellinghouses) (Notice Periods) Modification Regulations 2020, SSI 2020/270**, has anti-eviction provisions for private-sector residential tenancies, chiefly by changing the cases where the court 'must' grant decree in the landlord's favour to 'may' grant decree. This applies to tenancies under the Private Housing (Tenancies) (Scotland) Act 2016 (ie private residential tenancies), under the Housing (Scotland) Act 1988 (ie assured tenancies), and under the Rent (Scotland) Act 1984 (such as still exist). Notice periods are also extended. So for example in the case of private residential tenancies the standard notice period in respect of a landlord's notice to leave is extended from 84 days to six months, although, as in the previous law, the period can be shorter (eg where the tenant is in breach of the lease terms or has been entitled to occupy the property for six months or less).

Part 2 of sch 1 of the second Act introduces certain pre-action requirements where (i) the ground of eviction is rent arrears (of three or more consecutive months), (ii) all or part of the arrears relate to a period on or after 27 May 2020 (when the second Act came into force), and (iii) the application for an eviction order (or, in the case of assured or short assured tenancies an order for possession) was made on or after 6 October 2020. Despite the name, the requirements are not mandatory, but in considering whether it is reasonable to issue an eviction order (or an order for possession) against a tenant, the First-tier Tribunal is to consider the extent to which the landlord complied with the requirements before applying for the order. The pre-action requirements are set out in the **Rent Arrears Pre-Action Requirements (Coronavirus) (Scotland) Regulations 2020, SSI 2020/304** and are more or less identical for private residential tenancies and for assured and short assured tenancies. In relation to the former they are set out in reg 4(2)–(4), as follows:

(2) The provision by the landlord to the tenant of clear information relating to –
    (a) the terms of the tenancy agreement,
    (b) the amount of rent for which the tenant is in arrears,
    (c) the tenant's rights in relation to proceedings for eviction (including the pre-action requirements set out in this regulation), and
    (d) how the tenant may access information and advice on financial support and debt management.
(3) The making by the landlord of reasonable efforts to agree with the tenant a reasonable plan to make payments to the landlord of –
    (a) future payments of rent, and
    (b) the rent for which the tenant is in arrears.
(4) The reasonable consideration by the landlord of –
    (a) any steps being taken by the tenant which may affect the ability of the tenant to make payment to the landlord of the rent for which the tenant is in arrears within a reasonable time,
    (b) the extent to which the tenant has complied with the terms of any plan agreed to in accordance with paragraph (3), and
    (c) any changes to the tenant's circumstances which are likely to impact on the extent to which the tenant complies with the terms of a plan agreed to in accordance with paragraph (3).

These are loosely modelled on the pre-action requirements for enforcement of standard securities found in s 24A of the Conveyancing and Feudal Reform (Scotland) Act 1970.

Irritancy in commercial leases

For commercial leases, the focus of attention is on termination through irritancy. Under s 4 of the Law Reform (Miscellaneous Provisions) (Scotland) Act 1985, if a landlord wishes to irritate for non-payment of rent it must serve a notice with a 14-day ultimatum. That period is now changed from 14 days to 14 weeks by sch 7 paras 6 and 7 of the first Act. Furthermore, any notice which was served before 7 April 2020 (the date on which the first Act came into force) but in which the ultimatum had not expired by that date is treated as void and the landlord must serve a fresh notice with the new, much extended, ultimatum period. For discussion, see Kieran Buxton, 'An extension to an extension' (2020) 65 *Journal of the Law Society of Scotland* Oct/Online.

A UK-wide *Code of Practice for commercial property relationships during the COVID-19 pandemic*, available at www.gov.uk/government/publications/code-of-practice-for-the-commercial-property-sector, was published by the Ministry of Housing, Communities and Local Government in June 2020, and urges landlords and tenants to practise 'transparency and collaboration' in their dealings with each other.

Duration of planning permission

Planning permission generally has a three-year time limit within which the development must begin. That period is now extended by a year. More precisely, any planning permission which would normally have lapsed during the 'emergency period' (7 April 2020 to 31 March 2021) lapses instead at the end of the 'extended period' (30 September 2021) unless, before the end of the extended period, the development to which the permission relates is begun. See sch 7 paras 8–10 of the first Act, and **Town and Country Planning (Emergency Period and Extended Period) (Coronavirus) (Scotland) Regulations 2020, SSI 2020/254.**

Digital submission of deeds to the property register

More for the avoidance of doubt than anything else, paras 11–14 of sch 7 to the first Act make clear that a deed can be registered in the Land or Sasine Register by submission, not of the deed itself, but of a copy of the deed sent by electronic means. These provisions underpin the introduction by Registers of Scotland, in response to the pandemic, of the digital submission of applications for registration: see pp 78 ff below.

Digital submission of documents to the Register of Inhibitions

Similarly, the submission of documents to the Register of Inhibitions by electronic means was authorised by para 3 of sch 4 to the second Act. Instead of being signed in wet ink, the documents can be signed with an ordinary (as opposed to an 'advanced') electronic signature in the sense of s 7(2) of the Electronic Communications Act 2000 ('so much of anything in electronic form as (a) is incorporated into or otherwise logically associated with any electronic communication or electronic data; and (b) purports to be used by the individual creating it to sign'). Also sufficient is 'a version of an electronic signature which is reproduced on a paper document'.

Extension of period of effect of advance notices

Normally an advance notice expires after 35 days. All advance notices which came into operation during the pandemic, beginning on 24 March 2020 (the day on which Registers of Scotland closed their doors), were given a hugely extended life by paras 15–19 of sch 7 to the first Act. These are to last until 10 days after the day on which the Keeper declares the application record in the Land Register (or the Register of Sasines) fully open for the making of entries. On 3 December 2020 the Keeper nominated 1 March 2021 as the relevant date for full reopening. This means that all advance notices expired at the end of 11 March 2021 except for those which were sufficiently recent for the usual 35-day period still to be running. See further p 86 below.

Notarised documents

Although the provision is opaquely worded, the effect of para 9 of sch 4 to the second Act appears to be that, where a document requires to be authenticated by a notary, solicitor or advocate, the notary, solicitor or advocate does not, during the pandemic, need 'to be physically in the same place' as a person who signs the document, takes an oath, or makes an affirmation or declaration. This allows the process to be carried out using video technology. Examples of documents which are affected include the 'notarial' execution of deeds under s 9 of the Requirements of Writing (Scotland) Act 1995, and continuing and welfare powers of attorney. The provision does not, however, apply to the ordinary witnessing of deeds, as to which see p 83 below.

The Law Society has issued the following guidance on notarising documents (last revised on 17 June 2020):

Notarial acts using video technology

(a) A notary may, subject to the conditions set out in paragraph 4, use video technology to certify the execution of a document signed (including by electronic signature) by an individual by means of a notarial act.

(b) Both parties should begin the process by each having an unsigned version of the document, in relation to which notarial acts are to be performed, which can be transmitted one to the other via post, fax, email or other electronic means. The individual will require to provide the notary with documents necessary to satisfy the notary as to their identity having regard to the Coronavirus Guidance on Non Face-to-Face Identification and Verification published by the Society [reproduced on p 81 below] which provides guidance on client identity verification using video conferencing.

The notary can use free basic software products that enable video conferencing to assist with the identification and verification process. This is a more manual process and where personal or sensitive information supporting identity verification is sent by email or other electronic means, the notary should consider taking additional steps to mitigate security risks, including, where appropriate, encryption.

To undertake manual identification and verification, the notary should follow this process:

- Request that the individual sends a clear, legible colour image of their passport/ID document using a suitably secure means, such as encrypted email.
- Arrange to video call the individual. During this call, ask the individual to hold the passport/ID document to their face. By checking the digital copy along with capturing the image of the client with the passport/ID document, the notary should be satisfied that they are one and the same before proceeding.
- In addition to the passport/ID document, ask the individual to provide a digital copy of their valid proof(s) of address.
- The notary should ensure that the rationale for adopting revised identification and verification measures is documented in the client/matter level risk assessment and to risk grade the relationship accordingly.
- Policies, controls and procedures should be revised to take into account the new process.

Should the individual be unable to satisfy these requirements and/or present a higher risk of money laundering, the firm should ensure that they are satisfied that those risks are addressed before proceeding. This may include obtaining further verification of identity or undertaking other measures as stipulated under r 33(5) of the Money Laundering, Terrorist Financing and Transfer of Funds (Information on the Payer) Regulations 2017, SI 2017/692.

(c) Once both parties have an unsigned copy of the relevant document the notary should take steps during the video conference to ensure that the document that they have sight of is an exact copy of the same document that is before the individual. This can be done by, for example, having the individual read out the document or by having the individual share their screen.

Once the notary has confirmed that each document is the same, the notary should then either place the individual on oath or take the solemn affirmation or receive the statutory declaration and observe the signature or requisite act of the individual.

The signed document must then be sent to the notary to allow them to notarise it and this can be done in a number of ways:

(i) if the document is an electronic document and has been electronically signed by the deponent it can electronically notarised upon receipt;

(ii) if the document is a traditional, hard-copy document and has been signed by traditional means that document can be returned to the notary by post or courier for them to notarise;

(iii) in order to fulfil the intention behind the legislative change it will be acceptable for a traditional document that has been signed in a traditional manner to be scanned and returned to the notary to notarise upon receipt.

If option (iii) is considered the most appropriate or necessary process to undertake it would be best practice to request that the original, traditionally signed document is kept by the individual until such time as the current movement restrictions are no longer in place as this will allow for the document to be provided, when safe to do so, to the notary to form part of their file and audit trail.

The notary should also take care when producing a narration to ensure that if the process in (iii) is followed that it is clear that they have notarised a 'copy' rather than an 'original' document.

(d) If practicable the notary or where applicable the solicitor must, having obtained the prior consent of the individual, record the video conference and retain that recording for a period of 10 years.

(e) Where it is not practicable to record the video conference the notary shall, having obtained the prior consent of the individual, take screen capture photographs of the individual and his or her identity documents.

(f) The notary must use all reasonable endeavours to establish that this procedure will result in the acceptance of the document in the receiving jurisdiction. If the document will not be accepted in the receiving jurisdiction the notary must so advise the individual.

(h) The notary should not be considered, and should not be described as, a witness to the document certified under this guidance.

(i) The notarial certificate should narrate the exact procedure followed by the notary. The certificate must not state or imply that the notary was physically present with the individual when the document was executed. The procedure followed, including a description of the type of video technology used, should be recorded.

(j) Where the document has been sworn/declared before a notary by way of video conference rather than in person, appropriate wording should be inserted in the declaration to confirm that.

For example:

'Declared by way of video conference

Signed: [Signature of deponent]

This: _____ day of _____ 20XX

At: [*insert place of signing by deponent*]

before me [*insert name of person authorised to administer the oath/declaration*], via video conference which I attended from [my address at] [*insert address*].'

Corporate Insolvency and Governance Act 2020 (c 12)

The Corporate Insolvency and Governance Act 2020 was rushed through as Covid-related emergency legislation: the Bill was published on 20 May 2020, went at high speed through Parliament, received the Royal Assent on 25 June and (see s 49(1)) came into force the following day. It might be supposed that its provisions are temporary. Some of them indeed are. But others make permanent amendments to the Insolvency Act 1986, bringing about the most significant changes to corporate insolvency law since the Enterprise Act 2002.

The aspect of the Act relevant to conveyancing is the introduction of a new type of moratorium, which confers short-term protection for distressed companies against their creditors. The default period is 20 days but can, depending on the circumstances, be shorter or considerably longer: Insolvency Act 1986 s A9. During the moratorium there are various rules of relevance to conveyancing, such as no irritancy (1986 Act s A21(1)(b)), no enforcement of a standard security (1986 Act s A21(1)(b)), and certain restrictions on the ability to grant conveyancing deeds such as standard securities and dispositions (1986 Act s A26 and s A29). Provisions on these lines are not new – comparable provisions (equally full of obscure drafting) can also be found in other procedures in the 1986 Act. So from the standpoint of the conveyancer the new legislation does not represent an entirely new type of peril.

How is the conveyancer to know if one of these new moratoriums is in place? As with other procedures in the 1986 Act there is a duty to notify the Registrar of Companies (1986 Act s A8), so a normal search in the Companies Register should in theory do the trick. But the provisions do not inspire confidence. The directors are to notify the 'monitor' (an insolvency practitioner who has certain functions in a moratorium) 'as soon as reasonably practicable' (s A8(1)), and the monitor is to inform Companies House 'as soon as reasonably practicable' after hearing from the directors (s A8(2)). So in practice there will be plenty of scope for a search in the Companies Register to be clear even though in fact a moratorium is in place. There are other publicity requirements, such as a duty to give information on the company's website (1986 Act s A19(2)) but these are likely to be equally fallible.

Register of Persons Holding a Controlled Interest in Land

Section 39 of the Land Reform (Scotland) Act 2016, which obliges Scottish Ministers to make regulations setting up a public register of persons who have controlling interests in owners and tenants of land, was brought fully into force on 16 December 2020: see **Land Reform (Scotland) Act 2016 (Commencement No 11) Regulations 2020, SSI 2020/383**. On the following day, the Land Reform (Scotland) Act 2016 (Register of Persons Holding a Controlled Interest in Land) Regulations 2021 were laid before the Scottish Parliament and have now been passed: see p 93 below. The projected starting date for the register has been pushed back from 1 April 2021 to 1 April 2022. The Regulations will be considered in detail in next year's volume.

Right to buy land to further sustainable development

Part 5 of the Land Reform (Scotland) Act 2016 was brought into force on 26 April 2020 by the **Land Reform (Scotland) Act 2016 (Commencement No 10) Regulations 2020, SSI 2020/20**. Part 5 allows community bodies to apply to buy land for the purpose of furthering sustainable development. Unlike most of the community rights to buy (but not the right to buy abandoned, neglected or detrimental land), the right applies even where the owner of the land is not willing to sell it. For details, see Malcolm M Combe, 'Rights to buy: the new addition' (2020) 65 *Journal of the Law Society of Scotland* July/34.

In outline, the right to buy applies to most types of land though there are some exclusions such as owner-occupied homes (s 46). The right can only be exercised by 'community bodies' (s 49), defined as (i) companies limited by guarantee, (ii) Scottish charitable incorporated organisations (SCIOs), or (iii) community benefit societies under the Co-operative and Community Benefit Societies Act 2014. Alternatively the right can be exercised by a person nominated by such a body: s 54(1). An application to buy is made to the Scottish Ministers, having first been approved by the community by means of a ballot (ss 56(3)(h) and 57) and registered in a new register maintained by the Keeper, the Register of Applications by Community Bodies to Buy Land (s 52); the register can be consulted, free of charge, at https://roacbl.ros.gov.uk/. In reaching a decision, the Scottish Ministers have a broad duty to consult (s 5). At the time of writing, no applications under the right to buy legislation had yet appeared on the register.

In terms of the criteria set out in s 56(2), an application is not to be accepted unless the Scottish Ministers are satisfied that:

(a) the transfer of land is likely to further the achievement of sustainable development in relation to the land,
(b) the transfer of land is in the public interest,
(c) the transfer of land –
    (i) is likely to result in significant benefit to the relevant community (see subsection (11)) to which the application relates, and
    (ii) is the only practicable, or the most practicable, way of achieving that significant benefit, and
(d) not granting consent to the transfer of land is likely to result in harm to that community.

There is no definition of 'sustainable development'. Provision is made for valuation of the land being bought (s 65), and for the making of Government grants towards the purchase (s 68). There is a right of appeal to the sheriff court (s 69) or, in respect of the valuation, to the Lands Tribunal (s 70).

Some of the provisions of the Act are now fleshed out by statutory instrument, notably the snappily-named **Right to Buy Land to Further Sustainable Development (Eligible Land, Specified Types of Area and Restrictions on Transfers, Assignations and Dealing) (Scotland) Regulations 2020, SSI 2020/114**. This follows a public consultation launched on 26 June 2019 (see *Conveyancing 2019* p 107) which, surprisingly, resulted in a mere 20 responses: see the analysis of responses published on 7 February 2020 and available at www.gov. scot/publications/consultation-right-buy-land-further-sustainable-development-consultation-analysis/. A business and regulatory impact assessment was published at the same time, as well as impact assessments in respect of data protection and equality.

Regulation 3 amplifies s 46(2)(a) of the Act, which excludes from the right to buy 'land on which there is a building or other structure which is an individual's home unless the building or structure is occupied by an individual under a tenancy'. The definition of 'tenancy' is extended to include, for example, a right to occupy under a licence (as opposed to a lease) or under a liferent, or tied accommodation. Regulation 4 specifies certain pertinents of a home which are equally excepted under s 46(2)(b) (the Regulations refer, incorrectly, to para (a) of s 46(2)). These are:

(a) land that forms the curtilage of the individual's home,
(b) land that is used for one or more of the following purposes –

   (i) the storage of possessions kept by the occupants of the individual's home that are used for the maintenance, upkeep or subsistence of the individual's home or its occupants,

   (ii) the storage of vehicles that are used by the occupants of the individual's home,

   (iii) drainage, water supply or the provision of other services (such as media or electricity) for the individual's home,

   (iv) the growing of food which is principally for the subsistence of the occupants of the individual's home,

   (v) activities including recreation and leisure activities which are incidental to the use of the individual's home,

   (vi) the keeping of pets belonging to the occupants of the individual's home,

   (vii) access to the individual's home, if the land is owned by the same person that owns that home.

Regulation 6 specifies the types of area by reference to which a community may be defined under s 49(9)(a) of the 2016 Act – for example, electoral wards or postcode areas.

The rest of the Regulations are concerned with the 'restriction period', ie the period during which there are restrictions on dealing with land in respect of which an application to buy has been registered. Here s 61 of the 2016 Act makes only outline provision, and the details are now given in regs 7–11 of the 2020 Regulations. By reg 8 the restriction period begins on registration of the application in the Register of Applications by Community Bodies to Buy Land. The rules as to when the period ends are complex and depend on whether the application is accepted or refused. During the restriction period it is 'prohibited' to transfer the land which is the subject of the application, or land that includes the land, or even to advertise it for sale or enter into negotiations for a transfer (reg 8). If the application relates to the purchase of the interest of a tenant, there is an equivalent prohibition of assignation of the lease. No sanction is provided for breach of the prohibition. Is, for example, a disposition granted in breach of this prohibition void or voidable (and, if the latter, at the instance of whom)? We are not told. From a practical point of view, of course, a purchaser would not wish to proceed if a search of the register disclosed an application.

Not all transfers are caught by this prohibition. Among the exceptions listed in reg 9 are transfers by way of donation, transfers in implement of a court order (with some qualifications), and transfers between companies in the same group. A notable omission is transfers in implement of missives. So even where missives were concluded before the registration of the application, a transfer cannot go ahead during the restriction period and, if the right to buy goes through, cannot go ahead at all. If a transfer falls within one of the exceptions, and so can go ahead, the disposition must contain a declaration specifying which exception is being relied on (reg 10).

During the restriction period there is also suspended (i) any right of pre-emption, redemption or reversion, and (ii) any right conferred under Part 2 of the Land Reform (Scotland) Act 2003 in respect of the community right to buy (reg 11).

Further provision as to the mechanics of application is made by the **Right to Buy Land to Further Sustainable Development (Applications, Written Requests, Ballots and Compensation) (Scotland) Regulations 2020, SSI 2020/21**. A form is prescribed for applications (regs 2 and 3 and sch 1), and for the written request which must be made to the owner to transfer the land (reg 5 and sch 2). Other regulations deal with the conduct of the ballot (regs 8–13), with applications to Scottish Ministers for reimbursement of the cost of the ballot (regs 14–17), and with the procedure for compensation claims by the owner of the land and others (regs 19 and 20).

For the convenience of users, the forms and a series of guidance notes are available at www.gov.scot/collections/right-to-buy-land-to-further-sustainable-development-part-5/.

Registers of Scotland: change in rules for reserves

Up until now, Registers of Scotland have been able to retain and accumulate all surpluses made from registration and any other of their functions. But no longer. The provision under which accumulation was allowed, s 9 of the Public Finance and Accountability (Scotland) Act 2000, was repealed with effect from 31 March 2020 by the **Public Services Reform (Registers of Scotland) Order 2020, SSI 2020/92**. See p 90 below.

Adjustments to common parts for the disabled

The **Relevant Adjustments to Common Parts (Disabled Persons) (Scotland) Regulations 2020, SSI 2020/52**, lay down a procedure by which disabled persons can carry out alterations to the common parts of a building or development (typically a tenement). The agreement of a majority of owners of the common parts is necessary, and the disabled person is solely responsible for the cost of the works. See **Commentary** p 173.

Fees in the Lands Tribunal

Some small adjustments to fees in the Lands Tribunal are made by the **Lands Tribunal for Scotland Amendment (Fees) Rules 2020, SSI 2020/22**, amending the Lands Tribunal for Scotland Rules 1971, SI 1971/218.

PART III
OTHER MATERIAL

OTHER MATERIAL

Fair Rents (Scotland) Bill

This is a Members' Bill, introduced to the Scottish Parliament on 1 June 2020 by Pauline McNeill, a Labour MSP. The Bill applies to private rented housing and, as its name suggests, seeks to control rent levels by (i) preventing a landlord from increasing rent by more than a set amount (related to inflation), and (ii) allowing tenants to apply to a rent officer to have a 'fair open market rent' set for the property. In addition, landlords would have to include details of the rent they charge in the landlords' register. If enacted, the Bill would insert new provisions into the Private Housing (Tenancies) (Scotland) Act 2016 and the Antisocial Behaviour etc (Scotland) Act 2004. Thus far the Bill has made no progress in the Scottish Parliament, and is unlikely to do so because, at the start of July, the allocated committee, the Local Government and Communities Committee, decided that it was too busy to give proper time to scrutinising the Bill prior to the election in May 2021.

Heat Networks (Scotland) Bill

This Government Bill was introduced to the Scottish Parliament on 2 March 2020 and completed Stage 1 on 3 December. The Bill seeks to encourage greater use of heat networks. These are insulated pipes and heat generation systems which make heat, whether in the form of hot water or steam. The idea is to help reduce emissions from homes and other buildings. The heat network sector is currently unregulated, but this will be changed by the Bill. Only a licensed provider will be allowed to 'supply thermal energy by means of a heat network' (s 2(1)), and Part 1 of the Bill makes extensive provision for the necessary 'heat networks licence'. Furthermore, by s 17(1) 'a person must not construct or operate a heat network unless the person holds a heat network consent relating to (a) the construction of the heat network, or (as the case may be) (b) the operation of the heat network'. Part 2 provides detailed rules as to the necessary consent. Part 3 is concerned with 'heat network zones' – areas designated by a local authority or the Scottish Ministers as particularly suitable for the construction and operation of a heat network.

Not much of this touches on property law and conveyancing. But it is worth mentioning that licence holders have powers of compulsory acquisition, subject to authorisation by the Scottish Ministers (s 57). There is also provision for wayleaves ('network wayleave rights'), whether obtained by agreement or by compulsion (ss 58–63).

Airbnb and other short-term lets

Following a public consultation in 2019 (as to which see *Conveyancing 2019* pp 104–05), a statement was made to the Scottish Parliament on 8 January 2020 by the Minister for Local Government, Housing and Planning, Kevin Stewart, announcing the policy as to short-term lets to be adopted by the Scottish Government: see *Official Report*, 8 January 2020, cols 36–39. The new policy has three prongs. First, a licensing scheme for short-term lets is to be established under powers contained in the Civic Government (Scotland) Act 1982. Among other things, this is intended to inform local authorities as to which properties in their area are being used for Airbnb etc, and so allow monitoring for fire safety and the like. Secondly, local authorities will be able to introduce 'short-term let control areas' under powers contained in amendments made to the Town and Country Planning (Scotland) Act 1997 by the Planning (Scotland) Act 2019. The use of property for short-term lets in such areas will require planning permission. Thirdly, the Government will 'carefully and urgently consider the tax treatment of short-term lets' with the aim of ensuring 'that short-term lets make an appropriate contribution to local communities and support local services' (col 38). This is in addition to a proposed visitor tax ('transient visitor levy') for which legislation is planned.

Today, a year on, the issue seems less urgent than it did in January 2020. Within weeks of the Minister's announcement the Covid-19 virus had struck and tourism, especially foreign tourism, was badly hit. Shorn of visitors, flats and houses which had previously been used for Airbnb and the like reverted to ordinary residential use and, it is said, re-entered the private letting market. The pause, however, looks likely to be temporary. With tourism returning on the back of the various vaccines, the demand for short-term lets is likely to be restored and, in time, may even continue its previous upward trajectory. Whether supply will correspond to demand is perhaps less clear. Certainly, the proposed regulatory framework will increase costs for owners and is likely to dampen their enthusiasm to re-enter the market.

Despite Covid-19, there was rapid progress during 2020 on the first two of the proposed policy approaches, ie licensing under the Civic Government (Scotland) Act 1982 and the establishment of control areas under the Planning (Scotland) Act 2019. A further consultation was launched between 14 September and 16 October 2020, leading to the Scottish Government's *Consultation report on proposals for a licensing scheme and planning control areas for short-term lets in Scotland* which was published on 10 December. In implement of the report, two statutory instruments were laid before the Scottish Parliament on 14 December 2020. Assuming Parliamentary approval these will come into force on 1 April 2021. They were accompanied by an impact assessment: *Short-term lets: licensing scheme and planning control area legislation: Business and Regulatory Impact Assessment*. All of the above can be accessed at www.gov.scot/publications/short-term-lets/.

Of the two statutory instruments, the Civic Government (Scotland) Act 1982 (Licensing of Short-term Lets) Order 2021 is the more important. The use of accommodation for qualifying short-term lets will need to be licensed by the local authority under Part I of the Civic Government (Scotland) Act 1982 (modified in some respects by schedule 2 of the Order). The scheme is intended to be open for business from 1 April 2022, and 'hosts' will have until 1 April 2023 to apply for a licence (art 3). The scheme's scope turns on the definition of 'short-term let' in art 2(2). This means:

> the grant of an agreement in the course of business for the use of residential accommodation (or a part of the accommodation) by a guest, where all of the following criteria are met –
>
> (a) the guest does not occupy the accommodation as the guest's only or principal home,
> (b) the agreement is entered into for commercial consideration,
> (c) the guest is not –
>> (i) an immediate family member of a person granting the agreement,
>> (ii) sharing the accommodation with a person granting the agreement for the principal purpose of facilitating the provision of work or services by the guest to that person or other members of the household, or
>> (iii) sharing the accommodation with a person granting the agreement for the principal purpose of advancing the guest's education, as part of an arrangement made or approved by a school, college, or further or higher educational institution,
> (d) the accommodation is not provided for the principal purpose of facilitating the provision of work or services by the guest to the person who is granting the agreement or to another member of that person's household, and
> (e) the accommodation is not excluded accommodation (see schedule 1).

As can be seen, the definition contains a number of exclusions, and these are augmented by a further list in schedule 1. So a let is not a 'short-term let', for example, in the case of care homes, student accommodation, and accommodation provided for the purposes of work or for live-in domestic help such as au pairs. In what may turn out to be a significant exclusion, a let only falls within the definition if is granted 'in the course of business'.

Accommodation licensed for short-term lets is placed under a number of 'mandatory licence conditions' (art 3 and sch 3). So for example, the premises must be inspected annually for gas safety and every five years for electrical safety, and licence-holders 'must take all reasonable steps to ensure the accommodation is safe for residential use' (sch 3 paras 2 and 7). Details as to the cost of a licence and other administrative matters are still awaited.

The other statutory instrument, the Town and Country Planning (Short-term Let Control Areas) (Scotland) Regulations 2021, is intended to supplement s 26B of the Town and Country Planning (Scotland) Act 1997. Under s 26B a local authority can designate all or part of its area as a 'short-term let control area'. Where this is done, a change of use of a dwellinghouse to use for the purposes of providing short-term lets is deemed to be a material change of use and so constitutes 'development' under s 26 of the Act. That in turn means that planning permission is needed. This is in addition to the licence already mentioned. Among the exclusions are lets in cases where 'all or part of the dwellinghouse is the only or principal home of the landlord or occupier' (s 26B(3)(b)): the idea is that the requirement for planning consent should apply only to lets of whole properties and not to home-sharing. The new Regulations set out the designation procedure, with provision for public notification and consultation, and for approval by the Scottish Ministers. It remains to be seen whether local authorities will choose to exercise these powers.

The impact assessment acknowledges the regulatory burden on 'hosts' as well as on letting 'platforms' such as Airbnb, booking.com and Expedia, and accepts that the number of short-term lets is likely to fall. But this, it is said, will bring a number of benefits such as reduced costs on public services, a better functioning housing market, improved quality of life for neighbours, and, for hotels and B&Bs, a measure of regulatory equality.

Short-term lets can potentially be controlled by private law as well as by public law, and this aspect is explored further at p 196 below.

Coronavirus conveyancing

The closing of the registers

As part of the national lockdown, Registers of Scotland closed their doors on 24 March 2020, although staff continued to work remotely where this was possible. Postal applications – in effect, *all* applications – for registration were suspended, and all mail to RoS was returned undelivered. The immediate effect was to make it impossible to register deeds. In the course of the week the UK Government advised that people should not move house.

To this crisis RoS responded with impressive speed and skill. By the end of the week they had prepared provisions which appeared in the Coronavirus (Scotland) Bill which was published on 31 March, passed by the Scottish Parliament the following day, and given Royal Assent on 6 April, coming into force the following day. For details of the provisions, see p 63 above.

These provisions underpinned a two-part strategy. The ultimate aim was to enable registration by submission, not of the customary paper deed, but of a scanned copy of the deed. This was, in a sense, an extension of the 'tell me don't show me' procedure. The paper deed was not to be seen at all at RoS, at least in the ordinary case. Instead, it would be for the applicant's solicitor to scrutinise the original and then send a scanned copy to the Registers, along with an electronic application form. Arguably, there was nothing in the Land Registration etc (Scotland) Act 2012, or in the Land Register Rules, to prevent this form of registration but, to be on the safe side, para 12 of sch 7 of the Coronavirus (Scotland) Act 2020 added four subsections to s 21 of the 2012 Act. These make explicit that, for the purposes of applications for registration, 'submission by electronic means of a copy of the deed is sufficient evidence of the original for the purposes of accepting an application for registration'.

As RoS knew from the outset, it would take several weeks to build the computer systems which would allow digital submission of deeds to take place on a large scale (although in those few cases where a failure to register would put the applicant in potential peril, RoS could and did accept digital submission from the beginning). So there had to be a temporary fix to tide things over until then. This was based on advance notices. In most cases, applications for such notices were, of course, already submitted electronically. For cases where they were not – first registrations and transfers in part – electronic application was made available. So even during the period when applications for registration of deeds could not be made, it remained possible to apply for advance notices. Under the 2012 Act, advance notices expire after 35 days, but that was changed by sch 7 paras 15–19 of the 2020 Act. Advance notices would now last until 10 days after 'the Keeper declares the application record fully open for the making of entries'. The extended period applied to new advance notices, of course, but it applied also to any existing advance notices which were still live on 24 March 2020.

The new digital submission service for deeds was launched on 15 April 2020, initially on a phased basis, working from the oldest advance notice in the system forwards. Applications were also accepted where they required to proceed urgently but were unable to settle on the basis of an advance notice. There then followed a prolonged period of catch-up, but by the summer the system had sufficient capacity to deal with all applications.

Missives

Is it necessary for missives to contain Covid clauses? On this, the Law Society is not to be drawn:

> Our Property Law Committee have been asked for their view as to whether all missives should include contractual provisions to take account of the risks presented by the virus.
>
> Any such provisions would be a matter of negotiation between the respective parties and it is therefore for members to take their clients' instructions on this issue. Given the continuing uncertainties with the impact of Covid-19, and their impact on the particular circumstances of each transaction, we would stress the importance of tailoring each clause to the particular transaction and clients.
>
> Anyone considering negotiating such a clause should think very carefully about doing so and about covering the desired outcome during this time of uncertainty, and the practical issues of applying and enforcing such a clause. Such a clause could create unintended consequences depending on how circumstances change.

The ever-helpful Property Standardisation Group (www.psglegal.co.uk) has been more forthcoming in respect of commercial property transactions:

> During the restrictions on movement imposed by the Scottish Government, you may need to consider making some adjustments to the PSG Offers to Sell to accommodate some of the limitations on signing, delivery and changes to registration. Key considerations are timescales e.g. [10] Business Days in which to do something, and the Land Registration requirements and Post Completion time limits.

Pre-conclusion of contract

It is rare these days for contracts to be concluded subject to property due diligence being completed. Accordingly, it is unlikely that you will need to make any particular adjustment to missives to account for Covid-19 limitations for this stage. If you are required to conclude missives prior to conducting or completing due diligence, then make sure the time limits in Clauses 6.2/7.2 and 6.3/7.3 *Documents to be Disclosed* are sufficient. They currently stand at [15] Business Days, which still ought to be ample.

Conclusion of Missives

The Offers to Sell provide that both the missives letters themselves and any document referred to in the contract have to be 'duly executed', meaning they must be self-proving (i.e. 'meets the requirements of section 3 or sections 9B and 9C of the Requirements of Writing (Scotland) Act 1995'). Since strictly speaking missives do not require to be self-proving, and to reduce the signing burden on solicitors during restrictions, we suggest that the definition of 'Missives' be amended to read: 'means the contract constituted by this offer and all ~~duly executed~~ letters following on it validly executed in terms of section 2 or section 9B of the Requirements of Writing (Scotland) Act 1995', and to amend the provisions of Clause 19.1/23.1 *Formal Documentation Required* in a similar way.

Completion

Solicitors will need to determine how they are prepared to accept delivery of the documents for submission, on a case-by-case basis. Issues to consider include the availability of postal and courier services, the ability to scan and send pdfs of documents, and the ability to receive physical documents.

It is recommended that parties agree to adopt one of the PSG Digital Submission Protocols for completion of the transaction (see below). For ease, a new definition 'Digital Submission System' could be used:

> 'means the system for online submission of applications to register documents in the Land Register of Scotland [Register of Sasines] under the provisions of section 21 of the 2012 Act [section 6A of the Land Registers (Scotland) Act 1868];'

This reflects the changes that the Coronavirus (Scotland) Act 2020 made to permit the Keeper to accept submissions by electronic means.

Payment of the Price and handing over the completion items in terms of Clause 8/10 *Completion* should be able to proceed notwithstanding Covid-19 restrictions: advance notices, legal reports and charges searches are all available.

Post Completion

There are a number of documents where signing may need to be finalised post-Completion (e.g. assignations of rent deposits, guarantees and service charge contracts). Registration of the disposition and discharge (and other documents) also takes place post completion, and the Offers provide a number of time limits and timescales for these. The principal clauses are 7.8/8.8 *Land Register Requirements* and 9/11 *Post Completion*.

Land Register Requirements

Now that the Digital Submission System is fully operational for both Land Register and Sasine documents, completions ought to be able to take place as normal. There should be no need to amend the Offer, although until such time as the Keeper declares the application record fully open, there is no need to obtain further advance notices.

Post Completion

The obligation on the seller that the purchaser's title sheet will contain no adverse entries is dependent on the purchaser's solicitor presenting the disposition for registration prior to the earlier of 14 days after completion and the date of expiry of the last advance notice registered in relation to the Disposition. While the provisions of the Coronavirus (Scotland) Act 2020 apply, advance notices will have an open-ended duration. This means that the 14 day period will, until those provisions are either repealed or the Keeper declares the application record open, always be the earlier of the two dates (until the advance notice protection starts to count down from the date of the Keeper's declaration). The PSG does not consider that any amendment is currently necessary to this clause.

Time scales and time limits

A table [on the PSG website] identifies the clauses in the Offers where a time scale or time limit is imposed. Not all timescales will need to be amended. Those that relate to payment for example ought to be capable of being complied with, as most payments will be processed through the banking system in the normal way. Similarly, there seems to be no Covid-19-specfic reason to extend time limits for resilement, or for examination of title.

Identification and verification of clients

The Law Society has issued guidance on non-face-to-face identification and verification during the coronavirus crisis (updated on 1 May 2020). The guidance offers the following three options:

1. Client identity verification software

You can use client identity verification software which allows you to undertake client checks remotely and securely, making it easier to maintain records for audit. The service provider should be a reliable, independent digital ID system with appropriate built-in information security protocols which will help mitigate fraud risks.

2. Video conferencing tools

Alternatively, you can use free basic software products that enable video conferencing to assist with the identification and verification process. This is a more manual process and where firms request that personal or sensitive information supporting identity verification be sent by email or other electronic means, you should consider taking additional steps to mitigate security risks, including, where appropriate, encryption.

To undertake manual identification and verification, we suggest the following process:

- Request that the client sends you a clear, legible colour image of their passport/ ID document using a suitably secure means, such as encrypted email.
- Arrange to video call the client. During this call, ask the client to hold the passport/ID document to their face. By checking the digital copy along with capturing the image of the client with the passport/ID document, you should be satisfied that they are one and the same before proceeding.

- In addition to the passport/ID document, ask the client to provide you with a digital copy of their valid proof(s) of address.
- Ensure that you document the rationale for adopting your revised identification and verification measures in the client/matter level risk assessment and to risk grade the relationship accordingly.
- Policies, controls and procedures should be revised to take into account the new process.

Should the client and/or matter in question raise additional red flags and present a higher risk of money laundering, the firm should ensure that they are satisfied that those risks are addressed before proceeding. This may include obtaining further verification of identity or undertaking other measures as stipulated under r 33(5) of the Money Laundering, Terrorist Financing and Transfer of Funds (Information on the Payer) Regulations 2017, SI 2017/692.

3. Email and third-party validation

If you do not wish to adopt software and are unable to access video-conferencing, there is the option to use email and a third party to validate the necessary documents. It does rely on the third-party having access to their own filing systems. Where firms request personal or sensitive information be sent by email or other electronic means in support of ID&V/CDD, due consideration should be made to associated information security risks and requisite steps taken (including, where appropriate, encryption) to mitigate such risks.

1. Ask the prospective client to contact their accountant or another identifiable professional, such as another solicitor or a doctor, to enquire if they are willing to certify documentation on their behalf.
2. The prospective client emails the documentation, for example, copies of valid proof(s) of address and passport to the certifier.
3. The certifier reviews the details they hold on file for the prospective client to ensure that it is correct and matches up to new information provided.
4. If correct, the certifier emails both the client and a contact at the firm from their professional email address confirming:
   - their relationship to the client
   - how long they have known the client
   - that the details on the valid proof of address match the details they, in their professional capacity, hold on file
   - that the photograph in the valid passport bears a true likeness to the client
   - their job title, full name, address and contact numbers if not included in their email signature.
5. Conduct an online check to establish the identity of the certifier and their company/firm and retain a screenshot of the same for your records. Similarly, you can check online to see if the certifier is registered with the professional body they purport to be a member of.

If the certifier is using an Adobe pdf, they can use the 'fill and sign function' to certify that the copies they had sight of, mirror the details that they hold on file and include the information in the bullet points above.

You should amend your policies, controls and procedures accordingly to reflect the interim changes and to record the new procedure in their client/matter risk assessments.

Should the client and/or matter in question raise additional red flags and present a higher risk of money laundering, the firm should ensure that they are satisfied that those risks are addressed before proceeding. In higher risk situations, for example, further verification (including verification of source of funds/wealth) will likely be appropriate, along with other measures as stipulated under r 33(5) of the Money Laundering Regulations 2017.

It is important to note that the regulations have not been relaxed in the current situation. We hope our suggested procedure above is useful but solicitors should remember that if they cannot complete adequate due diligence they should not proceed with the transaction.

Please also see the latest Legal Sector Affinity Group (LSAG) Covid-19 Advisory Note for further UK legal sector-wide information.

Witnessing deeds by video-link

Can deeds be witnessed by video-link? The Coronavirus (Scotland) (No 2) Act 2020 sch 4 para 9 expressly allows this where a deed is to be notarised: see p 66 above. But for the witnessing of ordinary deeds, whether it is permissible is a matter of general principles and is not specifically covered by legislation.

The view of the Law Society is that witnessing by video-link is indeed permissible. In guidance issued on 25 March 2020 in relation to wills, the following is stated:

> It may be however that a suitable witness is not available and able to be physically present when the client is in a position to sign the will. It may then be feasible to arrange a video link with the client. If this can be done, the solicitor can witness the client signing ... or have someone else on the video call do so ... The will can then be returned to the solicitor. We consider that the witness, as long as they have seen the client actually sign each page, can on receipt of the signed will, legitimately sign and complete the signing details on receipt of the signed will. We would anticipate that this would be deemed to form one continuous process as required by the legislation.

If that is true for wills, it is equally true for dispositions and other conveyancing deeds because the legislative provision, s 3 of the Requirements of Writing (Scotland) Act 1995, is the same in both cases. But is this a correct reading of s 3? The answer is – possibly, but not certainly. The difficulty, as the guidance hints, is the requirement of s 3(4)(e) 'that the granter's subscription or, as the case may be, acknowledgement of his subscription and the person's signature as witness of that subscription were ... one continuous process'. The purpose of this requirement is to avoid the substitution of deeds between the time of the signature by the granter and that by the witness. A typical delay which has been permitted in normal times is 45 minutes (*Thomson v Clarkson's Trs* (1892) 20 R 59), but it may be that a more lenient rule would be applied in the peculiar circumstances of the Covid-19 crisis. Whether this would be sufficient to allow the granter to post the deed out to a solicitor is not entirely certain.

Another possibility would be for the granter, having signed the deed privately and sent it to his or her solicitor, to acknowledge the signature on the deed by video-link. 'That is my signature', the granter could say, after which the solicitor could sign. This avoids the issue of a delay between the event witnessed (in this case, the granter's acknowledgement) and the witness's signature, but it creates a difficulty of a different kind, because it is far from certain that granters can acknowledge a signature on a deed which is not available for their physical inspection.

Of course, if the witnessing is invalid, the deed is still properly executed under s 2 of the 1995 Act because it has been subscribed by the granter. But if the fatal time gap is apparent from the testing clause, as it may well be, then the deed would not be probative and so, on presentation for registration, would be rejected by the Keeper by virtue of ss 21 and 22(1)(c) of the Land Registration etc (Scotland) Act 2012. What all of this suggests is that witnessing by video-link should be used only as a last resort, where no other means of procuring a witness is available.

Settling transactions

The Law Society issued the following guidance, updated as of 19 August 2020, in relation to settlement:

> The interim measures have been put in place to provide a legal framework to allow certain transactions to settle, but any settlement would need to comply with the Government restrictions, and are designed solely to deal with one particularly important legal problem arising from the closure of the application record and Sasine Register to paper applications. A conveyancing settlement requires a number of different parties to be able to implement various legal and practical processes, which in the current circumstances are difficult to achieve.
>
> The current restrictions imposed by Government are for the protection of public health during a national and international emergency. Our guidance should be read in conjunction with the current and any future advice from Government and the safety of members, their staff, clients and the wider public should be the most important factor in deciding whether or not it is appropriate to proceed with settlement of a transaction in present circumstances. In particular, our members should refer to the 'Solicitors' section of the Scottish Government Coronavirus (COVID-19) guidance on moving home.
>
> Members should be careful to obtain clear instructions from clients, including lenders, to settle transactions in the above circumstances.
>
> Members should also be wary of the vulnerability of clients looking to purchase a home in the present circumstances and be careful to ensure that a client's informed consent to proceed is adequately obtained.
>
> None of the measures proposed should in any way be used to compel settlement of a transaction where someone is shielding from the virus. This is reflected in the Scottish Government guidance.

Digital submission protocols

In order to save the need for negotiation between law firms as to how a transaction is to be run, the Property Standardisation Group prepared a suite of six protocols, any one of which can be used and each of which sets out a set of procedures for dealing with delivery of documents and submission for registration. The protocols can be found at www.psglegal.co.uk/digital_submission_protocols. php.

Checking the physical deed

In using the digital submission service, the applicant's solicitor needs to be able to certify to RoS that the submitted document is valid. The Property Standardisation Group (www.psglegal.co.uk/) comments that:

> Many solicitors will want to receive the wet-signed hard copy document. Others will be prepared to accept confirmation from the solicitor holding the document that it has been validly signed. Either way, a qualified solicitor must check that the wet-signed hard copy document has been validly signed and witnessed eg: the signatures are in ink; the signatures have not been written on top of a label, on an erasure, or using a facsimile signature; the signatures are reasonably legible (ie they comply with section 7 of the Requirements of Writing (Scotland) Act 1995); and the signatures bear to be those of the parties signing.
>
> Acceptance of electronic delivery of a pdf document will depend on confirmation from the firm sending the pdf to the receiving solicitor that the original has been checked, is in the possession or control of the sending firm, and that it bears to have been validly signed. That confirmation should be given at the same time the pdf is being sent, and should be given by a partner of the sending firm. While best practice will be for the confirmation to be given by way of a signed letter on the firm's headed notepaper, giving this confirmation by email from a partner in the firm is as binding on the sending firm. Individual firms may have their own internal requirements on the giving of undertakings that may need to be adhered to.

Digital submission service: Land Register

Law Society guidance, updated as of 19 August 2020, explains that:

(a) Once submitted electronically, there is no need to submit the physical deeds once the application record is fully open. However, it is possible that Registers of Scotland may requisition any of the hard copy deeds, and so these deeds must be stored until, at least, completion of registration.

(b) If the plan is too big to be scanned in a single image, the plan can be scanned in sections. We are working with Registers of Scotland to generate further guidance on other acceptable ways of submitting plans which are too big to be scanned.

(c) Multiple transaction can be linked.

(d) Where the order in which related applications are taken on is significant, there is provision for uploading a covering letter to set out the order of registration.

In relation to (a), the ultimate fate of the originals of deeds depends on the law firm's policy on retention of papers. This is just a new version of the familiar issue of what, under the previous system, was done with deeds once they were returned by RoS.

In relation to (b), RoS now allow paper submission of a plan, which is tied in to the electronic application by means of a bar code.

Digital submission service: Register of Sasines

Law Society guidance, updated as of 19 August 2020, states that:

> The digital portal for electronic submission of applications for registration in the Register of Sasines was initially restricted to a limited range of applications,

principally section 75 agreements and unilateral undertakings and dual registrations, and with a daily limit on the number of such applications. Daily limits remain in place, but the digital portal has been opened up to all application types other than for assignations and discharges of standard securities being recorded in the Register of Sasines, ie where they are not part of a wider transaction triggering first registration, and some other less common deed types.

Registers of Scotland are still providing for other arrangements, where there are compelling reasons for a transaction to be submitted for registration which could not otherwise be submitted through the digital portal. Members should contact Registers of Scotland's Customer Services team …

For Sasines (and mixed Land Register and Sasines) applications transactions that require certainty for their registration date, we would recommend early contact with Registers of Scotland's Customer Services team, ahead of any proposed settlement date, to ensure that the process for submitting an application to RoS (either via the portal or as advised by the senior adviser) is agreed with RoS, allowing settlement to proceed.

Paper submission: Books of Council and Session

Digital submission is not available in respect of the Register of Deeds. (This is the main part of the Books of Council and Session, the other two parts being the Register of Judgments and the Register of Protests.) But paper submission resumed on 1 July 2020. Deeds could and can be sent by post to Register of Deeds, PO Box 24161, 153 London Road, Edinburgh EH7 9FZ. Alternatively, they can be sent by DX to Registers of Scotland, DX 555401, Edinburgh 15. Cheques are not acceptable for payment of the registration dues, and so it is important to include the FAS account number within the C&S1 Form.

Advance notices: the end of the extended period of validity

The generous extension of the 35-day period for advance notices was intended only as a temporary measure, until the registers got back on their collective feet by means of the digital submission service. The idea was that transactions should be able to settle, even where no deed had been registered or submitted for registration. With the help of UK Finance, a large number of lenders signed up to this system. But, almost from the beginning, RoS were planning to bring the system to an end. In terms of the Coronavirus (Scotland) Act 2020, an extended advance notice lasts until 10 days after 'the Keeper declares the application record fully open for the making of entries'. The application record has now been open for some time, although not 'fully open' in terms of the legislation. In deciding when it should be deemed to be 'fully open', RoS have been conscious of the restrictions imposed by the Scottish Government on working in non-essential offices (including solicitors). Ideally, the extended validity of advance notices would remain in place until the restrictions were lifted. In consultation with the Law Society, however, the Keeper announced on 3 December 2020 that the application record would become 'fully open' on 1 March 2021. This means that all advance notices expired at the end of 11 March 2021 except for those which were sufficiently recent for the usual 35-day period still to be running. According to RoS, deeds protected by such notices had to be submitted for registration by 10 March (or by 9 March if there were associated papers to be submitted via the non-digital documents process). Thereafter it will be business as before the crisis, with new advance notices subject to the 35-day period.

Scottish Government guidance on Covid-19

Throughout the Covid-19 crisis, the Scottish Government has published guidance on a large number of different topics, and updated it periodically. The guidance is available at www.gov.scot/collections/coronavirus-covid-19-guidance/. Of particular interest to those involved in conveyancing are the following:

- Guidance on moving home;
- Guidance on allocations for the housing sector;
- Guidance for private landlords and letting agents;
- Second homes guidance; and
- Advice for private tenants.

Land registration

Completion of the Land Register

As of 31 March 2020, 39.2% of Scotland's land mass had reached the Land Register, equating to 1,855,213 titles: see Registers of Scotland, *Annual Report and Accounts 2019–20* p 24. This was a little short of target. Voluntary registration continues to be an important vehicle for completion of the Register. Forestry and Land Scotland have now submitted all of their registration applications, accounting for 7% of Scotland's land mass. Certain local authorities and certain landowners – including 10 of the 20 largest – are also engaging with voluntary registration. By contrast, less progress has been made with registration of farms, not least because of the number which are held by corporate vehicles.

It is no longer expected that Keeper-induced registration (KIR) will make a large contribution to completion of the Register. Currently it is being used in association with social landlords for the registration of public-sector housing. A possible future use would be to catch the last few units in a private housing estate. The earlier use of KIR for private housing estates has been abandoned, having achieved around 65,000 registrations (against a one-time target of between 500,000 and 600,000). Attempts to automate the process having come to nothing, it did not bring the expected economies of scale and was too resource-intensive to continue. Mistakes were also sometimes made, which led to requests for rectification and a demand that RoS pay the costs. For this or other reasons, some solicitors viewed KIR title sheets with suspicion and treated the next transaction as a quasi-first registration for which it was necessary to look behind the title sheet.

More generally, there must be serious doubt as to whether the target of completion of the Land Register by 2024 can be met. Insofar as completion is intended to simplify conveyancing, a failure to finish by 2024 may not matter very much, because most properties which are regularly traded will already have changed hands by then and so will be on the Land Register. But insofar as completion is intended to supply the answer to 'Who owns Scotland?', such a failure would be more serious, and it may be that other means will be needed to supply this information. In a blog dated 17 September 2020, the Keeper did some thinking out loud on this topic:

> [T]he Sasines register already contains data on property ownership; the thinking we have developed over the past few months is whether we could unlock that data and make it more accessible. We would seek to do this by collating spatial data to provide a visual representation on a map of where that property is, and its approximate extent, then link it to the Sasines data that provides ownership information. Doing this would enable us to provide information for most of the land in Scotland well ahead of it formally transferring from the Sasine to the Land Register.
>
> Unlocking Sasines would enable us to provide an enhanced level of information on the likely ownership of areas not yet on the Land Register with a high degree of certainty … We anticipate that the spatial data gathered on indicative extents of properties will also make it quicker and easier for RoS staff to identify the relevant Sasines search sheets. Allowing us to 'match' the spatial data to the textual description of the land in Sasines and enabling us to access the information on the last recorded proprietor.
>
> Whilst this unlocked Sasines data will not have the same certainty as a fully registered title, it will be a very useful addition to inform policy relating to land ownership and could be easily accessible to the general public. Effectively, allowing us to fill in the gaps to allow us to help answer the question – who owns Scotland?

More on this can be found at https://insideros.blog/2020/10/30/unlocking-sasines-your-questions-answered/ and https://insideros.blog/2020/11/30/unlocking-the-sasine-part-1/.

Meanwhile, the Register of Sasines remains open for business and there are no immediate plans to close it. Today it is used mainly for discharges of standard securities, and for deeds and documents presented by someone other than the owner or a person taking a deed from the owner. In theory it would be possible to make such deeds a trigger for first registration (as has been done, for example, for standard securities); there is power to do so in s 48(3) of the Land Registration etc (Scotland) Act 2012. But the current thinking is that to do so would involve the parties in unreasonable trouble and expense.

Registration arrears

In a letter published in the March 2020 issue of the *Journal of the Law Society*, J Keith Robertson took RoS to task for the continuing delays in registration, and especially in first registrations:

> In June 2018, in response to publicity about title registration arrear, Registers of Scotland (RoS) accepted in a post still on its website, that an arrear then standing at 40,000 was unacceptable, and indicated that the whole arrear of first registration (FR) and transfer of part (TP) applications would be cleared by June 2019. The deadline was then amended to August 2020 … According to the latest RoS figures, the

February 2020 arrear stands at 57,581, an increase of 43.95% on the 'unacceptable' 2018 figure.

Mr Robertson pursued this topic at greater length in an article ('Registers of Scotland: an organisation in crisis?') in the *Scottish Law Gazette* published in the same month.

Further details as to the position as at March 2020 are given on p 23 of the *Annual Report and Accounts 2019–20* of Registers of Scotland. They are unlikely to satisfy Mr Robertson or, no doubt, many others. In the previous 12 months, RoS completed 10,079 cases that were older than two years. What was then left to complete was some 73,533 cases, comprising:

Year of application	Number of uncompleted cases
2016	424
2017	11,735
2018	26,386
2019	34,988

The hope that the arrears might be cleared off in the course of 2020 had to be abandoned when the Covid-19 crisis made other priorities more pressing.

Meanwhile, a mechanism is available to prioritise the most urgent cases. This is the Expedite Request Service which was first introduced in October 2018: see www.ros.gov.uk/support/contact-us/expedite-requests. Requests are assessed against three criteria:

- delays to the application will result in financial loss or hardship;
- delays to the application will result in the loss of future transactions; and
- delays to the application will result in personal loss or hardship.

According to the *Annual Report and Accounts 2019–20* p 22, 2,193 requests were received in 2019/20 of which a little over half (1,321) met the criteria and were fast-tracked.

Continuation of the digital submission service?

Improvised in haste to cope with the closure of RoS offices at the outbreak of Covid-19 (see above), the digital submission service has proved its worth. Once the Covid emergency is over, a decision will need to be made as to whether digital submission should continue, either as an option or in place of paper registration. Should, in other words, the improvisation become permanent? Now that practitioners have become used to it, the digital system can be seen to have certain advantages, including the flexibility of being able to register deeds at any time of the day or night, as well as the provision of a digital audit. If it is to continue, it could be seen as a stepping stone to the full digital registration that, at one time, seemed so close.

On 22 December 2020 RoS launched a consultation on putting digital submission of deeds on a permanent footing: see www.ros.gov.uk/about/publications/consultations-and-surveys/2020/digital-submissions-2020/consultation-paper. What is being proposed is digital submission as the default rule but, as currently with advance notices, with provision for paper submission in cases of need. It would not, say RoS, be cost-effective to run a full system for paper applications alongside the digital submission service.

It is also proposed to open up the Register of Deeds and Probative Writs (ie the main part of the Books of Council and Session) to 'true' electronic documents, ie those authenticated by way of qualified electronic signature. Since the purpose of this Register is to hold originals of deeds and not copies, it is not feasible to allow (mere) copies of deeds to be registered digitally.

The consultation closed on 1 February 2021.

Digital registration

Meanwhile, digital registration has continued for discharges of standard securities. According to p 34 of the RoS *Annual Report and Accounts 2019–20*, 55,315 discharges were signed and submitted through the 'digital discharge service' representing 43% of all discharges. Most were in respect of residential property. 500 solicitors and 16 lenders are now using the service. Most discharges (some 80%) were processed without manual intervention, in what was a significant saving of staff time.

Against the background of this new technology, some very old technology has stumbled on. ARTL continues to be used for some re-mortgages and statutory notices, but in small numbers. The cost of maintaining such a dated system is becoming hard to justify in view of the low level of usage.

Surrender of RoS reserves

With effect from 1 April 2020, Registers of Scotland were reclassified by the Office of National Statistics as a central government body. This, apparently, is because their surpluses derive from a monopoly. Over the years, those surpluses have been accumulated for a rainy day, or indeed for two possible rainy days, namely a downturn in the property market (which would affect RoS income) or an extra-large claim for compensation. But now, rainy days or not, surpluses can no longer be kept. More than that, reg 3 of the Public Services Reform (Registers of Scotland) Order 2020, SSI 2020/92, provides, starkly, that: 'The Keeper of the Registers of Scotland must pay any accumulated reserves held on the day this Order comes into force [31 March 2020] into the Scottish Consolidated Fund.' We hope that, in the manner of lottery winners, an outsize cheque was handed over by the Keeper to the First Minister. It was certainly for an outsize amount, of £50 million. In future, if there is an unexpected drop in income or increase in liabilities, RoS will have to bid for money to the Scottish Government. And, according to RoS projections, the first such bid will need to be made in the current financial year due to a sharp fall in income from registration during the Covid-19 crisis (projected as a fall of between 25% and 60%).

Fee increases

In terms of art 4 of the Registers of Scotland (Fees) Order 2014, SSI 2014/188, the Keeper is empowered to increase (or reduce) fees by up to £10. But an increase is only permissible where it is 'necessary to prevent material damage to the Keeper's financial position' and also where 'that damage arises from conditions which cannot be otherwise mitigated by action by the Keeper'. In the light of the fall in income from registration during the Covid-19 crisis, the Keeper exercised her power to impose a £10 increase, with effect from 5 October 2020.

Under the 2014 Order, the £10 increase cannot last for more than two years. Long before the expiry of that period, however, there will be a new Fees Order, with increased fees. To that end a consultation on fees was launched by RoS in October 2020. Apart from the recent £10 increase, fees (with minor exceptions) have remained unchanged since 2011. They now need to be increased, the consultation document said, partly because of increased staff costs, only partly offset by efficiency improvements, and partly because of the loss in registration income, actual and projected, due to Covid-19. Under the proposals the fee for registration of a disposition for a consideration of between £150,001 and £200,000 will be increased from £370 to £400. Comparable increases will be made throughout the fee table with, at the very top, the cost of registering a disposition for a consideration of more than £5 million increasing from £7,510 to £8,250. Following the consultation, the Registers of Scotland (Fees) Amendment Order 2021 was laid in the Scottish Parliament and, if approved, will come into force on 1 April 2021. For all details, see www.ros.gov.uk/about/publications/consultations-and-surveys/2020/fee-review-2020. Assuming that that happens, and assuming also that the market recovers to 90% of its pre-crisis level, RoS forecast that income would cover costs as well as leaving a small surplus needed for investment in future projects and services.

Buying from volume builders: a problem with legal reports?

In an article entitled 'Only "part of" the story', published at (2020) 65 *Journal of the Law Society of Scotland* Dec/36, William MacRae raises an interesting issue about searches. Volume builders generally refuse to provide legal reports. Search firms in such cases typically offer to buyers only so-called 'part of' legal reports, which do not confirm that the plot in question, or part of it, has not been already conveyed to another purchaser. If that has indeed happened, it will be discovered only after settlement, when the registration application is bounced by the Keeper. While a legal report that provides detailed assurance can be obtained, it is likely to be expensive, and perhaps slow, because non-standard. Mr MacRae concludes his article by asking: 'Why should conveyancers have to choose either to pay an extraordinary amount, or to risk a potentially large claim, to cover arguably the most basic point in the conveyancing process – ensuring the seller owns what they are seeking to sell?' We think that this article merits consideration by residential conveyancers.

Scottish Housing Market Review 2020

Divided into quarterly returns, the Scottish Housing Market Review for 2020 (www.gov.scot/publications/scottish-housing-market-review-2020/) contains a great deal of useful information in respect of the period from 1 October 2019 onwards. This draws together data from a number of sources including Registers of Scotland, the Scottish Government, UK Finance and the Bank of England. The results of the corresponding Review for 2019 were summarised in *Conveyancing 2019* pp 99–100. Some of the more important findings of the 2020 Review are given below.

Sales

In the full calendar year 2019, there were 102,930 residential property sales registered in Scotland, up by an annual 2.1%.

There were 29,065 residential property sales registered across Scotland in the fourth quarter of 2019 ('Q4 2019'), which is an annual increase of 1.0%. This was followed by a significant drop in sales activity after Scottish Government advice to delay home moves was issued on 31 March 2020 (advice that was not lifted until 29 June). The number of residential LBTT returns fell by an annual 67% in April and May combined, while sales registered in Scotland fell by an annual 81% over the same period (although the latter may have been affected by a temporary pause in registrations). Thereafter activity picked up strongly.

Prices

In the calendar year 2019, the average (mix-adjusted) house price in Scotland increased by an annual 1.8%, while the average (non mix-adjusted) Scottish house price increased by an annual 1.2%

The average (mix-adjusted) house price in Scotland stood at £153K in Q4 2019, up by an annual 2.2%.The average house price in Scotland increased by an annual 2.5%, to £152K in Q1 2020 and by an annual 1.8%, to £154K, in Q2. House prices have continued to fall in Aberdeen/shire and Moray; over the last five years, the average house price has fallen by 1.1% per annum.

Lending

The mean LTV ratio for new mortgages advanced to first-time buyers stood at 82.5% in Q4 2019, which was higher than levels seen just prior to the 2008 financial crisis. Following the introduction of strict stay-at-home measures to reduce the spread of Covid-19 in late March 2020, the number of mortgage products available fell by approximately half. Since then, there has only been relatively modest recovery in the mortgage market.

The average fixed mortgage rate on new lending stood at 1.76% in July 2020, down only nine basis points since January 2020 (in the context of a 65 basis point fall in Bank Rate, to 0.1%, in March 2020). High LTV mortgages became relatively more expensive. In August 2020, the spread between the average advertised two-year fixed 90% LTV and 75% LTV mortgage rate was nearly double the amount in January 2020 (now 120 basis points). However, this is not out of line with the long-term spread since 2010.

Lenders offered to residential and buy-to-let mortgage customers who had been affected by Covid-19 a mortgage payment holiday, and enforcement actions were stopped. On 22 May 2020 the FCA announced that customers yet to request a payment holiday would have a further three months to do so (until 31 October) and, for those already taking a mortgage payment holiday and unable to resume full payments, their lender should offer them a further full or partial payment deferral for three monthly payments. The FCA also expected all lenders to stop enforcement action until 31 October 2020, regardless of whether borrowers' income was affected by Covid-19.

House-building

A total of 9,317 affordable homes were completed in 2019, up by an annual 0.7% (+61). Meanwhile, there were 10,765 starts in 2019, up by an annual 3.7% (+380). All-sector new-build completions in 2019 increased by an annual 11.4% to 22,386, Scottish Government statistics show. This data does not yet cover the post-Covid-19 period.

Residential LBTT

There was a sharp fall in residential LBTT revenue. From April to August 2020, residential LBTT liabilities (excluding ADS) totalled £55m, down 56% on the same period in 2019–20. This was due to the slowdown in housing market activity, as well as the Scottish Government raising the zero rate threshold for all buyers to £250,000, which took effect on 15 July 2020.

Transparency in property ownership

Since 6 April 2016 UK-registered companies have had to maintain a public register (the 'PSC register') of those who have 'significant control' over the company: see Small Business, Enterprise and Employment Act 2015 Part 7 and sch 3, inserting ss 790A to 790ZG and sch 1A into the Companies Act 2006. (Connoisseurs of statutes will savour a section numbered as '790ZG'.) It is intended to apply a similar regime to 'overseas entities', and accordingly a draft Bill (Westminster) was published in 2018: the Registration of Overseas Entities Bill: for discussion see *Conveyancing 2018* pp 174 ff. The original expectation had been that this Bill would be passed before the end of 2019, with commencement planned for 2021. Brexit and Covid have prevented progress, but we understand that the project is postponed rather than abandoned. Possibly the legislation will be passed in 2021 with commencement in 2022. As and when that takes place the effect on conveyancing involving overseas entities will be substantial.

Side by side with the London initiative there is an Edinburgh initiative, which was likewise intended for commencement in 2021 and which likewise has been blown off course, by Covid, but which likewise has not disappeared. See *Conveyancing 2018* pp 174–81 for background. And whereas nothing in 2020 has happened with the London initiative, there have been developments in 2020 in Edinburgh, as to which see p 69 above. In particular, the Land Reform (Scotland) Act 2016 (Register of Persons Holding a Controlled Interest in Land) Regulations 2021 were laid before Holyrood on 17 December 2020, re-laid on 15 January 2021, and have since been passed. The intention is that the Regulations, if approved, will come into force on 1 April 2022. The Regulations will be covered in next year's annual volume. The publication of the Regulations was accompanied by an *Explanatory Document* (www.gov.scot/publications/register-persons-holding-controlled-interest-land-explanatory-document/) and by a trio of impact assessments (Equality, Data Protection, and Business and Regulatory Impact Assessments).

One unusual aspect of the new Regulations may be mentioned now. Regulation 16(1) provides that:

> An associate who is an individual may, at any time, make a declaration that the inclusion in the RCI of one or more of the associate's required details would put the associate or an individual connected with the associate at risk of violence, abuse, threat of violence or abuse, or intimidation (a 'security declaration').

The Keeper, applying a reasonableness test, can either accept or reject such a declaration; if the latter there is a right of appeal to the Lands Tribunal; and in the event that an appeal is made, the appeal *must* be heard in private – a unique direction for the Tribunal. The relevant provision is the Lands Tribunal for Scotland Rules 2003, SSI 2003/452, r 15(2) as substituted by the Lands Tribunal for Scotland (Miscellaneous Amendments) Rules 2020, SSI 2020/443, r 3.

In summary, it is possible – we cannot put it higher than that – by the end of 2022 Scotland will have three 'transparency' regimes, namely: (i) the existing PSC regime, which is UK-wide; (ii) the Registration of Overseas Entities Act 2021 (maybe), also UK-wide; and (iii) the Land Reform (Scotland) Act 2016 (Register of Persons Holding a Controlled Interest in Land) Regulations 2021 (probably).

Price transparency

The CMA study

In the course of a wide-ranging research report on *Legal Services in Scotland*, which was published in March 2020 (www.gov.uk/cma-cases/scottish-legal-services-research#research-report), the Competition and Markets Authority examined whether information as to the cost of legal services was readily available to consumers, and whether consumers could make meaningful comparisons on price and quality as between different law firms. The CMA's conclusion was that much more needed to be done on this front (paras 3.30–3.32):

> We find that there is generally limited transparency in price information provided by solicitors in Scotland.

First, only a minority of Scottish solicitor firms display prices of services. Of the 160 solicitor firms who responded to the CMA's survey, only 6% said they currently advertise prices on their website and a further 4% said they intended to do so in the future. 72% of firms said they had no plans to advertise prices on their website and 18% said that they had no website. Further, only 16% of all solicitor firms responded that they had used any other method to advertise price, such as print and television methods of advertising.

Second, it is apparent that price is not seen as an important parameter of competition by solicitor firms in Scotland. Only 3% of solicitor firms mentioned price transparency when asked what is important for winning clients. Moreover, only 22% of solicitor firms mentioned that price level was important for winning business, which is not in line with consumer preference as noted in paragraph 3.21

An important effect of this absence of price transparency, the CMA said, was to restrict competition and consumer choice. On conveyancing, the CMA found that, while the median fee charged for selling a house was £700, fees ranged from £600 to £800. Yet how was a consumer to know which firms charged £600 and which £800? This information, said the CMA (paras 3.35–3.37), was simply not available:

The lack of information available online, together with the limited meaningful uptake on DCTs [digital comparison tools, ie price-comparison websites] by firms, means that consumers have limited readily accessible information to compare prices. To do so they must instead contact and discuss their case with each solicitor directly, which increases search costs ... For consumers to shop around effectively, it is important that they have access to information about the prices of multiple providers, based on which they can choose a specific solicitor. We note that the LSS has required, since 2005, that all solicitors provide a letter of engagement prior to being instructed which includes an estimate of price. The rules that impose this requirement specify that either a total cost or the basis on which the fee is to be charged must be provided to the client. However, during stakeholder engagement, concern was raised that such letters were not assisting consumers in shopping around and comparing prices of multiple providers before engagement, as the letter is issued only after the solicitor has been instructed.

From the evidence above, we can see that providers do not typically make price information available to consumers in an accessible manner. The limited information made available by providers exacerbates the complexity of legal services and poses a significant barrier for consumers to shop around, especially in light of their limited experience and knowledge of the legal sector.

'In conclusion', said the CMA (para 3.49):

the large dispersion of prices for the commonly used Scottish legal services we examined support the view that there is a lack of price competition in the sector. This in part reflects the lack of accessible price information available to consumers, and the fact that providers do not have an incentive to depart from the status quo where they enjoy a degree of information asymmetry over consumers. We consider that regulatory intervention is required to address this asymmetry. While we recognise that information transparency alone does not remove all barriers for consumers to engage given the inherent complexity of the legal sector, it is an important starting point for increasing the competitive pressure on providers.

More precisely (paras 3.63 and 3.64):

> Consumers should be able to obtain an indicative cost for a case in any area of law. This should take the form of usable indicators of price or the charging model that can assist in comparisons between providers. Consumers should be able to identify this information without having to discuss the details of their case with a provider, ideally through a website. Consumers should also know the details of the service they would receive for the indicative price.
>
> The form in which such indicators of costs can most effectively be provided may vary by type of service. Firms should be required to provide a minimum level of information on the price for a service. Where the process is standardised, such as the purchase or sale of a house, including the price of any additional services and outlays, it may be that a fixed price can be provided. However, where a case is complex and not easily priced without understanding the details of a case, there are a variety of ways in which information about price can be given.

Price, the CMA acknowledged, was not the only factor relevant to consumer choice. The quality of the service provided and advice given was already important. But here, too, there was little information for the consumer. While, on the basis of the CMA's survey, 82% of Scottish law firms had a website, only 16% included third-party business listings such as Google or Facebook on their site which would allow for ratings and reviews to be added by clients, and only 34% published reviews of previous clients (para 3.52). In the CMA's view, change was needed (paras 3.70 and 3.71):

> Consumers should also have information on the quality of a firm's service and advice when purchasing legal services. This is important to enable consumers to judge the value of a firm's offering. Many consumers rely on personal recommendations. However, these are based on subjective experience and since they often come from one-off purchasers of legal services, they are not based on a review of what the whole sector has to offer.
>
> We therefore recommend that the regulator should look to identify appropriate signals of quality in the sector. For example, it could encourage providers to engage with independent review and rating platforms and consumers should be passed details of where to leave reviews and feedback … Additionally, indicators of quality of advice such as quality marks or findings of adverse conduct should be communicated clearly to consumers.

The Law Society's guidance on price transparency

A few weeks ahead of this onslaught from the CMA, and alerted to what was likely to be said by the equivalent *Legal Services Market Study* for England and Wales which had been published by the CMA in 2016, the Law Society, for the first time, issued guidance on price transparency. Matters were then delayed by the Covid-19 lockdown and the commencement of the guidance was postponed until 31 January 2021. The key parts of the guidance are the following:

2. Publishing price information

2.1 When to provide price information

There are two points where price information should be provided to consumers:

1. When the consumer is searching for a price. At this point the consumer may wish to obtain a general idea of price to make an informed choice across several practice units. The price information should be available upfront, for example on a website and this guidance is relevant to this stage.
2. The second point is at the instruction stage. This is where the consumer contacts and engages with a practice unit direct, providing further details of the legal matter in question. At this point mandatory compliance with Practice Rule B4 (Client Communication) requires solicitors to provide the following information in writing to clients:
   - an outline of the work to be done;
   - an estimate of the total fee or the basis upon which the fee will be charged including VAT and outlays;
   - details of any contribution towards Legal Advice and Assistance or Legal Aid and details of the effect of preservation or recovery of any property if relevant;
   - who will do the work and
   - who the client should contact if they have any concerns or complaints.

2.2 Where to publish

Practice units should make information on the services they offer, and their relative prices, as readily available as possible to consumers, in a manner which is timely, meaningful, accessible, easy to understand and which allows the consumer to compare information across providers. The consumer should be able to access price information without being required to supply personal data (such as names or contact details).

Where the practice unit has a website then price information should be published in a prominent location which is clearly signposted and without the need to provide detailed information to access this.

Where the practice unit does not have a website, then price information should be readily available in another format which can be provided to the consumer, again without the need for the consumer to provide detailed information. For example, price information leaflets could be available in public facing parts, in a reception area, of practice unit premises, via social media or by a web-based online quote calculator.

2.3 Form of price information

Price information should be provided in a suitable and understandable form. However, it is for the practice unit to decide on the most appropriate form to suit their business model. Different formats may be suitable for different services. For example, practice units may choose to provide information that:

   - sets out the hourly chargeable rates for each level of fee earner,
   - provides fixed fees price,
   - sets out scenario fees or the price of a typical case.

When publishing a total price (fixed fees, scenario or typical price) the guidance relating to Practice Rule B3 (Advertising and Promotion) should be complied with.

Prices for consumers should be shown as VAT inclusive. Where VAT inclusive pricing is used, this should be made clear. For example, 'Prices inclusive of VAT at 20%'.

Where VAT exclusive prices are given, it must be made clear that the price does not include VAT. This must be stated along with the current applicable rate. For example: 'Prices do not include VAT. VAT will be charged at the rate of 20%'.

2.4 Clear and meaningful language

Language within the price information must be clear and in words which are understandable to the consumer, avoiding the use of legal terms wherever possible. Guidance on this can be obtained from the Plain English Campaign. The language should not be ambiguous in any way. Practice units must have regard to compliance with Practice Rule B3 (Advertising and Promotion).

2.5 Price information to be provided

This guidance is not intended to place an obligation to publish price information which is a binding quote. The price information published only needs to be an average or typical price.

It is acknowledged that it may not be possible to publish an accurate price for every service in every scenario, or to anticipate unusual complexities, but the published information should be an average or typical price to allow consumers to have an informed understanding of the likely cost of the services offered, and of the factors which may influence the final cost. As far as possible, the price information provided should be complete and contain enough information to allow the consumer to understand the price that is relevant to their circumstances.

When publishing price information this should include:
details of the services included;

- details of any services that a consumer may reasonably expect to be included, given the nature of the work, but which are not, in fact, included;
- where hourly chargeable rates are applied, information about the level(s) of fee earner(s) who will undertake different parts of the work;
- where you publish a range of prices, the basis of your charges, and the types of factors which will determine the final price;
- a description of any likely outlay and its likely cost – or the method by which such cost is calculated;
- whether any fees or outlays attract VAT – and how this is calculated.

Where appropriate, the price information should make it clear, that the price is an average or typical price only and the final price will be dependent on the circumstances of the legal matter.

2.6 Additional information

When publishing price information, the practice unit may choose to publish other information which allows consumers to be able to assess value for money, for example the level and quality of service to be provided.

Where a practice unit chooses to publish additional information on quality of service, then they must be mindful of compliance with Practice Rule B3 (Advertising and Promotion).

2.7 Additional complexities

The very nature of legal matters often gives rise to unforeseen complexities and additional work. This guidance does not require practice units to provide or publish binding price information or to pre-empt complexities arising. However, where complexities arise or the nature of the client's instructions change, then the practice unit should inform the client of this and provide revised price information.

Nothing in this guidance removes the responsibility of the practice unit to provide in writing the specific information required in Practice Rule B4 (Client Communication) when tendering for business or at the earliest opportunity upon receiving instructions to undertake any work on behalf of a client.

The guidance then goes on to give a series of examples. The only example which relates to conveyancing is for a fixed fee for the sale of residential property:

Our fees cover all of the work required to complete the sale of your current property including the marketing of your property, dealing with any offers and subsequent missives, ordering searches, repaying any secured loans and registering any deeds at Registers of Scotland and paying any funds to you.

Fees and outlays

- Legal fee £{insert amount}
- VAT payable £{insert amount}
- Estate Agency Fee £{insert amount}
- Home report fee £{insert amount}
- Property Search fees £{insert amount}
- Registers of Scotland – fee for registering Discharge £{insert amount}
- Advance notice registration fee for Discharge £{insert amount}
- Electronic money transfer fee £{insert amount}

Estimated total: £{insert amount}

Outlays are costs related to your matter that are payable to third parties, such as Registers of Scotland and Search Companies. We handle the payment of the outlays on your behalf to ensure a smoother process.

Stages of the process

The precise stages involved in the sale of a residential property vary according to the circumstances. However, below we have suggested some key stages that you may wish to include:

- Take your instructions and give you initial advice.
- Carry out required Anti Money Laundering checks.
- Arrange home report.
- Market the property.
- Receive offers on property and take your instructions.
- Obtain redemption statements from current lender (the amount required to repay your mortgage).
- Order Title Deeds.
- Receive and advise on missives (contract).
- Carry out property searches as required.
- Obtain further planning documentation if required.
- Revise draft documents received from purchasers' solicitors.
- Conclude missives (and notify you that this has happened).
- Issue completion statement.
- Complete sale.
- Repay any mortgages and pay any outlays due.
- Prepare the discharge of the standard security and submit this to the Registers of Scotland.
- Paying any surplus funds due to you.

Is guidance enough?

For the moment at least, the Law Society's recommendations on price transparency take the form of guidance rather than binding rules. In its report on *Legal Services in Scotland*, the Competition and Markets Authority doubted whether this was enough. The CMA's formal recommendation (para 3.69) was for:

> the LSS to carry out an assessment of the impact that the existing guidance has had within a year of its introduction. This should examine whether the guidance has driven any change in solicitors' approach to providing relevant pricing and service information, and whether it has resulted in changes in consumer behaviour. Assuming that it has not driven the sort of change in transparency that we would like to see, we recommend that the LSS adopts a set of mandatory rules

Anti-money laundering guidance

A new edition of *Anti-Money Laundering: Guidance for the Legal Sector* was issued in March 2020. It is prepared by the Legal Sector Affinity Group (which includes the Law Society of Scotland) and runs to some 156 pages. Among the changes in law and practice which it takes into account are the amendments made to the Money Laundering, Terrorist Financing and Transfer of Funds (Information on the Payer) Regulations 2017, SI 2017/692, with effect from 10 January 2020, by the Money Laundering and Terrorist Financing (Amendment) Regulations 2019, SI 2019/1511 (as to which see *Conveyancing 2019* p 88).

In addition, the Legal Sector Affinity Group (LSAG) issued an advisory note in April 2020 (www.lawscot.org.uk/media/368664/covid-19-lsag-advisory-note-14420.pdf), highlighting key AML risks and challenges for the legal profession associated with the Covid-19 crisis. Further advice from the Law Society can be found at www.lawscot.org.uk/news-and-events/law-society-news/amlroundupjune20/.

Cladding of external walls and EWS1 certificates

The fire risks created by certain types of cladding used for external walls have become a major issue following the devastating fire at Grenfell Tower in London on 14 June 2017. On 30 March 2020, Scottish Ministers agreed to set up a Technical Working Group to develop a *Scottish Advice Note* to determine the fire risk posed by external wall systems in existing multi-storey residential buildings. This is intended to bring clarity to the different legislative requirements and guidance in Scotland, and to take account of the key findings from fire-testing of external wall cladding systems carried out by the UK Government. Further details can be found at www.gov.scot/collections/external-wall-cladding-systems-advice/.

For owners and tenants, and potential owners and tenants, the question of personal safety is, obviously, paramount. But there is also a valuation, and hence a conveyancing, dimension because of the importance of determining whether any cladding on a property which is being bought or sold is safe from the point of view of fire. In response to this issue, lenders have issued instructions to their panel valuers that, without satisfactory certification from a suitably qualified professional confirming that the cladding does not pose a fire risk, valuers are to place a £0 value on the property. A standard-form certificate has been agreed for this purpose by the Building Societies Association, RICS and UK Finance (see eg www.ukfinance.org.uk/policy-and-guidance/reports-publications/external-wall-fire-review). This is the External Wall Fire Review, better known as an EWS1 certificate.

EWS1 certificates

The requirement for an EWS1 applies to all buildings in excess of 18 metres high (measured from ground level to the carpet level of the top floor property). Some lenders may also require an EWS1 for buildings under 18 metres, and in its *Advice for Building Owners of Multi-storey*, issued in January 2020, the (UK) Ministry of Housing, Communities & Local Government emphasised the fire risks to such lower buildings. New-build properties are affected as well as older buildings. Grenfell Tower had Aluminium Composite Material (ACM) cladding, but other types of cladding may also be combustible. The issue extends beyond cladding in the strict sense to include external wall systems generally, including, for instance, wooden balconies.

At only a single page, form EWS1 seems reassuringly straightforward. But it raises many issues, only some of which have been resolved. Helpful guidance from the Law Society can be found at www.lawscot.org.uk/news-and-events/law-society-news/cladding-update/ and again at www.lawscot.org.uk/news-and-events/law-society-news/externalwallsystems/.

In completing form EWS1, the fire-safety expert must choose between option A and option B. The first certifies that external wall materials are unlikely to support combustion. The second is for where combustible materials are present in the wall, whereupon the expert must certify either that 'the fire risk is sufficiently low that no remedial works are required' or that 'an adequate standard of safety is not achieved'. To make an option B certification requires a higher degree of expertise than option A so that, if option A turns out to be inapplicable, the person conducting the inspection may finish up recommending that another person with the appropriate expertise be engaged. On this topic, the notes to the form say that:

> For Option A, the signatory would need the expertise to identify the relevant materials within the external wall and attachments and whether fire resisting cavity barriers and fire stopping have been installed correctly. However, this would not necessarily include the need for expertise in fire engineering. The signatory should be a member of a relevant professional body within the construction industry. For Option B the signatory would need expertise in the assessment of the fire risk presented by external wall materials and should be a member of a relevant professional body that deals with fire safety in the built environment. This could be a Chartered Engineer with the Institution of Fire Engineers or equivalent.

In Scotland there is a shortage of people with the necessary qualifications, and obtaining a certificate is likely to take some time. It will also be expensive. In excess of 1,000 buildings have now had inspections carried out. The Law Society reports, anecdotally, that the fail rate for buildings inspected may be about 30%.

If the building fails the inspection – if, in other words, the EWS1 concludes that 'an adequate standard of safety is not achieved' – the flats in the building are likely to be unmarketable unless or until the necessary remediation works are carried out. That in turn will require the agreement of the owners, or at least of the percentage of owners who can authorise acts of maintenance under the title deeds or, if the deeds are silent, under the Tenement Management Scheme. In the case of the latter, the owners of a majority of flats can authorise maintenance: see TMS rr 2.5 and 3.1(a). It is probable, though perhaps not quite certain, that the remediation works would fall within the definition of 'maintenance' in r 1.5. Significant sums of money will be involved.

Although almost all affected buildings are blocks of flats, a EWS1 certificate can only be prepared for the owner of a single flat and not for all the owners in the building. This is at the insistence of the PI insurers of the fire-safety experts, in order to limit potential liability. In support of this approach, the form contains the stern warning that:

> This review is for the sole and exclusive use of the client organisation named below. No responsibility is accepted to any third party for the whole or any part if its contents. For the avoidance of doubt, the term 'third party' includes (but is not limited to): any lender who may see the review during the process through which they come to make a loan secured on any part of the Subject Address; and any prospective purchaser who may see the review during the process through which they come to purchase an interest in any part of the Subject Address.

Although there has been some loose talk of the seller who instructs an EWS1 'assigning' its benefits to the purchaser and the purchaser's lender, it is apparent that (assuming the limitation of liability just quoted to be valid and enforceable) the expert signing the form has no duty of care to such third parties, and that such a duty can only arise if it is voluntarily assumed by the expert. That is why note 4 to the form states that: 'Should there be a desire for a third party to rely on this form, they should contact the signatory's organisation.' Such extended liability, if it can be agreed upon, will not be free of charge.

The role of solicitors

On the role of solicitors the Law Society's website contains some useful pointers. In the first place, solicitors should seek to ascertain whether the home report surveyor is identifying potential EWS1 issues in the single survey (in the absence of an agreed RICS approach to reporting). For this purpose, the whole home report should be scrutinised.

Secondly, and assuming an EWS1 to exist:

> A purchaser's solicitor does not have either the technical knowledge or the PI cover to advise on the terms of an EWS1 other than to confirm that one exists and the terms thereof and should make that clear to the client either in letter of engagement or at the time the issue arises. A purchaser should be advised that if they wish further advice they would need to consider engaging a suitably qualified person to provide that. If a buyer does proceed where an EWS1 exists it will be good practice to record the client's wishes in a file note or email to the client.

Thirdly, solicitors can and should check that the firm or individual issuing the EWS1 is a member of the professional body they purport to be and that they have current and adequate PI cover, perhaps with confirmation from the PI provider that it extends to the specific EWS1 in question. EWS1 certificates should not be accepted at face value because of the risk of fraud. Ideally, solicitors should call the party purporting to have issued the certificate and seek a letter of provenance as to its authenticity.

Fourthly, assuming the EWS1 to be in order, solicitors acting for the purchaser should ensure that the signatory's duty of care is extended to the purchaser (and, if appropriate, the lender).

Fifthly, the risk of buildings insurers declining to renew cover or withdrawing cover should be considered when advising a client about buying a flat with cladding, particularly where the terms of the EWS1 are not straightforward.

Amalgamation of the Land Court and Lands Tribunal?

On 27 July 2020 the Scottish Government opened a consultation on the possible amalgamation of the Scottish Land Court and the Lands Tribunal for Scotland: see www.gov.scot/publications/consultation-future-land-court-lands-tribunal/. Primary legislation would be needed. If an amalgamation were to go ahead, this would be likely to involve the Lands Tribunal, as the younger and less senior body, being subsumed into the Land Court.

The two bodies have shared the same head (respectively Chairman and President) since 1978. Perceived advantages of amalgamation include reduced administrative costs, the flexibility of being able to deploy the same judges across the two jurisdictions (useful given the small staffing levels of both bodies), and the opportunity to add other aspects of land law – such as the litigation generated by the substantial body of legislation on land reform – to the jurisdiction of the combined body. We would warmly support the last of these suggestions. The Lands Tribunal has brought an admirable degree of expertise and consistency to applications under the Title Conditions (Scotland) Act 2003 and the Land Registration etc (Scotland) Act 2012, and much else besides. No doubt the same could be said of the Land Court (though we lack the knowledge to comment). As the consultation paper notes in relation to the right-to-roam legislation (which has to be litigated in the ordinary courts), 'the present arrangements mean that individual sheriffs are unlikely to gain extensive expertise in the determination of such cases and there is, consequently, a risk of lack of consistency of approach' (para 50). No major disadvantages of amalgamation are mentioned in the paper other than to say that both bodies work very well as things are and are valued by their users.

The opportunity was taken to consult on one or two other matters, including whether the Land Court should continue to be required to have a Gaelic-speaking member, and whether, in the interests of access to justice, s 103 of the Title Conditions (Scotland) Act 2003 (which, broadly speaking, provides for expenses to follow success) should be amended.

The consultation closed on 19 October 2020.

Scottish Barony Register

One by-product of the abolition of the feudal system on 28 November 2004 was for barony titles (ie the dignity of baron including the right to use the title 'baron') to be severed from the land to which they had formerly been attached: see Abolition of Feudal Tenure etc (Scotland) Act 2000 s 63. As a result they could no longer be registered in the Land Register or Sasine Register – or, officially, anywhere else (other than the Books of Council and Session). In response, a private register was set up under the direction of Alistair Rennie, a former Deputy Keeper of the Registers. Now that baronies were to be transferred by assignation and not by disposition, the idea was, and is, that the assignation should be registered in the new register, known as the Scottish Barony Register.

As a matter of law, of course, a transfer is already complete when an assignation is delivered (2000 Act s 63(2)); but the further step of registration is intended to reassure future purchasers that the same barony has not been sold twice, and in practice an unregistered assignation may not be accepted as a good title. In addition, certification from the 'custodian' of the Register is accepted by the Lord Lyon as evidence of title in dealing with a petition for arms based on ownership of a named baronial dignity. A note on p 37 of the *Journal of the Law Society of Scotland* for December 2020 gives something of the background:

> It was obvious from the start that no absolute guarantee could be given by the register as to the validity of any claim, because there would be a number of things that the Custodian could not know. Equally obviously, there could be no compulsion to register, so why would people do so? The answer lay in setting terms and conditions as regards evidence that would make it difficult for any fraudster to comply with, and establishing a rigorous examination process to ascertain, as far as possible, that the evidence submitted is credible. As a further protection, the register will only accept applications from solicitors registered to practise in Scotland.

It is thought that every transfer of the dignity of baron occurring since 2004 has been registered, and the Register contains details of transfer of 170 different dignities, some of which have been transferred more than once.

After 16 years, Mr Rennie is retiring as custodian of the Register. His successor, from 1 December 2020, is Alastair Shepherd, a former partner in Coulters. He can be contacted at 1 Monkrigg Steading, Haddington EH41 4LB or by email at custodian@scottishbaronyregister.org. A new website has been set up with all relevant information including forms and fees: see www.scottishbaronyregister.org.

Land Use Strategy

The first two Land Use Strategies

The first Land Use Strategy was laid before the Scottish Parliament in 2011, in implement of s 57 of the Climate Change (Scotland) Act 2009. The Strategy comprised a Vision, Three Objectives, and Ten Principles for Sustainable Land Use. They are reproduced in full in *Conveyancing 2011* pp 75–76. That, however, was far from being the end of the matter because s 57(6) of the Act requires that a revised Land Use Strategy be prepared every five years. In 2016 it was decided to carry the 2011 Strategy forward for a further five years but with the addition of Nine Policies (reproduced in *Conveyancing 2016* pp 104–05).

Progress on the second Strategy was reviewed in a Scottish Government document published on 16 July 2020: *Getting the best from our land – a land use strategy 2016 to 2021: first annual progress report*. This explained (at p 2) that:

> How we use and manage our land in Scotland is critical to tackling both the climate and environment crises. The importance of land use for mitigating and adapting to climate change has been highlighted by the UK Committee on Climate Change in their advice on setting an economy-wide net-zero emissions target for 2045 and in their recent *Land Use: Policies for a Net Zero UK* report. The Scottish Government recognises this, and actions taken to fulfil commitments within the Land Use Strategy 2016–2021 in areas such as Agriculture and Forestry continue to contribute to the on-going drive to reduce net emissions from sources in Scotland. The Scottish Government is also clear that in parallel to moving towards net-zero emissions we need to restore and enhance Scotland's wider natural capital, including its biodiversity.
>
> The pivotal importance of land in these efforts is reflected in the 2018 *Climate Change Plan: Third Report on Proposals and Policies 2018–2032* (RPP3), which set out indicative emissions envelopes for the Land Use, Land Use Change and Forestry (LULUCF) as well as agriculture sectors to meet the previous, less challenging, target of an 80% reduction in emissions by 2050. Land use will remain a cornerstone of the forthcoming recasting of the Plan in the context of the new target of reaching net-zero by 2045 and of a green recovery from COVID-19.

Progress towards meeting the aims of the Land Use Strategy is reviewed under a number of headings: natural capital, land reform, agriculture, and forestry. One subject on which little progress has so far been made is regional land use partnerships, and a 'key priority over the coming year is to ensure that partnerships emerge locally during 2021' (p 5).

Regional land use partnerships

Meanwhile, the Scottish Land Commission (https://landcommission.gov.scot) has been carrying out scoping work on regional land use partnerships, culminating in its publication in 2020 of *Advice to Scottish Government on the Establishment of Regional Land Use Partnerships*. Such partnerships had first been proposed in the second Land Use Strategy, of 2016. The idea is to build on existing forms of community empowerment by encouraging 'plan-based action'. Analogous in some respects to National Parks, some 12–15 regional land use partnerships would be set up, to 'engage widely on the land use opportunities, choices and priorities and drive a collaborative approach to land use decision making in the public interest' (7). Each partnership would consist of an appointed board. Their remit would be 'to deliver on the objectives of the Land Use Strategy and the principles of the Land Rights and Responsibilities Statement' (10) (for the latter, see *Conveyancing 2017* pp 95–96). An initial task would be to produce a Regional Land Use Framework; these 'should be indicative spatial plans which identify opportunities, choices and priorities for all land use, including forest and woodland strategies, in order to stimulate delivery and be accessible to all within a region' (13). Although there is to be 'a clear focus on the delivery on the ground' (4), it is unclear, as yet, what this actually amounts to, or indeed how the proposed new bodies are to fit in with existing bodies without merely adding another layer of bureaucracy.

The third Land Use Strategy

A third Land Use Strategy is now under preparation and a consultation document – *Scotland's Third Land Use Strategy 2021–2026: Consultation and Draft Strategy* – was published on 2 December 2020. Rather than offering new policy proposals, the third Land Use Strategy intends to bring together 'key strands of Scottish Government policy that affect land use, and sets out how these various policy areas fit together on the ground' (4). The consultation closed on 17 January 2021. It will be followed by an 'overarching strategic document' which will be laid before the Scottish Parliament in March 2021. A more detailed delivery plan will then be published in the next Parliamentary session. 'The focus of our recovery from COVID-19', the consultation paper says, 'is a green one that seizes on the opportunities for creating sustainable jobs. It is imperative that the Green Recovery is part of our just transition to net-zero that leaves no one behind.'

Scottish Crown Estate: strategic management plan

The Crown Estate is owned by the Crown but administered by others. Until 1 April 2017 it was under the direction of the Crown Estate Commissioners; today, in terms of the Scottish Crown Estate Act 2019, it is administered by Crown Estate Scotland (*Oighreachd a' Chrùin Alba*), and management of particular assets can be further devolved to local authorities, harbour authorities, other public authorities, community organisations, or even to the Scottish Ministers: for details, see *Conveyancing 2018* pp 88–89.

For as long as the Crown Estate in Scotland was administered by the Crown Estate Commissioners, there was a statutory duty, under s 1(3) of the Crown Estate Act 1961, 'to maintain and enhance its value and the return obtained from it'. The equivalent provision in the Scottish Crown Estate Act 2019, s 7, qualifies that duty by requiring the 'manager' – whether Crown Estate Scotland or some devolved body – to (a) 'act in the way best calculated to further the achievement of sustainable development in Scotland', and also to (b) 'seek to manage the assets in a way that is likely to contribute to the promotion or the improvement in Scotland of (i) economic development, (ii) regeneration, (iii) social wellbeing, and (iv) environmental wellbeing'.

A certain amount of flesh is put on these bones by the *Strategic Management Plan* published by the Scottish Government on 31 March 2020 (www.gov.scot/publications/first-strategic-management-plan-scottish-crown-estate/). This had previously been the subject of public consultation: for an analysis of the responses, published on 25 February 2020, see www.gov.scot/publications/consultation-analysis-report-draft-strategic-management-plan-scottish-crown-estate/. The plan, which is to run for five years, comprises a 'vision' and 22 'objectives, priorities and policies'. The vision is that (para 46):

The Scottish Crown Estate is managed sustainably, responsibly and fairly, and in a transparent and inclusive manner, to deliver long term financial and wider social, economic and environmental wellbeing benefits for Scotland and its communities.

The 'objectives, priorities and policies' (set out in Annexe A and extensively glossed in paras 50–157) are:

1. Scottish Crown Estate assets should be managed for the benefit of Scotland and communities, with market value being charged for sales or leases, unless the manager of the asset can demonstrate that wider benefits of equivalent scale will be delivered.

2. In order to realise the benefits potential, and in recognition that some land and property has been acquired over time for specific investment purposes, there are likely to be sales of assets or parts of assets over the five year period of the Plan, particularly on land or at the coast in response to requests for public benefit purposes or opportunities to increase value to Scotland, recognising that the seabed is a national strategic asset that Scottish Ministers do not wish to become fragmented.

3. Strategies and Plans for Scottish Crown Estate assets should consider the potential for delivering benefits to island communities and assessment of possible impacts will be completed as required under the Islands Act 2018.

4. Managers should consider the potential to contribute to wider policies on land reform and community empowerment by offering opportunities to own or manage these assets directly, and as part of strategies to consider the wider value of the existing land assets remaining part of the Scottish Crown Estate.

5. By 2025, the balance between activity related to management of coastal and marine assets is likely to have grown compared with the rural land assets, to reflect the new opportunities that can be realised, but the Scottish Crown Estate is likely to still include a significant amount of land and property assets.

6. Managers should consider the potential for investments that contribute to the achievement of Scotland's Climate Change Plan and Climate Change Adaptation Plan, and consider the potential for increased investment activity for the purpose of regeneration for community or national benefit, including land on the coast around ports, harbours and other infrastructure, to realise opportunities for Scotland and local economies, and for these investments to normally be prioritised over other new commercial property investments.

7. Investments in the Scottish Crown Estate should not be limited to the land or property that currently forms part of the Estate, if returns or wider benefits to the Estate and Scotland can be realised. For example, to make it possible to deliver benefits to communities living on the coast adjacent to parts of the seabed contained in the Estate.

8. The diversity of the Scottish Crown Estate means that a one-size-fits-all approach to management is not practical and there are potential benefits of local control, management or enhanced input to decision-making within the national governance framework provided by the Scottish Crown Estate Act, and this framework provides the potential for different approaches in different parts of Scotland.

9. It is anticipated that by the end of the five year period there may be a variety of managers of Scottish Crown Estate assets with individual assets managed at the appropriate level and opportunities through either transfers, delegations or pilots for councils, communities and other eligible organisations to contribute to or control decisions on how assets are managed and used.

10. Scotland's seabed is a national strategic asset and should be managed at the national level but Scottish Ministers will keep the arrangements under review to

determine whether it is most appropriate for assets to be managed at the national or local level.

11. Scottish Ministers will run an initial round to invite proposals for transfer or delegation of management of an asset, or parts of an asset to local parts of Scotland, and will consult in advance on draft guidance on what proposals should include and the criteria for assessing proposals received including potential benefits and value for money.

12. All managers should exercise functions when managing a Scottish Crown Estate asset in a way that is transparent, accountable, inclusive and consistent with any other principle of good governance.

13. Scottish Ministers will develop guidance or directions on the manner in which a manager is expected to comply with the requirements of the Scottish Crown Estate Act relating to furthering sustainable development and seeking to manage assets in a way that is likely to contribute to wider benefits to Scotland, including relevant considerations when exercising the powers in section 11 of the Act.

14. Scottish Ministers will develop directions or guidance on other requirements for managers including accounting requirements and any charging requirements under section 13 of the Act.

15. The net revenue will be used for the benefit of Scotland and communities with appropriate arrangements to co-ordinate funding for programmes and projects that cannot be undertaken by a single community or council.

16. The net revenue from marine assets out to 12 nautical miles should demonstrably benefit coastal communities and all arrangements for the use of net revenue should be transparent and accountable with opportunities for communities to express views on how the revenue is used.

17. The Scottish Government will work with COSLA to complete a review of the future arrangements for net revenue from marine assets out to 12 nautical miles. The review will take account of the management requirements of the estate, how future revenue can be increased through strategic funding, the potential for other communities of interest to be managers and the case for these organisations to directly benefit from the net revenue.

18. Local organisations interested in management of a Scottish Crown Estate asset should consider how they could take on the function and liabilities for the longer term and manage the asset in a way that delivers added value, transparency and efficiency and which is compatible with their core remit.

19. Scottish Ministers have a preference for shared services approaches to administration of the assets in order to maximise efficiency and hence net revenue available to Scotland and local communities.

20. An organisation that wishes to take on direct management will normally be expected to manage the associated liabilities, including those arising from their decisions on the management, and cover the associated costs from the income generated from the asset.

21. Crown Estate Scotland staff rights will be respected and protected in the reform of the management of the Scottish Crown Estate and they will have opportunities to contribute their views.

22. Crown Estate Scotland will assist Scottish Ministers in implementing the Strategic Management Plan and will develop new roles in contributing to the co-ordination of the management of the wider Scottish Crown Estate, facilitating delivery of the Plan and realisation of potential benefits, including piloting new partnership working models and potentially including joint ventures.

A full list of assets of the Scottish Crown Estate is given in Annexe C. This comprises:

Asset	Definition
George Street	The property at 39 to 41 George Street, Edinburgh
Seabed	The seabed from 0–12nm in Scottish Territorial Waters
Storage Rights (Seabed)	The rights out to 200nm of: (1) unloading gas to installations and pipelines; (2) storing gas for any purpose and recovering stored gas; and (3) exploration with a view to use for (1) and (2)
Energy rights (Seabed)	The rights, out to 200nm, of exploitation, exploration and connected purposes for the production of energy from wind or water
Mineral Rights (Seabed)	The right to exploit the Seabed and its subsoil other than for hydrocarbons out to 200nm
Cables (including interconnectors)	The right to install all or part of a distribution or transmission system on or under the Seabed out to 200nm
Pipelines	The right to install pipelines out to 200nm
Whitehill Estate	The Whitehill Estate in Midlothian
Glenlivet Estate	The Glenlivet Estate in Moray
Applegirth Estate	The Applegirth Estate in Dumfries & Galloway
Fochabers Estate	The Fochabers Estate in Moray
Aquaculture Rights (Seabed)	The right to shellfish and finfish farming operations
Mooring Rights (Seabed)	The right to lay and use permanent moorings in foreshore which is deemed to form part of The Scottish Crown Estate
Foreshore	(1) In Orkney and Shetland, lying between mean high water springs and lowest ebb tide; and (2) In the rest of Scotland, lying between mean high and low water
Internal Waters	
Salmon Fishing	The right to fish for salmon in rivers and coastal waters where the right belongs to the Crown
Gold and Silver (onshore minerals)	The right to naturally occurring gold and silver except where the right has been has been granted away in formal deeds from the Crown to another party. The Crown's statutory ownership of the right to gold and silver mining in Scotland stems from legislation in the 15th and 16th centuries
Reserved Minerals	All the reserved mineral rights owned by the Crown in Scotland other than on the Seabed
Rights beyond 12 nautical miles	Rights to natural resources on the continental shelf (excluding fossil fuels) under the Continental Shelf Act 1964; Rights to offshore renewables and the transportation and storage of natural gas and carbon dioxide on the continental shelf under the Energy Act 2008.

Asset transfer requests: evaluation

Under Part 5 of the Community Empowerment (Scotland) Act 2015, which came into force on 23 January 2017, community bodies are able to request a whole range of public bodies to sell or lease heritable property to them (s 79). These bodies, listed in sch 3 of the Act, include local authorities, the Scottish Government, the Scottish Police Authority, Scottish Natural Heritage, Scottish Water, and VisitScotland. In considering such an 'asset transfer request', the public body is required to assess the community body's proposals against the current use or any other proposal, and must agree to the request unless there are reasonable grounds for refusal (s 82). Among the factors that it must take into account are whether agreeing to the request would promote economic development, regeneration, public health, social wellbeing or environmental wellbeing, and whether it would be likely to reduce inequalities of outcome which result from socio-economic disadvantage. For further details, see *Conveyancing 2015* p 76, *Conveyancing 2016* pp 88–89, and *Conveyancing 2017* pp 86–88.

An evaluation of the operation of the legislation in the period to the end of 2019, carried out for the Scottish Government by Glasgow Caledonian University, was published on 30 July 2020: see www.gov.scot/publications/asset-transfer-requests-evaluation-part-5-community-empowerment-scotland-act-2015/. This finds that a total of 139 asset transfer requests were made during this three-year period, mainly to local authorities. 81 were agreed to and 10 refused; the fate of the other 48 requests is unclear. Typical purposes for the requests are for community hubs or community parks or woodlands. Some local authorities were described as being 'hostile or obstructive' in dealing with requests (2).

Scottish Land Commission papers

The Scottish Land Commission (*Coimisean Fearainn na h-Alba*) continues to commission and publish papers and documents on topics within its remit, all of which are available on the Land Commission's website (https://landcommission.gov.scot). Apart from those mentioned elsewhere in this volume (pp 105 and 117), the main papers published in 2020 were those mentioned below.

Review of the first three years

The Scottish Land Commission was established in April 2017 and issued a three-year strategic plan in September of that year. A review of the first three years of the Commission's operation has been published as *Making More of Scotland's Land: Our progress so far*.

Alternatives to community ownership?

In a thoughtful chapter in an important new book, *Land Reform in Scotland: History, Law and Policy* (eds Malcolm M Combe, Jayne Glass and Annie Tindley, 2020), Malcolm Combe speculates as to why the land reform agenda in Scotland has placed so much emphasis on community land ownership (175):

Did we think this through, or did it just happen because an organic movement which reacted to problems that existed in parts of Scotland caught the imagination of legislators, at just the right time and when there was some precedent for community land ownership on the statute books to adapt? … This is not to criticise or praise where Scotland sits, but there are times when Scotland seems to be on something of an accidental community land ownership journey which is not really replicated elsewhere.

What happens elsewhere is considered in a paper commissioned by the Scottish Land Commission and published in April 2020: R McMorran et al, *Review of International Experience of Communal and Municipal Ownership of Land*. This is, of course, an enormous subject, and it is inevitable that a paper which is relatively brief (105 pages, half of which are given over to case studies) and which, presumably, was produced at speed, should take a somewhat scattergun approach. For reasons which are not fully explained (though see pp 19–20), the paper chooses to consider four categories of 'community tenure' as exemplified in England and Wales, in four countries from Continental Europe (France, Germany, Italy and Norway), in North America, and in Kenya and South Africa. The four categories are:

- *Collective properties and commons*: includes examples where the rights of the legal owner are restricted and other people hold beneficial use rights over land.
- *Municipal ownership and commonage*: includes examples where local government authorities manage land in the public interest, and where land is co-owned by the state and community with varying degrees of community input.
- *Third sector and community land trusts*: includes examples where non-profit organisations own land with the primary aim of community benefit.
- *Customary tenure and indigenous groups*: includes examples where land is owned/ managed by indigenous people.

On the basis of the research, the paper draws certain 'lessons for Scotland'. These include (pp 8–9):

- Learning from experience in England and the USA, there is an opportunity to investigate further the potential application of the Community Land Trust model to deliver affordable housing in Scotland.
- In Scotland, anchor organisations (predominantly development trusts) play a critical role in community asset ownership and management. International experience from Community Land Trusts highlights the importance of developing bridging or 'umbrella' organisations at a regional level to oversee anchor organisations and provide co-ordinated guidance and support, as well as a conduit into national policy processes.
- Municipal ownership may offer considerable potential in Scotland, however, the existing local authority framework (and specifically the large scale of local authorities relative to municipal structures in some European countries) represents a key challenge for implementation.
- Partnership or 'hybrid' models of landownership involving communities (of place and of interest), non-governmental organisations, private landowners and the state deserve further attention. Existing partnership models developed in Scotland

under the National Forest Land Scheme for shared delivery of community forest management offer a starting point.
- Collective private models of ownership, equivalent to the state incentivised model of collective private forest ownership in France, may have potential in a Scottish context.

A brief 'Land Focus' paper on this topic, *International Experience of Community, Communal and Municipal Ownership*, has also been published.

Land for housing and development

A paper commissioned from the University of Reading, *Residential development land prices and house prices*, considers the relationship between land prices and house prices, and concludes that each affects the other. But whereas the housing market affects the land market rapidly, the land market affects house prices more slowly. 'This indicates that a policy that reduced housing development land prices by increasing land supply in a competitive environment would reduce house prices over the long-term' (p 21). But this would have to be done on a sufficient scale to keep up with demand for housing which, in Scotland, has been caused by rising living standards rather than by demographic change. At the same time, there has been a long-run decline in housing output since the 1970s due to the relative decline of housing built by the public sector: today Scotland relies on the private sector to provide the majority of new homes (p 2). As supply has reduced and demand increased, so house prices have risen: by approximately 590% since 1980, or approximately 54% in real terms.

One reason sometimes given for the reduced supply of housing is 'land banking', by which (it is said) commercial builders hold on to land for which they have planning permission in order to inflate prices. This issue is investigated in a paper written for the Scottish Land Commission by Paul Chamberlain and Chris Walker of ChamberlainWalker Economics Ltd, *An Investigation into Land Banking in Scotland*. They conclude that land banking of this kind is not a major issue and that, insofar as commercial builders develop land in phases (thus drip-feeding new-build homes on to the market), they do so due to market 'absorption constraints', ie to stop house prices falling due to over-supply. This, says the paper, is for the protection of a legitimate commercial interest rather than mere profiteering. Land banking can also occur in relation to land for which planning permission has not, or not yet, been obtained ('raw' and opposed to 'permissioned' land), and this topic is said to require further research.

The cost and availability for land for building are different as between rural and urban areas. In *The Role of Land in Enabling New Housing Supply in Rural Scotland*, Savills downplay both the cost of land (typically small) and its availability (typically quite good). The main difficulty is that in rural areas building costs tend to be higher than the value of the house once built. This stark fact largely excludes commercial builders, and especially volume builders, from the market. Instead, the provision of new housing relies to a considerable extent on not-for-profit organisations supported by public-sector subsidies. More stable public funding would improve matters: at present there is reliance on the short-term budgets of the Rural Housing Funds and the Scottish Land Fund. So would greater assistance for community and other bodies seeking to engage in the, inevitably complex, business of building houses. The creation of a Scotland-wide database of rural land transactions would help landowners to address quickly the issue of land price.

On the basis of detailed case studies from the Netherlands, Germany and Switzerland, a research team from the Universities of Glasgow and Liverpool make recommendations in relation to land allocation and assembly for housing. In *Housing Allocation, Assembly and Delivery: Lessons from Europe* they suggest that land assembly should be undertaken by public development agencies, whether through purchase (a pre-emption right for public bodies would help here) or by temporary acquisition with the idea that the land is returned to the owners. The public body would install basic infrastructure before selling plots or, as the case may be, returning the land to its original owners.

Finally, a briefing paper in the Scottish Land Commission's 'Land Focus' series, *Land for Housing & Development*, considers some of the main issues and summarises some of the research carried out on behalf of the Land Commission.

Land rights and responsibilities protocols

As part of its 'Good Practice' programme (for which see *Conveyancing 2019* pp 111–12), the Scottish Land Commission has been preparing a number of short 'protocols'. These are intended to support the practical implementation of the Scottish Government's Land Rights and Responsibilities Statement (reproduced in *Conveyancing 2017* pp 95–96) by indicating its 'application to real world scenarios'. The first protocol, on *Community Engagement in Decisions Relating to Land*, was published in 2019, and a further six were published in 2020: *Transparency of Ownership and Land Use Decision-Making*; *Land Ownership by Charities*; *Land Ownership by Private Trusts*; *Diversification of Ownership and Tenure*; *Good Stewardship of Land*; and *Common Good Land*. The protocols are developed in association with the members of the Good Practice Advisory Group: Community Land Scotland, Development Trusts Association Scotland, National Farmers' Union Scotland, Scottish Land and Estates, and Scottish Property Federation.

Shared equity schemes

The First Home Fund is one of a number of shared equity schemes run by the Scottish Government: for others, see *Conveyancing 2019* p 105. The First Home Fund is a £200 million pilot scheme to provide first-time buyers with up to £25,000 to help them buy a property. It is open to all first-time buyers in Scotland and can be used to help buy both new-build and existing properties. A whole suite of documents on the scheme is now available, some for potential buyers, others for solicitors and other professionals: see www.gov.scot/collections/first-home-fund/; and see also Gillian Cogan, 'First Home Fund: how does it work' (2020) 65 *Journal of the Law Society of Scotland* Feb/Online.

Meanwhile on 11 June 2020 the Scottish Government published an evaluation of three other such schemes, Help to Buy (Scotland) (HtB), New Supply Shared

Equity (NSSE), and Open Market Shared Equity (OMSE): see www.gov.scot/publications/evaluation-scottish-government-shared-equity-schemes/. NSSE and OMSE were introduced to improve access to housing for lower-income households. HtB was more specifically focused at supporting the recovery of the new-house building industry after the economic crisis of 2008 by assisting with the 'deposit barrier' faced by borrowers who were no longer able to access high loan-to-value lending. The schemes have supported more than 32,000 households since their introduction in 2005, nearly half of these via the HtB scheme since 2013/14.

In summary, the evaluation found that:

Buyers through the three shared equity schemes were typically relatively young in age profile (71% were under 40), most were first-time buyers (73%), most commonly moving from private (39%) or social renting (12%), and the great majority were in employment (98%) … The majority of buyers had considered home ownership as their only tenure option (91% of HtB, 80% of NSSE and 76% of OMSE). This was consistent with qualitative findings that the decision to use shared equity did not have a significant impact on the types and sizes of properties being considered by buyers. Rather, the option of buying with shared equity appeared to have allowed buyers to bring forward their decision to buy, to consider properties that better suited their needs, and/or to buy in their preferred areas …

Just over a tenth of respondents (11%) had increased their equity stake since buying with shared equity. Just over half (52%) of all respondents expressed an interest in increasing their equity stake over the next five years, although just under three quarters (73%) of those who would like to increase their stake felt they were likely to do so. This most commonly reflected affordability concerns, although a lack of clarity around the process was evident …

The evaluation has considered the 'additionality' delivered by the three shared equity schemes, in terms of the number of households buying a home who would have been unable to do so in the absence of the three schemes (demand-side additionality) and the number of new homes built as a direct result of the schemes (supply-side additionality) … Our estimate of the demand-side additionality generated by each of the three schemes is:

- 20% of HtB buyers have been additional (around 3,000 buyers).
- 39% of NSSE buyers have been additional (around 1,850 buyers).
- 47% of OMSE buyers have been additional (around 6,000 buyers).

Further analysis shows differences in the 'additionality rate' across key buyer groups. In particular, lower income households, those in social or private rented accommodation, single parents, those buying smaller and lower value homes, those aged 40+ and first-time buyers were most likely to be additional. The profile of additional buyers also suggests that the schemes have had some success in supporting households who typically have more difficulty accessing home ownership …

Consideration of supply-side additionality was largely confined to HtB. HtB has comprised a substantial share of overall private sector output, but it remains very difficult to place a figure on the extent to which this supply is additional, primarily due to a lack of available small area house price or construction data. Our estimate of supply-side additionality is therefore based on survey results, and indicated that

5% of all new build sales (around 3,000) from 2013/14 to 2018/19 were 'additional' as a result of HtB ...

A substantial proportion of those supported by the schemes, particularly HtB, may have feasibly been able to access home ownership without assistance. Furthermore, relaxation of lending restrictions and deposit requirements in the last 2–3 years are likely to mean that the HtB scheme as it is currently operating is likely to continue to be accessed by a substantial proportion of households who could feasibly buy without assistance. The OMSE, and to lesser extent NSSE, schemes appear to have been more effective in enabling lower income households to overcome price and deposit constraints to access homeownership.

Scottish House Condition Survey 2019

Key findings from this informative annual study (published in December 2020: www.gov.scot/publications/scottish-house-condition-survey-2019-key-findings/) include the following in relation to housing conditions:

- Disrepair to critical elements, central to weather-tightness, structural stability and preventing deterioration of the property, stood at 52% in 2019. Less than half of these (19% of all dwellings) required urgent repair to critical elements and just 1% had extensive disrepair (covering at least a fifth of the element area) to critical elements.
- Overall, this is an improvement of 5 percentage points on 2018, when 57% of dwellings had disrepair to critical elements, with 20% having critical elements in urgent need of repair and, again, just 1% having extensive disrepair to critical elements. The 2019 rate has returned to a level similar to 2017 (50%).
- 18% of dwellings had disrepair only to non-critical elements, with 3% of dwellings requiring some urgent repair and 1% with extensive disrepair to non-critical elements, similar to 2018.
- Levels of damp and condensation were similar to those seen in 2018: 91% of properties were free from any damp or condensation.
- 2% (or 40,000) of all dwellings fell below the Tolerable Standard in 2019, similar to 2018. Longer term this represents an improvement of 2 percentage points since 2012.
- The Scottish Housing Quality Standard (SHQS) failure rate in the social sector was 41%, not allowing for abeyances and exemptions, which is similar to 2018. This has fallen from 60% in 2010. Failures of the Energy Efficient criterion were the biggest drivers of failures overall. In 2019, 31% of social sector properties did not meet the Energy Efficient criterion.
- The failure rate in the private sector overall is similar to that seen in 2018 (44%, compared to 43%) and is also driven by failures of the Energy Efficient criterion. Nevertheless, whilst private owners and landlords are currently under no obligation to bring their properties up to this standard, long term improvement is being made in the private sector overall.
- The majority of dwellings falling below the SHQS failed on a single criterion; this accounted for more than 8 out of 10 failures in the social sector and overall.
- For 69% of social homes failing the SHQS this was due to falling short on a single one of the 55 elements which make up the standard. Most frequently these were cavity wall insulation, pipe and tank insulation, full and efficient central heating,

effective loft insulation, at least six kitchen sockets, and safe common front and rear doors.

- In 2019 around 51,000 households lived in overcrowded accommodation (2%) under the bedroom standard, similar to 2018.

The equivalent survey for 2018 was published, slightly later than usual, on 21 January 2020: see www.gov.scot/publications/scottish-house-condition-survey-2018-key-findings/.

Vacant and derelict land (1): Scottish Survey 2019

The Scottish Government conducts an annual survey of vacant and derelict land based on returns from local authorities. 'Vacant' land is land which is unused for the purposes for which it is held and is viewed as an appropriate site for development; the land must either have had prior development on it or preparatory work must have taken place in anticipation of future development. 'Derelict' land (and buildings) is land which has been so damaged by development that it is incapable of development for beneficial use without rehabilitation. The annual surveys are being watched with greater attention following the introduction of a community right to buy abandoned, neglected or detrimental land by s 74 of the Community Empowerment (Scotland) Act 2015, which came into force on 27 June 2018, and also in the light of the work of the Scottish Land Commission (for which see below).

Key findings from the 2019 survey (published on 28 April 2020: www.gov.scot/collections/planning-statistics/) include:

- The total amount of reported derelict and urban vacant land in Scotland decreased by 164 hectares (1.5%) from 11,090 hectares in 2018 to 10,926 hectares in 2019. The net decrease is the result of 311 hectares being brought back into use, 32 hectares recorded as naturalised, the addition of 167 hectares in new sites and a net increase of 12 hectares as a result of changes to existing sites and removal of sites that do not meet the required definitions.
- Of the 10,926 hectares of derelict and urban vacant land recorded in the 2019 survey 2,060 hectares (19%) were classified as urban vacant and 8,866 hectares (81%) were classified as derelict.
- There has been an annual decrease in the total recorded area of derelict and urban vacant land since 2014.
- Four authorities have more than 1,000 hectares of derelict and urban vacant land, 52% of the total area across Scotland. East Ayrshire has the largest area (16% of the Scotland total). Glasgow City has the largest area of the City Authorities (9% of the Scotland total).
- For those sites where the previous use is known, 29% of derelict and urban vacant land had been previously used for mineral activity, 20% for manufacturing and a further 13% for defence. For urban vacant land, manufacturing (15%) and residential use (15%) had the largest areas.
- Of the 167 hectares of new derelict and urban vacant land reported in 2019, the largest area had previous land uses related to defence activity (69 Ha, 44% of new land reported).

- Just over 7,800 Ha of derelict and urban vacant land, where the development potential was known, was reported to be developable, 71% of total area. 24% of all reported derelict and urban vacant land was considered developable in the short term (within five years).
- Overall 28% of the population were estimated to live within 500 metres of a derelict site, though there were differences across the country. Shetland and Orkney had the lowest percentage, both less than 1%. North Lanarkshire had the highest with 75%.
- 311 hectares of land was reclaimed or brought back into use in 2019. An additional 32 hectares were recorded as naturalised. Almost a third of the 311 hectares of derelict and urban vacant land brought back into use in 2019 were listed as solely private sector funded. 24% involved some form of public funding, either a full or partial contribution.

Vacant and derelict land (2): the Scottish Land Commission taskforce

Together with the Scottish Environment Protection Agency (SEPA), the Scottish Land Commission has been organising a taskforce for vacant and derelict land. The idea is to challenge all government and economic sectors in Scotland to help bring back such land into productive use. After carrying out an initial phase of work in 2019 (summarised in *Conveyancing 2019* pp 117–19), the taskforce completed its work in 2020. All publications are available on the Scottish Land Commission website (https://landcommission.gov.scot).

The taskforce's final report, *Transforming Scotland's Approach to Vacant and Derelict Land*, was published in October 2020. Among its recommendations are that:

- The Vacant and Derelict Land Register should be reformed to provide a clear focus on sites that have significant barriers to reuse.
- Planning and other policies should give greater prominence to 'place-based regeneration'.
- More funding should be provided for bringing vacant and derelict land back into use.
- Measures should be taken to prevent land from becoming vacant and derelict in the first place.
- A 'national green infrastructure investment programme' should be set up to rehabilitate 'stuck sites'. 'The Programme should be built around four pillars of action: urban green spaces, community-led regeneration, low carbon housing and renewable energy.'

Other publications in 2020 by the Scottish Land Commission reinforce this message. Some case studies of land brought back into use are highlighted in *Not so pretty vacant*. A paper commissioned from Biggar Economics – *Guidance on Assessing the Full Economic Benefits of the Productive Reuse of Land* – recommends that, in addition to considering the economic and fiscal benefits of bringing land back into use, it is also necessary to consider the well-being benefits, which are analysed (pp 8–24) under a number of headings such as communities, environment, poverty, health, education, human rights, and culture. A *Community Impact Tool* lists and scores eight questions designed to elicit how members of the public feel about local sites and their impact on matters such as health, well-being, and crime.

Partly in response to this flow of publications the Scottish Government announced, on 19 December 2020, that £50m would be spent over the next five years to help bring disused land back into use. In a press release it was said that:

> Sites that will benefit from the funding will offer opportunities for reuse that help tackle climate change, such as: low carbon, quality, affordable housing; woodland and other greenspaces; low carbon commercial and industrial developments; flood prevention measures; district heating and other community renewables projects.

Private-sector rent statistics

Private sector rent statistics: 2010–2020, published on 24 November 2020, gives both all-Scotland figures and figures by area. In respect of the year from 1 October 2019 to 30 September 2020:

- Average 2 bedroom rents increased above CPI inflation of 0.5% in 11 out of 18 areas, with the largest increase being 4.0% in East Dunbartonshire. Five areas saw little change in average rents compared with the previous year, with annual changes within +/-0.5%. Average rents decreased by more than 0.5% in the Ayrshires (–0.6%) and West Dunbartonshire (–1.3%).
- These regional trends combine to show an estimated 1.1% increase in average 2 bedroom monthly rents at a Scotland level.
- At a Scotland level there were also estimated increases in average rents for 1 bedroom (1.8%), 3 bedroom (2.2%), 4 bedroom (2.0%) and 1 bedroom shared properties (2.5%).

Taking the 10-year period from 2010 to 2020:

- Lothian and Greater Glasgow have seen average rents increase above the rate of inflation between 2010 and 2020 across all property sizes.
- Forth Valley and Fife have seen average rents rise above the rate of inflation for all property sizes except 1 bedroom properties.
- 5 Areas (Ayrshire, Dumfries and Galloway, North Lanarkshire, South Lanarkshire and West Dunbartonshire) have seen average rents rise less than the rate of inflation across all property sizes between 2010 and 2020.

Books

Malcolm Combe, Jayne Glass, and Annie Tindley (eds), *Land Reform in Scotland: History, Law and Policy* (Edinburgh University Press 2020; ISBN 9781474446853; £19.99)

Andrew Foyle, *A Practical Guide to the Law of Prescription in Scotland* (Law Brief Publishing 2020; ISBN 9781912687640; £39.99)

William M Gordon and Scott Wortley, *Scottish Land Law*, 3rd edn, Vol II (W Green 2020; ISBN 9780414017832; £100.00)

John MacLeod, *Fraud and Voidable Transfer* (Edinburgh Legal Education Trust, Studies in Scots Law vol 9, 2020; ISBN 9781999611842; £30.00)

Alisdair D J MacPherson, *The Floating Charge* (Edinburgh Legal Education Trust, Studies in Scots Law vol 8, 2020; ISBN 9781999611828; £30.00)

Hector L MacQueen, *MacQueen and Thomson on Contract Law in Scotland*, 5th edn (Bloomsbury Professional 2020; ISBN 9781526513830; £45.00)

Alasdair Peterson, *Prescriptive Servitudes* (Edinburgh Legal Education Trust, Studies in Scots Law vol 7, 2020; ISBN 9781999611811; £30.00)

Kenneth G C Reid and George L Gretton, *Conveyancing 2019* (Edinburgh Legal Education Trust 2020; ISBN 97811999611835; £28.00)

Adrian Stalker, *Evictions in Scotland*, 2nd edn (Edinburgh University Press, 2020; ISBN 9781474482165; £85.00)

Ann Stewart and Euan Sinclair, *Conveyancing Practice in Scotland*, 8th edn (Bloomsbury Professional 2019; ISBN 9781526509468; £95.00)

Articles

Zia Akhtar, 'Private residential tenancies and notice periods in eviction' (2020) 166 *Greens Property Law Bulletin* 3

Jan Berger and Stewart Brymer, 'Secure digital signatures: moving forward in a crisis' (2020) 65 *Journal of the Law Society of Scotland* May/34

Jan Berger and Stewart Brymer, 'The future is digital: the future is now' (2020) 165 *Greens Property Law Bulletin* 1

Stewart Brymer, 'Are you who you say you are? A consideration of unique personal identification and title registration' (2020) 169 *Greens Property Law Bulletin* 2

Stewart Brymer, 'Conveyancing 2023: a discussion paper' (2020) 165 *Greens Property Law Bulletin* 2

Stewart Brymer, 'E-missives' (2020) 167 *Greens Property Law Bulletin* 3

Stewart Brymer, 'Risk management in a digital world' (2020) 164 *Greens Property Law Bulletin* 4

Stewart Brymer, 'The home report: next steps' (2020) 168 *Greens Property Law Bulletin* 1

Kieran Buxton, 'An extension to an extension' (2020) 65 *Journal of the Law Society of Scotland* Oct/Online (considering pre-irritancy notices in the light of the temporary increase of the notice period from 14 days to 14 weeks under the Coronavirus (Scotland) Act 2020)

Kieran Buxton, 'Common good and consultation: *Guild v Angus Council*' (2020) 168 *Greens Property Law Bulletin* 5 (considering *Guild v Angus Council* [2020] CSIH 50, 2020 SLT 939)

Kieran Buxton, 'Management of "amenity areas" and the validity of real burdens revisited' 2020 *Juridical Review* 75

Kieran Buxton, 'Tenements, the duty of shelter and necessity: *Lacey v McConville & Carton*' (2020) 169 *Greens Property Law Bulletin* 6

Mat Campbell, 'Unjustified enrichment and statute' (2020) 24 *Edinburgh Law Review* 400 (considering *Pert v McCaffery* [2020] CSIH 5, 2020 SC 259)

Gillian Cogan, 'First Home Fund: how does it work' (2020) 65 *Journal of the Law Society of Scotland* Feb/Online (answering some questions on the new shared equity scheme for first-time buyers which will run until March 2021)

Malcolm M Combe, 'Development of common grazings under s 50B of the Crofters (Scotland) Act 1993' 2020 SLT (News) 239

Malcolm M Combe, 'Rights to buy: the new addition' (2020) 65 *Journal of the Law Society of Scotland* July/34 (considering the newly introduced community right to buy to further sustainable development)

Iain Doran, 'Capital allowances – plant and machinery fixtures' (2020) 165 *Greens Property Law Bulletin* 5

Derek Francis, 'The missing co-owner and jurisdiction' 2020 SLT (News) 57 and 63

Lila Gailling, 'E-signatures: silos, concerns and top tips' (2020) 65 *Journal of the Law Society of Scotland* Oct/34

John Gallacher, 'Lease, but not as we know it' (2020) 65 *Journal of the Law Society of Scotland* June/34 (considering alternative leasing models such as fixed-rent leases, turnover-rent leases, and factory-outlet leases)

Jonathan Hardman, 'Clarificatory evolutionary reform – the importance of the Scottish Law Commission's "Discussion Paper on Heritable Securities: Pre-Default"' 2020 *Juridical Review* 96

Stephanie Hepburn, 'Case law review: servitude rights and car parking in Scotland' (2020) 169 *Greens Property Law Bulletin* 4

Stephanie Hepburn, 'The Lewis crofters' victory overturned – *Highlands and Islands Airports Ltd v The Committee for the Combined Common Grazings of Melbost and Branahuie*' (2020) 167 *Greens Property Law Bulletin* 1

Jim Hunter, *Repeopling Emptied Places: Centenary reflections on the significance and the enduring legacy of the Land Settlement (Scotland) Act 1919* (Scottish Land Commission, 2020)

S King, 'Implied enforcement of real burdens under a common scheme' (2019) 193 *Scottish Planning and Environmental Law* 54.

Hannah Leslie, 'Time to bin the *Irvine Knitters* principle? Court of Session revisits access rights' (2020) 168 *Greens Property Law Bulletin* 4 (considering *Ruddiman v Hawthorne* [2020] CSIH 46, 2021 SLT 111)

John A Lovett and Malcolm M Combe, 'The parable of Portobello: lessons and questions from the first urban acquisition under the Scottish community right-to-buy regime' (2019) 80 *Montana Law Review* 211

Megan McDonald, '*GCN (Scotland) Ltd v Gillespie* [2019] CSOH 82' (2020) 164 *Greens Property Law Bulletin* 6

Tim Macdonald, 'Amnesty notices' (2020) 165 *Greens Property Law Bulletin* 6 (considering the amnesty for agricultural tenants' improvements contained in ss 112–118 of the Land Reform (Scotland) Act 2016)

Tim Macdonald, 'Crofting law reform consultation: tinkering around the edges' (2020) 166 *Greens Property Law Bulletin* 1

Tim Macdonald, 'LBTT on lease extensions: have we all been paying too much tax?' (2020) 167 *Greens Property Law Bulletin* 5

Stephen McGowan, 'System overload? Licensing short-term lets' (2020) 65 *Journal of the Law Society of Scotland* Feb/20

Charlie MacKay, '*Royal Bank of Scotland v Jamieson:* Another brick in the protective framework for residential debtors in enforcement of standard securities' (2020) 24 *Edinburgh Law Review* 405 (considering *Royal Bank of Scotland v Jamieson* [2019] SAC (Civ) 29), 2019 SLT (Sh Ct) 203)

H L MacQueen, 'Cohabitants, unjustified enrichment, contract and subsidiarity: *Pert v McCaffrey*' (2020) 165 *Family Law Bulletin* 4

William MacRae, 'Only "part of" the story' (2020) 65 *Journal of the Law Society of Scotland* Dec/36 (considering the dangers of accepting a 'part of' search in the purchase of a new-build plot)

Gillian Mawdsley and Alison McNab, 'Whose legal problems are short term lets?' 2020 SLT (News) 1

J Keith Robertson, 'Registers of Scotland: an organisation in crisis?' (2020) 88 *Scottish Law Gazette* 2

Jill Robbie, 'Living with water' (2020) 65 *Journal of the Law Society of Scotland* April/36 (considering the protection of properties against flooding)

Andrew J M Steven, 'Real burdens in Scots law: an environmental perspective', in S Demeyere and V Sagaert (eds), *Contract and Property with an Environmental Perspective* (2020) 143

Scott Crichton Styles, 'Contracts and coronavirus part 1: principles of frustration' 2020 SLT (News) 99

Scott Crichton Styles, 'Contracts and coronavirus part 2: frustration of leases on grounds of illegality in Scotland and England' 2020 SLT (News) 109

Chris Stuart, 'Legal tech: claiming back the benefits' (2020) 65 *Journal of the Law Society of Scotland* Feb/33, followed by a response by Jennifer Henderson, Keeper of the Registers of Scotland

Ken Swinton, 'A destination to a negligence claim' (2020) 88 *Scottish Law Gazette* 9 (considering *Ford v W & A S Bruce* [2020] SC KIR 9, 2020 Rep LR 56)

Ken Swinton, 'Cohabitation claims and unjustified enrichment' (2020) 88 *Scottish Law Gazette* 12 (considering *Courtney's Exrs v Campbell* [2016] CSOH 136, 2016 GWD 31-564 and *Pert v McCaffrey* [2020] CSIH 5, 2020 SC 259)

Ken Swinton, 'Smart homes and dumb contracts' (2020) 88 *Scottish Law Gazette* 1

Ken Swinton, 'Yet another a non domino case' (2020) 88 *Scottish Law Gazette* 14 (considering *Ardnamurchan Estates Ltd v Macgregor* [2020] SAC (Civ) 2, 2020 SLT (Sh Ct) 49)

Andrew Todd, 'Property law and diversity – can we do more?' (2020) 169 *Greens Property Law Bulletin* 1 (arguing for greater diversity of gender and race in respect of those who write about property law)

PART IV
COMMENTARY

COMMENTARY

SERVITUDES

Dominant tenements as a bridge

The problem

I own two contiguous areas of land – let's call these 'site 1' and 'site 2'. Site 1 is accessed by a private road, owned by my neighbour, over which I have a servitude right of way. Site 2 is accessed by a different route not involving servitudes.[1] Can I use my servitude over the private road in order to reach site 2? Of course, the dominant tenement is site 1, not site 2. But can I use the servitude in order to reach site 1 and, having arrived there, cross over to site 2?

In principle the answer is no. If the dominant tenement is site 1, then the servitude can only be used for the benefit of site 1. It cannot also be used for the benefit of site 2. Yet, as Professor Roderick Paisley has pointed out in an important article,[2] the rule cannot be an absolute one. Otherwise (to take a couple of his examples):[3]

> It would preclude anyone using the servitude of access to access the dominant tenement and then moving outside the boundary wall to conduct a simple operation such as painting the outside face of the fence on the boundaries of the dominant tenement. It would preclude the taking of access into the dominant tenement by means of a servitude of way and leaving the dominant tenement by means of a second servitude of way as the *solum* of the second servitude would be outside the dominant tenement.

It would mean that, if I wanted to go from site 1 to site 2, I would have to (i) retrace my steps back down the private road over which I have a servitude and then (ii) enter site 2 using the independent means of access to that site. I could not simply walk over the boundary from site 1 to site 2. Awkward at the best of

1 There will always be some means of access to site 2. At worst, if site 2 is landlocked, access will be available under the principle of necessity developed in *Bowers v Kennedy* 2000 SC 555.
2 Roderick R M Paisley, 'The Use of Praedial Servitudes to Benefit Land outside the Dominant Tenement', in Frankie McCarthy, James Chalmers and Stephen Bogle (eds), *Essays in Conveyancing and Property Law in Honour of Professor Robert Rennie* (2015) 203. This book is in print form but can also be downloaded at www.openbookpublishers.com/product/343. It was written in honour of a much loved and admired professor of conveyancing, whose death on 6 January 2021 has deprived us, and many others, of a greatly valued friend and colleague.
3 Paisley, 'The Use of Praedial Servitudes to Benefit Land outside the Dominant Tenement' 220–21.

times, this is particularly awkward if I have built a house which straddles the two sites. If the rule were to be applied strictly, it might take a long time, and the exposure to a great deal of weather, to pass from, say, the kitchen (built on site 1) to the sitting room or the bathroom (both built on site 2).

Yet while common sense suggests that there *must* be qualifications to the rule,[1] there is little sign of this in the case law.

The cases

Certainly the leading modern case is largely uncompromising. This is the well-known decision of the First Division in *Irvine Knitters Ltd v North Ayrshire Co-operative Society Ltd*.[2] The Co-op in Irvine was built partly on site 1 and partly on site 2. Only site 1 had the benefit of a servitude of access, over a lane. The Co-op's practice was to take goods into the building by means of the lane leading to site 1 and then to move them immediately into that part of the store which was on site 2. This was held to be unlawful. It was a misuse of the servitude to treat site 1 simply as a 'bridge' into site 2. In the words of the Lord President, Lord Emslie:[3]

> [T]he defenders as proprietors of the dominant tenement are entitled to use the lane for traffic of all kinds which is intended to serve, and which in fact serves, any lawful purpose to which they may choose to devote the dominant subjects. Putting the matter in another way the defenders are entitled to obtain access to the dominant tenement in connection with the purposes for which they elect to use it and to facilitate the carrying on of those purposes. What they may not do, however, is to use the way, or permit its use by others, to obtain access to subjects other than the dominant tenement, whether or not they happen to be heritable proprietors of those other subjects. They may not, in short, increase the scope of the right of access, and in particular they may not use the way for the purpose of securing access for persons or goods to subjects contiguous to the dominant tenement by using the dominant tenement merely as a bridge between the end of the lane and the non-dominant subjects.

This whole issue has now been re-examined by the First Division in a new case, *Ruddiman v Hawthorne*.[4] Over a number of years, the defenders in *Ruddiman* had been seeking planning permission to build on site 2 but, although it had an independent access, the intention was to make use of the access to the adjacent site 1, which also belonged to the defenders.[5] The access to site 1 was by means of a private driveway belonging to the pursuer and in respect of which the defenders had a servitude of access. All too conscious of the rule set out in cases such as *Irvine Knitters*, the defenders proposed to get round it in the following way. The car-parking for the development on site 2 would

---

1 Or, to conceptualise these in a different way, cases in which the rule is inapplicable.
2 1978 SC 109.
3 At 117.
4 [2020] CSIH 46, 2021 SLT 111. For the facts of the case and for other aspects of the decision, see p 12 above.
5 Latterly site 2 had become the property of the defenders' children, but the change in ownership was immaterial for the purposes of the litigation.

be situated on site 1. Owners of, or visitors to, the development would utilise the servitude road to reach site 1. Having parked their cars they would proceed on foot to site 2. The question was whether they would be entitled to do this. The Lord President, Lord Carloway, was clear that they would not be so entitled:[1]

> The defenders' use of the dominant tenement (Site 1) as a means of allowing persons or goods, which are destined for Site 2, to pass over the driveway on the servient tenement (the red area) is not permitted under the principle set out in *Irvine Knitters*. The use of a device, whereby a car park is created on the dominant tenement and to which the persons or goods would initially be going, does not alter matters. The dominant tenement would still be being used as a bridge to a non-dominant tenement. The question is: at the point when the persons or goods enter the driveway, are they destined *in bona fide* for the dominant tenement (Site 1) or a non-dominant tenement (eg Site 2)? If it is the latter, the use of the servitude is unlawful because it increases the burden on the servient tenement, whereby its owners are not merely allowing access across their land to the dominant tenement but to a third tenement beyond it and which has no equivalent right.

A glimmer of hope?

At first reading, *Ruddiman v Hawthorne* just looks like *Irvine Knitters* mark 2, a new recording of the same old song. But there is, just perhaps, a glimmer of hope for those who view the current rule as too restrictive. The difficulty in *Ruddiman*, as the Lord President said, was that those proceeding up the servitude road to park their car on site 1 were not 'destined *in bona fide* for the dominant tenement'. In reality they were destined for site 2, and the provision of a car-park on site 1 rather than on site 2 was no more than a ruse to evade an inconvenient rule (as indeed it was). Thus the Lord President's analysis seems to leave open the possibility of cases where (i) access to site 1 is taken for its own sake and in good faith, but equally (ii) at some point later on those taking access to site 1 might, quite legitimately, move on from site 1 to site 2. If that is correct – and it may be reading too much into the Lord President's remarks[2] – the crucial question would be whether the initial access to site 1 was taken for a purpose properly connected with site 1.[3]

Another way of framing the question is to ask whether there is one journey or two.[4] On the facts considered in *Ruddiman* there was a single journey from the

---

1 Paragraph 21.
2 This was the first significant case on this issue for 40 years, ie since *Irvine Knitters* itself. It may be another 40 years before the next one, for Scotland suffers from a serious shortage of cases. It is therefore to be regretted that the First Division did not take the opportunity to explore the limits of the rule – for limits there must be. Professor Paisley's article, which would have been of considerable assistance in this respect, was unfortunately not mentioned; we do not know whether it was cited to the court.
3 Paisley, 'The Use of Praedial Servitudes to Benefit Land outside the Dominant Tenement' 220 sees this as the 'distinction between the servitude linked not [merely] to the dominant tenement but the purposes of the dominant tenement'.
4 For a full analysis of the possibilities here, see Paisley, 'The Use of Praedial Servitudes to Benefit Land outside the Dominant Tenement' 220–34.

public road (via the servitude road) to site 1 (for car-parking) and then straight on to site 2 (always the intended destination). The position might be different if there were two separate journeys, one to site 1, and a second from site 1 to site 2 – for the second of those journeys, if distinct from the first, would not involve the use of the servitude. There was a hint of this possibility in Lord Cameron's judgment in *Irvine Knitters* where he seemed to regard it as permissible for the Co-op to use site 1 as a store or distribution centre from which goods might be taken – though not immediately taken – from site 1 to site 2 and indeed elsewhere.[1] As this example suggests, one of the ways of distinguishing two journeys from a single journey is the length of time which elapses between the component parts. Another might be the frequency with which the full journey is taken: do all journeys to site 1 end, ineluctably, with a journey to site 2? If so, that would suggest a single journey. A third factor might be whether the second journey involves a different mode of transport from the first – although, admittedly, the transition from car to feet did nothing to save the situation in *Ruddiman*. An example which combines all of these factors is given by Professor Paisley:[2]

> A house with attendant garage is built on a dominant tenement benefited by a vehicular servitude of access. A part of the garden to the house, comprising the lawn, is held on a separate title not benefited by the servitude of access. If the owner of the house comes home from work in her car she will park it in the garage. After entering the house to change clothing she may take a mower from the same garage and proceed to cut the lawn. The second journey outside the dominant tenement is made on foot.

Here there is the passage of time, a change in mode of transport, and an activity (cutting grass) which is not done every day. Is that in breach of the *Irvine Knitters* rule? One might think, and hope, not.

Practitioners, however, will want certainty, not speculations. The only safe approach is to assume the worst. Hence if a property is held on two (or more) separate titles, and depends on a servitude for access, it will be important to check that both (or all) parts of the property are dominant tenements for the purposes of the servitude. With properties in the Land Register this may not always be immediately detectable, because a site which comprised two (or more) Sasine titles is likely to be represented on the Land Register as a single plot. Care must be taken that any access servitude mentioned in the A (property) section serves the whole site and not merely the land which comes under one of the Sasine titles.

In time, positive prescription is likely to cure the problem. So if a servitude route which was granted in favour of site 1 only is in fact used, for 20 years, to reach site 2, a second servitude will usually be constituted in favour of site 2 by prescription.

---

1 1978 SC 109 at 122. It is not, however, clear from this passage whether Lord Cameron envisaged the goods being carried (after an interval) directly from site 1 to site 2, or whether it would be necessary to take them back down the servitude lane and into site 2 by a different access.
2 Paisley, 'The Use of Praedial Servitudes to Benefit Land outside the Dominant Tenement' 231.

Servitudes of use?

All servitudes involve using the servient tenement to some degree,[1] whether it be for access or the laying of pipelines, or for some other purpose.[2] But can there be a servitude which allows general, unspecified use? This is not really one question but two, because there are different rules as to the permitted content of servitudes depending on whether (i) the servitude was created by registration on or after the appointed day (28 November 2004) or (ii) it was not so created.[3] Servitudes in the second category are restricted to the traditional 'known' servitudes, or to rights analogous to them. Servitudes in the first category are not so restricted but are still subject to the general requirements which apply to all servitudes, namely that they are positive in nature, praedial, and are not so extensive as to be repugnant with ownership.

Cusine and Paisley are firmly of the view that servitudes of general use are not permitted:[4]

> Occasionally a grant includes a 'right to use' something, for example a garage or a garden. This is too inspecific to be a servitude or a real burden and further it is not so akin to an existing servitude that it could be regarded as a new species or as an adjunct of an existing one.

To this it may be added that, to the extent that a right of use purported to be exclusive, it would be repugnant with ownership and hence disqualified as a servitude on that ground also.

Judicial consideration of servitudes of general use has been rare but has taken the same line.[5] There is now, however, a new case, and for once the issue was a central focus of the decision. In *McCabe v Patterson*[6] one of the arguments used to defend an application for interdict against use of the pursuers' property was that the defenders had, by prescription, acquired a servitude right of general use. In the event, the defence failed due to the frailty of the pleadings, but the sheriff[7] took the opportunity to express her view on the law:[8]

> [A]s I was addressed on whether a general servitude right of use could exist, I should record that I have little difficulty in concluding that it cannot and should not. Put simply, such a servitude is too unspecific (Cusine & Paisley at paragraph 3.77). How is one to judge whether such a servitude is repugnant to ownership? How is the servient proprietor to understand what possessory rights are enjoyed

---

1 It was not always so because at common law servitudes could be negative, eg the servitude *non aedificandi*. Since 28 November 2004, however, it has ceased to be possible to create negative servitudes, and on that day all existing negative servitudes were converted into real burdens: see Title Conditions (Scotland) Act 2003 ss 79 and 80.

2 Another case from 2020, *Christie v Carroll* 2020 GWD 31-401, raised but did not decide whether there could be a servitude for recreational purposes. On that question, see *Conveyancing 2018* pp 169–74.

3 For discussion, see eg *Conveyancing 2016* pp 138–41.

4 D J Cusine and R R M Paisley, *Servitudes and Rights of Way* (1998) para 3.77.

5 Cusine and Paisley cite *Leck v Chalmers* (1859) 21 D 416 and *Moffat v Milne* 1993 GWD 8-572.

6 [2020] SC GLA 14, 2020 GWD 11-155. For the facts of this case, see p 9 above.

7 Sheriff Aisha Y Anwar.

8 Paragraph 79.

by the dominant proprietor, with which the servient proprietor must not interfere? By what measure would one determine whether the servitude was being exercised *civiliter*? There is no recognised general servitude of use, nor is such an expansive right akin to any known servitude. Each of the known and recognised servitudes involves some use of the servient tenement; each is limited to a particular specified and identifiable activity. I am not persuaded that a general servitude of use requires to be recognised in response to any development in society; the position in Scots law on this issue remains as stated by the Inner House, in particular by Lord Cowan in *Leck v Chalmers*.[1]

Both this decision, and the passage by Cusine and Paisley, were written in the context of type (ii) servitudes, but there can be little doubt that the position is the same in respect of servitudes of type (i) (ie those created by registration on or after the appointed day).

Access for repairs as a servitude of necessity?

Background

Servitudes must normally be created by (i) registered deed, (ii) by positive prescription or, occasionally and grudgingly,[2] (iii) by implication in a split-off conveyance. But is there a fourth possibility?[3] Can a servitude materialise out of nowhere on the basis that it is not only convenient (the test for implied servitudes) but is actually necessary? According to the decision in *Bowers v Kennedy*[4] back in 2000, access comes into that category, at least if the property is landlocked and if it was formerly a part of the neighbouring property over which access is now claimed.[5] But does access exhaust the possibilities, or do others exist?

In our annual volume for 2017[6] we noted a case which, though decided in 1958, had only just come to light.[7] This was *Brydon v Lewis*[8] in which the owner of the lower flat in a tenement was held to have a servitude right – born, apparently, of necessity[9] – to take access over her upstairs neighbour's garden in order to repair one of the external walls of her flat. As an unreported decision of a sheriff in which the result proceeded on a concession, this could not be regarded as

---

1 In *Leck v Chalmers* (1859) 21 D 416 the court rejected the idea of a servitude of *exclusive* use. The sheriff in *McCabe v Patterson* expressed a similar view as to the existence of a general servitude of storage: see para 82.
2 For a high point of judicial grudging, see *ASA International Ltd v Kashmiri Properties (Ireland) Ltd* [2016] CSIH 70, 2017 SC 107, discussed in *Conveyancing 2016* pp 133–38.
3 Or indeed yet other possibilities, as to which see D J Cusine and R R M Paisley, *Servitudes and Rights of Way* (1998) ch 11.
4 2000 SC 555, discussed in *Conveyancing 2000* pp 52–54.
5 Strictly, the court in *Bowers* found the right to be an intrinsic aspect of the ownership of the dominant tenement rather than a servitude in the strict sense; but other than in fending off negative prescription (which was at issue in *Bowers*) it is hard to see any point of difference.
6 *Conveyancing 2017* pp 162–65.
7 Due to perseverance on the part of Professor Roderick Paisley.
8 12 February 1958 (debate) and 26 August 1958 (proof), Edinburgh Sheriff Court.
9 It is, however, possible to regard a servitude of this kind as a 'natural' servitude, as to which see Cusine and Paisley, *Servitudes and Rights of Way* para 1.07.

high authority.[1] But it was at least suggestive of a way in which the law might, just possibly, develop.

A new case

That suggestion, if that is what it was, is firmly discarded in a new case, *Soulsby v Jones*,[2] a decision of Lady Carmichael in the Outer House. The parties owned adjoining houses in Elie, Fife. Between the houses was a narrow strip of land sufficient to allow maintenance to be carried out. For some of its distance, the strip was a passageway, owned in common by both parties. For the rest, the strip was on land which belonged solely to the defenders. The dispute concerned the latter part of the strip. Narrow at the best of times, it had been made narrower still by the erection of an extension to the defenders' house. Although the pursuer had objected to the extension at the time, the building work had gone ahead. Arguing that he had a servitude over the strip for the purposes of carrying out repairs, the pursuer sought the removal of the extension to the extent that it was built on the strip. The case was argued mainly on the basis that a servitude had been established by prescription (an argument which failed on the evidence),[3] but there was a second-string argument to the effect that there was a servitude by necessity – that a servitude arose by virtue simply of the fact that repairs could not be carried out in any other way.

The facts of *Soulsby* raised starkly an issue which was only touched on in *Brydon v Lewis*. It is one thing to say that a neighbour can use your ground to carry out repairs if that ground is available and unbuilt-on. It is quite another to say that, because there is a right to carry out repairs, your ground *cannot* be built on either now or in the future. Yet that is the obvious implication of the right being classified as one of servitude. And it was the foundation of the pursuer's case in *Soulsby*: if there was a servitude for repairs, the defenders could not build; and having built, in breach of the servitude, they must now remove the building.

As we had pointed out in our discussion of *Brydon*, such a servitude would sterilise the servient property – a consequence so severe that we speculated whether, exceptionally, the servient proprietor might be allowed to build, but at his or her own risk, so that if repairs were needed to the neighbour's wall, and those repairs could only be carried out from the servient tenement, the servient proprietor would have to accept the inconvenience and expense of demolishing part of the building. No doubt such risk could be reduced or even eliminated by building in a way that protected the neighbour's wall from the elements; indeed it would be a valuable incentive to behave with due regard for one's neighbour.

Lady Carmichael's solution, however, was more radical. Such a servitude, she said, should not be recognised at all. Courts should avoid 'an expansive approach to the constitution of off-register rights, including servitudes of

---

1 It also had the speciality that the owner of the ground-floor flat was subject to a real burden requiring that maintenance be carried out. Whether that factor is entitled to any weight is a matter on which opinions have differed.
2 [2020] CSOH 103, 2021 SLT 286.
3 For this aspect of the case, see p 9 above.

necessity'.[1] And in the particular case of servitudes for repair, the resulting sterilisation of the land created 'considerable' difficulties in practice.[2] With the second of these reasons we would certainly agree. Indeed, as Lady Carmichael went on to point out:[3]

> the logical consequence of the pursuer's argument is that by building right up to the boundary of his property, a proprietor may create a servitude right of access for the purpose of maintenance, which sterilises the neighbouring property to the extent of preventing its proprietor from exercising the liberty to build on his own land. There would in effect be a race to be first to build to the boundary, and the unilateral imposition of a servitude right.

The first reason, however – the avoidance of off-register rights – seems open to question. It comes from a decision of the Inner House on the topic of implied servitudes.[4] But there is a great deal of difference between a servitude imposed by law and one created by implication or indeed by prescription. The latter is a bespoke arrangement between two particular properties. Being bespoke, and therefore unpredictable, it is desirable (if not always possible) that it should appear on the property register. But the former is a universal rule, imposed by law. All properties are potentially subject to it. It need no more appear on the register than any other universal rule such as, say, the rule that to build on land requires a grant of planning permission or the rule that land must be used in such a way as to avoid causing nuisance to a neighbour.

Lady Carmichael's decision in *Soulsby* has been reclaimed.

A residual right of access for repairs?

Just as important as what *Soulsby v Jones* decides is what it does not decide. It does not challenge servitudes of access for repair as such. Even if they cannot arise by force of law, as a matter of necessity, they can at any rate be created by registered deed or by prescription.[5] Nor does the case decide whether a neighbour's land can be used to carry out repairs, if the land happens to be available for such use (typically by being unbuilt on)[6] and if the repairs cannot reasonably be carried out in any other way.[7] That issue remains to be determined on another day. The only authority on the question, however – and one quoted in full by

---

1 Paragraph 355.
2 Paragraph 354. At this point Lady Carmichael quotes from *Conveyancing 2017* p 164. The compromise suggested there, of being permitted to build at one's own risk, is dismissed by Lady Carmichael as 'not logically compatible with the existence of servitude', a view which may underestimate the flexibility of the law of servitudes.
3 Paragraph 355.
4 *ASA International Ltd v Kashmiri Properties (Ireland) Ltd* [2016] CSIH 70, 2017 SC 107.
5 That they can be created by prescription was the working assumption in the detailed consideration in the case as to whether there had been sufficient prescriptive possession.
6 Though, as was pointed out in the course of evidence in *Soulsby v Jones*, even where land *has* been built on, it may be possible and indeed necessary to use the building to launch the repair.
7 As Lady Carmichael was careful to say (at para 356), 'I do not require in this process to determine what rights a proprietor such as the pursuer may have regarding access to inspect, maintain or repair, or what may be the juridical character of any such rights.'

Lady Carmichael without apparent disapproval[1] – is decidedly in favour. This is a passage from the lectures of Baron David Hume, delivered to his students at Edinburgh University in the academic year 1821–22:[2]

> [A]n owner's interest must yield sometimes to the immediate interest even of an individual where this is out of all proportion to the owner's interest in preventing the interference, or where the matter in question, though immediately concerning an individual, does at the same time, in its consequences, though remotely, concern the neighbourhood too ... On the like [ie this] ground I think it may be maintained with respect to conterminous properties in a Burgh, which in many instances, owing to the crowded situation of the building, cannot be repaired without some temporary interference, as by resting ladders on the next area, or suspending a scaffold over the next area, that this slight and temporary inconvenience must be put up with, from the necessity of the case.

What we now know, following *Soulsby v Jones*, is that such a right, assuming it to exist, is not part of the law of servitudes.[3]

Servitude conditions

The general idea

Even if nothing is said in the constitutive deed, the exercise of a servitude is subject to a number of well-known restrictions. Servitudes must, for example, be exercised *civiliter* (ie without encroaching unduly on the rights of the servient proprietor). The burden of a servitude is not to be increased beyond the level set at the time of creation. And only the stipulated dominant tenement can take benefit. Such restrictions can be viewed either as freestanding rules of law or, alternatively, as implied terms of the servitude itself, albeit terms implied 'in law' rather than 'in fact'.[4] Probably the classification chosen does not matter very much. At any rate, however these restrictions are viewed, they can be added to[5] by agreement of the parties. *Implied* servitude conditions – if that is what they are – can thus be augmented by *express* servitude conditions. By adroit drafting, a servitude can thus be fine-tuned to the wishes and needs of the parties.

In this respect there is a distinction, which the drafting may or may not make overt, between (i) the grant of the servitude, in the narrow sense, and (ii)

---

1 At para 347.
2 *Baron David Hume's Lectures 1786–1822* vol III (ed G Campbell H Paton; Stair Society vol 15, 1952) 206–07. In argument the pursuer also quoted an equivalent passage from a Roman-Dutch writer, Johannes Voet, who has had considerable (if mainly indirect) influence on Scots law. This was Voet's *Commentarius ad Pandectas* (1707) 8.2.14, quoted in the standard English translation by Percival Gane (*The Selective Voet* (1955–58) vol 2, 455): see para 336 of Lady Carmichael's judgment.
3 The most plausible attribution is common interest: see K G C Reid, *The Law of Property in Scotland* (1996) para 359(9).
4 For different kinds of implied term, see eg W W McBryde, *The Law of Contract in Scotland* (3rd edn, 2007) paras 9–03 to 9–07. A term is implied 'in fact' when it is implied in response to the particular circumstances of the case.
5 They can also be subtracted from, although whether there are limits on this is not entirely clear.

the conditions which regulate its exercise. This is the difference between what you are allowed to do and the manner in which you are allowed to do it. The distinction seems especially clear when a servitude condition seeks to impose an affirmative obligation on the servitude-holder, such as an obligation to contribute to the maintenance of a road over which access is to be taken. Indeed affirmative (but not negative) servitude conditions are included by the Title Conditions (Scotland) Act 2003 among the conditions which can be varied or discharged by the Lands Tribunal.[1]

Nonetheless, there is a certain fuzziness in the boundary between the core servitude and the conditions which regulate its exercise, and this has tended to impede the development of a coherent body of law as to the latter. Case law on servitude conditions has been sporadic and not especially helpful, and the subject has rarely been litigated in modern times. Insofar as there are recognised rules at all, they are largely the result of two pioneering chapters in Cusine and Paisley's *Servitudes and Public Rights of Way.*[2] Cusine and Paisley propose rules for the creation and extinction of servitude conditions. They also deal with permissible content, perhaps the most important and perplexing issue of all. That content must be restricted in some way is obvious; in that respect servitude conditions can hardly expect to be different from servitudes themselves. But the rules are largely unclear. Plausibly, Cusine and Paisley see a close analogy with real burdens, and seek to borrow the well-established rules which govern the content of real burdens. In particular, Cusine and Paisley take the view that servitude conditions, like real burdens, must concern the property right itself rather than the person who happens, for the time being, to hold the right – must, in other words, be praedial rather than personal. It is precisely that praediality which provides the justification for servitude conditions to run with the servitude.

We return to the praedial rule shortly, but before we do so we should mention one other important limitation.[3] Servitude conditions, at least on the analysis offered by Cusine and Paisley, are burdens on the holder of the servitude (ie the dominant proprietor), enforceable by the owner of the land burdened by the servitude (ie the servient proprietor). They do not work the other way around. This view is in accordance with the long-settled rule – a rule indeed of Roman law – that a servitude cannot impose an affirmative obligation on the servient proprietor. Servitudes, as is sometimes said, operate *in patiendo* and not *in faciendo*.[4] Whether it might be possible, through servitudes, to impose a supplementary[5] *negative* obligation on servient proprietors is unclear and, in

---

1 This is achieved by including such affirmative conditions as part (c) of the definition of 'title condition': see Title Conditions (Scotland) Act 2003 s 122(1). For the thinking behind this, see Scottish Law Commission, *Report No 181 on Real Burdens* (2000) para 6.31.

2 D J Cusine and R R M Paisley, *Servitudes and Rights of Way* (1998) chs 13 and 14.

3 Other limitations suggested by Cusine and Paisley (paras 14.09–14.19) are that servitude conditions must not (i) be illegal or contrary to public policy; (ii) be vexatious or *in aemulationem vicini*; (iii) be so severe as to be inconsistent with the right of servitude; or (iv) restrict juridical acts.

4 Ie in the passive acceptance of restriction rather than the active performance of duties.

5 Ie supplementary to the core servitude itself.

the modern law, may not matter very much, because obligations of all kinds (including affirmative obligations) can be imposed on the servient proprietor by means of real burdens.

The new case

There is a new case on servitude conditions. After a prolonged drought, some rain has finally fallen. The servitude which was litigated in *Duncan v Glasa LLP*[1] was granted in the following terms:[2]

> IN CONSIDERATION of certain good and onerous causes but without any consideration being paid to the Burdened Owner by the Benefited Owner, the Burdened Owner grants the Servitude Rights but subject always to the Servitude Conditions.

The 'Servitude Rights' were set out in part 1 of the deed and the 'Servitude Conditions' in part 2. This clear separation of the two helped focus the issues, and was no doubt one reason why the validity of the conditions was considered on its own.

The servitudes in part 1 of the deed comprised, in respect of the same or different properties, (i) a right of access including access for the purpose of laying, constructing, and repairing a road; (ii) a right to widen roads; (iii) a right of access including access for the purpose of erecting and installing a bridge and a new section of road; and (iv) a right to lay, inspect and repair water pipelines.

Of the five servitude conditions in part 2 of the deed, only the last caused serious difficulty. This imposed an (affirmative) obligation on the servitude-holder to pay for the cost of certain categories of tree-felling. The dominant tenement had changed hands since the servitude was created and the current servitude-holder, Glasa LLP, was a singular successor of the original grantee. Condition 5 could not be binding on Glasa as a matter of contract, because there was no contract between Glasa and Mr Duncan, the granter of the servitude.[3] If, therefore, Mr Duncan was to enforce condition 5 against Glasa, it could only be on the basis that it was a servitude condition which, running with the servitude, was binding on Glasa as the current holder of the servitude. The point to be determined by the court, therefore, was whether condition 5 was a valid servitude condition; and that in turn involved a consideration as to whether it complied with the content rules which apply to such conditions.

---

1 [2020] CSOH 26, 2020 SCLR 821. This was one of three linked cases, the others being *Kildermorie Partnership v Glasa LLP* [2020] CSOH 25 and *Kildermorie Partnership v SSE Generation Ltd* [2020] CSOH 27. The judgment, by Lord Ericht, is given in [2020] CSOH 26.

2 This was one of two servitudes with terms which were similar or identical, but with different parties to reflect the different ownership of the land. The commercial background was a joint venture for a hydroelectric dam and turbine on the Kilmorie Estate in Ross-shire (as to which see www.kildermorie.co.uk/history.html). The litigation arose out of the failure of the project.

3 The position was different in respect of the second servitude, where the original parties to the deed were still in place.

The praedial rule

Of the content rules which might potentially apply, it was accepted that the critical one was the praedial rule, mentioned earlier. In the words of the Lord Ordinary (Lord Ericht):[1]

> To be enforceable against a singular successor, a servitude condition must be praedial. The test for whether a servitude condition is praedial is two-fold, and is conveniently set out[2] by Cusine and Paisley in *Servitudes and Rights of Way* at paragraph 14.08 as follows:
>
> > 'Because it is connected with the underlying servitude, the servitude condition must have a praedial nature. This rule also has two aspects. First, a servitude condition must not impose a personal obligation upon the dominant proprietor which is unrelated to the exercise of the servitude. Secondly, the servitude condition must confer a benefit on the servient tenement and not just the then proprietor.'

This passage is of significance in two respects. In the first place, it accepts the view, put forward by Cusine and Paisley, that servitude conditions, like real burdens and indeed servitudes themselves, are subject to a praedial rule. In the second place, it accepts the formulation of that rule as set out in Cusine and Paisley's book. These are important clarifications.

As for the rule itself, the formulation by Cusine and Paisley, now adopted by the court in *Duncan v Glasa LLP*, follows quite closely the established rule for real burdens, which today is set out in s 3(1)–(3) of the Title Conditions (Scotland) Act 2003. The rule is in two parts. From the viewpoint of the dominant proprietor, a servitude condition must relate to the servitude of which the proprietor is the holder.[3] And in addition, from the viewpoint of the servient proprietor, the benefit of the condition must be one which is associated with the (servient) property which the proprietor owns.[4]

The rule applied

The praedial rule having been affirmed, it then fell to the court to apply it to servitude condition 5. The condition was in two parts of which only one was found to pass muster. This was an obligation to pay compensation to the servient proprietor for trees felled and removed 'from pipelines, cables, the power house and access routes'. In the view of the court, the trees in question were directly 'related to the exercise of the servitudes' granted in part 1 of the deed (notably the right to take access and to lay pipelines).[5] Accordingly, the condition satisfied the praedial rule in respect of the dominant proprietor in the servitude. The

---

1 Paragraph 70.
2 The words 'conveniently set out' understate the degree to which the analysis by Cusine and Paisley is novel.
3 Compare the rule for real burdens, in s 3(1) of the Title Conditions (Scotland) Act 2003: 'A real burden must relate in some way to the burdened property'.
4 Compare the rule for real burdens, in s 3(3) of the Title Conditions (Scotland) Act 2003: 'In a case in which there is a benefited property, a real burden must … be for the benefit of that property.'
5 Paragraph 72.

rule was equally satisfied in respect of the servient proprietor – which is also required – because the condition 'deals with paying the owner of the land in respect of trees removed from the land in order to exercise the servitude rights ... Payment to a landowner in connection with the felling of trees on the route of a servitude ... is payment to the owner in his capacity as owner and not in a personal capacity'.[1]

The other obligation in condition 5, however, fell short of the requirements of the praedial rule. Again the obligation was one to pay the servient proprietor in respect of the felling of trees. But whereas the trees in the first obligation stood in a direct relationship with the servitudes granted, the relationship in the case of the second obligation was no more than indirect. In terms of condition 5, the trees in question were to be felled 'for the purposes of carrying out the construction of the new bridge and road'; but, as the Lord Ordinary pointed out, the relevant servitudes were only servitudes *of access* for the purpose of constructing a bridge and road, as opposed to actual servitudes of construction of the bridge and road. The relationship between condition and servitude was thus indirect rather than direct:[2]

> The servitude rights of access merely facilitate the construction by allowing the owner of the dominant tenement to have access over the servient tenement for the purposes of carrying out construction. In these circumstances the felling of trees is not for the purpose of exercising the servitude right of access but for the collateral purpose of construction and is unrelated to the exercise of access under the servitude.

If, to some eyes, this may seem an overly strict application of the law, it serves as a timely warning to those involved in the drafting of servitude conditions. A direct relationship between condition and servitude is needed. Anything less risks invalidity of the condition.

Implied ancillary rights – again

Introduction

In last year's volume we discussed implied ancillary rights – the additional rights that can sometimes be implied into servitudes – in the light of two new cases.[3] These were almost the first cases since the idea of ancillary rights was presented in a fully developed form by the House of Lords in *Moncrieff v Jamieson* in 2007.[4] In one of the cases, the court recognised a right to park as ancillary to an express servitude of access;[5] in the other, also concerning an express servitude of access, the court turned down the idea that the servitude-holder might make use of the road's verges as passing places.[6] There has been more authority in 2020. The first

---

1 Paragraph 73.
2 Paragraph 71.
3 *Conveyancing 2019* pp 146–52. Ancillary rights are, in a sense, the opposite of the servitude conditions considered above. Servitude conditions restrain the servitude-holder; ancillary rights give the holder additional powers.
4 [2007] UKHL 42, 2008 SC (HL) 1.
5 *Johnston v Davidson*, 29 August 2019, Forfar Sheriff Court.
6 *Macallan v Arbuckle*, 11 June 2019, Dundee Sheriff Court.

of last year's cases, *Johnston v Davidson*, was appealed to the Sheriff Appeal Court, and there has also been a new decision on whether a servitude of parking can be supplemented by a right to lock a gate.

We will come to these cases shortly. Before we do so, however, we should summarise the test for implying ancillary rights which emerged from the detailed discussion by the House of Lords in *Moncrieff*. The test has two limbs.[1] For an ancillary right to be implied it must be 'necessary for the convenient and comfortable use and enjoyment of the servitude'.[2] That is the main requirement. But in addition, according to Lords Hope and Neuberger in *Moncrieff*, the right must also have been in the reasonable contemplation of the parties at the time when the servitude was created.[3] This is because, in implying rights, the court must consider the terms of the servitude itself and the circumstances surrounding its creation. As the court is putting words into the mouths of the parties, so it must try to gauge the parties' original intentions. To some extent the second limb may rein in the first. Admittedly, as Lord Hope emphasised in *Moncrieff*, a right may be within the parties' contemplation even if it is not in fact exercised at the time of the servitude's creation, for '[a]ctivities that may reasonably be expected to take place in the future may be taken into account as well as those that were taking place at the time of the grant'.[4] But parties – and especially the servient proprietor – cannot be taken to have contemplated activities for which there was no obvious need at the time of creation.

Parking

We now turn to the cases. Like *Moncrieff v Jamieson*, the right sought to be added by implication in *Johnston v Davidson*[5] was a right of parking. The facts were these. The pursuer (and respondent) owned number 16 Fox Street, Carnoustie, Angus, and the defenders (and appellants) number 14. These were semi-detached cottages within a single building. Neither house had direct access to Fox Street, both being reached by (i) a private roadway followed by (ii) a concrete path which led from the roadway to number 14 and then beyond to number 16. In the late 1990s both properties came into the ownership of local builders who renovated the cottages and sold them. First to be sold was number 16, the house which was later to belong to the pursuer. The disposition, in 1998, conferred in respect of the roadway 'a heritable and irredeemable servitude right of access in common with … (the) proprietors of [number 14]'. Ownership of the roadway, however, remained with the builders and in due course was conveyed as part of number 14. In the result, therefore, the pursuer, as owner of number 16, had an access servitude over the roadway, which was the sole property of the defenders. The wording did not specify whether access was to be by vehicle or by foot alone,

---

1 For a discussion, see *Conveyancing 2007* pp 111–17.
2 Paragraph 29 per Lord Hope.
3 Paragraph 30 per Lord Hope and para 113 per Lord Neuberger.
4 Paragraph 30.
5 [2020] SAC (Civ) 22, 2021 SCLR 17. The Opinion of the Court was delivered by Sheriff Principal D L Murray.

but the sheriff was ultimately to decide that access was vehicular, a conclusion that was not disturbed by the Sheriff Appeal Court.[1]

Number 16 itself could not be reached by vehicles but there was room on the roadway to park up to four cars. For many years, the pursuer availed himself of this possibility, first of all from 2004 until he moved to Thailand in 2007, and then again, on his return from Thailand in 2012. By 2007, however, the defenders had started to challenge the pursuer's right to park and, in his absence abroad, they divided the roadway in two by erecting a fence, and also planted a fast-growing conifer tree. In February 2019 they went further, erecting lockable bollards between Fox Street and the roadway, and refusing to give the pursuer a key. The effect was to make it impossible for the pursuer to park, or indeed to take access by car at all.

In this action the pursuer sought declarator of his right to park on the roadway, and interdict against obstruction by the defenders. Parking, admittedly, was not mentioned in the pursuer's servitude, but the pursuer argued that a right to park was included within the access servitude by implication on the basis of the decision of the House of Lords in *Moncrieff v Jamieson*.

The facts of *Moncrieff* had been, to say the least, unusual. The successful pursuers owned a house which faced the sea and which could only be reached, from the landward side, by a private road over which they had a servitude of way. Due to a steep fall in the land, it was not possible to take a car from the end of the road on to the pursuers' property, and the road was too narrow for a vehicle to turn. Accordingly, the pursuers' practice was to use part of the defenders' land for turning and parking. A dispute arose as to their entitlement to do so. If the pursuers were not allowed to park, they would plainly suffer inconvenience, even hardship. As Lord Hope explained:[2]

> For the owners, use of their own vehicles would involve walking a distance of about 150 yards, in all weathers and in times of darkness as well as in daylight, over what the sheriff has described as a significantly steep descent or climb in open and exposed country. In the case of a mother with very young children, for example, this would mean leaving them unattended and unsupervised in the house while parking or collecting her vehicle, or alternatively taking her children with her on foot in such conditions to and from the place where she had to park her vehicle. Owners who had no difficulty in driving but found walking difficult because they were disabled or elderly would have to do this too, as the restriction on parking for which the defenders argue applies to everyone … In my opinion it is impossible to reconcile such hardships with the use that might reasonably have been expected to be made of the servitude right of vehicular access for the convenient and comfortable use of the property. It would mean, as Lord Philip said in the Extra Division, para 90, that the proprietor's right of vehicular access would effectively be defeated.

Against this background, the House of Lords was willing to concede that a right of parking existed by implication. Yet it was a close-run thing. Lord Rodger

---

1 Although the sheriff's reasoning was strongly criticised. The different analysis offered by the Sheriff Appeal Court is not itself beyond reproach: see p 146 below.
2 Paragraph 34.

virtually dissented, while Lord Neuberger too had doubts.[1] Throughout the speeches, it was emphasised that the circumstances in *Moncrieff* were 'particular and unusual'[2] being based on 'unusual topography'[3] and amounting to 'unusual facts'.[4] The question to be considered in *Johnston v Davidson*, therefore, was whether these 'unusual facts' were replicated in the present case – whether, in other words, Carnoustie was like Shetland.

Following a proof, the sheriff held that it was. There could be no parking on the pursuer's own property. Nor could there be parking in Fox Street itself because it was too narrow and there were double-yellow lines. Finding a parking space elsewhere would not necessarily be easy. Meanwhile the house in Carnoustie, like its counterpart in Shetland, was suitable for a couple with young children, and children could not be left unattended while their parent tried to find somewhere to park the family car.

The Sheriff Appeal Court had little to add to the sheriff's judgment. Surprisingly (but in line with the sheriff at first instance), the court made no mention of the second limb of the test in *Moncrieff* (ie that a right to park must have been in the reasonable contemplation of the parties at the time when the servitude was created). For the Sheriff Appeal Court, as previously for the sheriff, the only question was whether a right of parking was necessary for the comfortable use and enjoyment of the servitude. And, like the sheriff, the Sheriff Appeal Court thought that the answer was plainly yes:[5]

> [W]e find there is sufficient evidence, and no contrary evidence,[6] to allow us to concur with the view of the sheriff that there is an ancillary right to park a vehicle on the disputed area. The property is residential and particularly attractive to families – the pursuer has a young family; the configuration of the location is important – it is virtually impossible to park in the street with the consequence that, without the right to park, the right becomes limited to drop off only and therefore to render the servitude of very limited value; it was always intended that it be used for parking and was so used until the defenders took steps to obstruct it[7] – that suggests the right to park was seen as an integral part of the enjoyment of the subjects; the defenders use the disputed area for parking and have gone to some lengths to stop the pursuer from doing the same thing – they clearly consider it beneficial to them. We therefore accept having regard to the test endorsed by the majority in *Moncrieff* that an ancillary right to park is necessary for the comfortable enjoyment of the property given the benefits it brings and the issues around alternative available parking.

The pursuer was perhaps fortunate to have succeeded in this case. Those who live in towns cannot necessarily expect to have on-site parking, and the law

---

1 Paragraph 125.
2 Paragraph 36 per Lord Hope.
3 Paragraph 101 per Lord Mance.
4 Paragraph 124 per Lord Neuberger.
5 Paragraph 34.
6 It appears that the defenders chose not to give evidence.
7 Earlier, at para 31, the court had emphasised the relevance of the parties' behaviour immediately following the grant of servitude. Again, though, there was no mention of the second limb of the test in *Moncrieff*.

should hesitate before conferring parking rights at the expense of a neighbouring owner. Lord Rodger's observations in *Moncrieff*, even if made in the course of a quasi-dissent, seem particularly apt in this context:[1]

> Especially in cities, there are many flats or houses without any adjacent land on which cars can be parked. That feature is often a significant factor for people when deciding whether to buy the flats or houses and, if so, at what price. Those who own such properties can get to them by car, but are very familiar with the need to drop off their shopping and passengers before trekking off to search for a resident's parking space some streets away. Those with young children and no one to watch them have to take the children to the parking place and then trail them back home, whether up or down a steep hill, whether through icy rain or in blistering sun. These are simply the inevitable everyday consequences of the owners' decision to buy the house or flat in question ... Unlike your Lordships, I am, accordingly, utterly unmoved by the supposedly intolerable sufferings of owners of Da Store [the house in question] who might face that dire modern dilemma of leaving their children unsupervised or taking them on foot, back and forward, up or down a significant slope in open and exposed country.[2]

Gate-locking

In the second case, *McCabe v Patterson*,[3] the defenders claimed a servitude of parking over the pursuers' land which, said the defenders, had been constituted by positive prescription. On that issue the sheriff allowed a proof.[4] As ancillary to the alleged servitude the defenders also claimed a right to lock the gates which gave access to the pursuers' land by means of a combination padlock. The gates were elderly but the padlock was new, so that the right to use it could not be established by prescription – hence the claim based on an implied ancillary right. The facts on the ground were that the land in question, although belonging to the pursuers, was used exclusively by the defenders for parking their vehicles and for other purposes. The justification for the lock was to keep the vehicles safe. In a spirit of neighbourliness, the defenders offered to disclose the combination number to the pursuers, so that they could take access to their own land.

An initial question was whether ancillary rights could be implied into a servitude (ie the alleged servitude of parking) which had been constituted, not by grant, but, or so it was averred, by prescription. *Moncrieff v Jamieson*[5] and the cases that followed it had all concerned servitudes by grant, and in

---

1 Paragraphs 85 and 86. As the owner of a flat in Dublin Street in Edinburgh's New Town, Lord Rodger was speaking from personal experience.
2 To this one might add Lord Hope's comment (at para 34) that: 'The situation in this case ... is far removed from the urban situation to which Lord Rodger refers where people who buy flats or houses without adjacent car parking just have to put up with it.' Carnoustie, in this context, is also an 'urban situation'.
3 [2020] SC GLA 14, 2020 GWD 11-155. For the facts of this case, see p 9 above.
4 Paragraphs 71–74. On freestanding servitudes of parking, see most recently Stephanie Hepburn, 'Case law review: servitude rights and car parking in Scotland' (2020) 169 *Greens Property Law Bulletin* 4.
5 [2007] UKSC 42, 2008 SC (HL) 1.

Moncrieff itself there was a strong suggestion that ancillary rights were to be viewed as implied terms of a grant.[1] If, therefore, there was no grant – if the servitude was constituted by prescription and not by grant – it might appear to follow that the issue of ancillary rights could not arise. Instead, the scope of the servitude would be determined by the possession actually taken, on the basis of the maxim *tantum praescriptum quantum possessum*. This difficulty, if difficulty it was, was brushed aside by the sheriff[2] without discussion: she could 'see no reason' why the test for ancillary rights 'should not be applied to servitudes created by prescription'.[3]

That test, in the form laid down in *Moncrieff v Jamieson*, has two limbs, as we have seen. For an ancillary right to be implied it must be 'necessary for the convenient and comfortable use and enjoyment of the servitude',[4] and it must also have been in the reasonable contemplation of the parties at the time when the servitude was created. As the second limb presupposes a servitude by grant, it was disregarded – indeed not mentioned – by the sheriff in *McCabe v Patterson*. But looking just at the first limb, she had little difficulty in rejecting the argument of the defenders:[5]

> The question of what ancillary rights are necessary for the comfortable use and enjoyment of the servitude, will be guided by practical considerations (Lord Hope, *Moncrieff* at paragraph 26). The practical considerations averred by the defenders arise, it is said, from the need to protect vehicles from vandalism and theft. While the defenders refer to the need to protect stock and property, such a need is not referable to the right to park vehicles. However, the question is not whether an ancillary right is desirable or presents the least costly means of enjoying a servitude right. The defenders' need to protect vehicles could of course be addressed by other security measures such as the installation of CCTV cameras, use of security guards, warning signs, wheel clamps or steering wheel locks, none of which would involve the assertion of further rights against the servient proprietor. The defenders fail to set out why the locking of a gate and thus the controlling of entry and egress to the servient tenement is necessary for the reasonable and comfortable use of the dominant tenement. I have little difficulty concluding that it is not; it does not strike the right balance between the interests of the servient and dominant proprietors.

But there was another ground of decision as well. The sheriff took from the reasoning in *Moncrieff* that a right could not be ancillary to a servitude unless it was capable of existing as a servitude in its own right: thus, 'a right to lock a gate as an ancillary right to park would be difficult to accept if a right to lock a gate as a servitude in its own right is unacceptable'.[6] Expressed in this way,

---

1 See in particular Lord Neuberger's statement of the underlying principle as being 'that the law will imply a term into a contract, where, in the light of the terms of the contract and the facts known to the parties at the time of the contract, such a term would have been regarded as reasonably necessary or obvious to the parties': see [2007] UKHL 42 at para 113.
2 Sheriff Aisha Y Anwar.
3 [2020] SC GLA 14 at para 90.
4 [2007] UKHL 42 at para 29 per Lord Hope.
5 [2020] SC GLA 14 at para 92.
6 Paragraph 93.

this thought goes too far.[1] Even in *Moncrieff* itself, it was not finally determined that the ancillary right recognised in that case – a right to park – could exist as a freestanding servitude,[2] although it has since been decided that it can.[3] What can, though, be accepted is that a right cannot be ancillary to a servitude unless it complies with the characteristics required of all servitudes. In particular, an ancillary right, like the servitude which it augments, must be praedial in nature, and must not be so far-reaching in effect that it is repugnant to the ownership of the servient proprietor.

It was repugnancy that concerned the sheriff in *McCabe v Patterson*. If the defenders were permitted to lock the gate, then they, and they alone, could control access to the land. But that was the privilege of an owner and not of a person whose right was only one of servitude. An ancillary right to lock a gate was thus quite different from the ancillary right to park which had been recognised in *Moncrieff*:[4]

> [W]hile the servient proprietor may build over the servient tenement, build under it and advertise on hoardings around it without interfering with a servitude right of parking, access to any such buildings or hoardings would be controlled by the dominant proprietor, if a servitude of locking a gate were to be recognised ... Moreover, were the servient proprietor [ie the owner of the land] to undertake any activity upon his property (as simple as perhaps providing a bench for community use), which involved allowing members of the general public access to the servient tenement, provided he does not interfere to any material extent with the reasonable exercise of the dominant proprietor's servitude rights, there would be obvious practical difficulties in supplying all such persons with the combination for the padlock to the gates. A servitude right to lock a gate would represent an unwarranted interference with the servient proprietor's rights of ownership.

Final thoughts

A few final thoughts on these cases. First, the failure to have regard to the second limb of the test in *Moncrieff* (that the ancillary right was in the reasonable contemplation of the parties at the time when the servitude was created) is both striking and surprising. Quite why it was thought possible to take one part of the decision of the House of Lords but not the other is unclear and is not explained. At the same time, the second limb of the test can be criticised as difficult to operate, especially in the case of older servitudes, and also as tending to impose an artificial limitation on what can and cannot be recognised as an ancillary right. Secondly, if any trend can be read into the cases it is that the current judicial attitude towards ancillary rights is one of generosity. Thirdly, and by way of qualifying what has just been said, it is probably a mistake to

---

1 In *Moncrieff*, Lord Hope (at para 26) described ancillary rights as 'rights which, although they would not qualify on their own as servitudes, are necessary if the dominant proprietor is to make reasonable and comfortable use of the property'.
2 For discussion, see *Conveyancing 2007* pp 108–11.
3 *Johnson, Thomas and Thomas v Smith* [2016] SC GLA 50, 2016 GWD 25-456; for discussion, see *Conveyancing 2016* pp 141–44.
4 [2020] SC GLA 14 at para 99.

read too much into individual decisions. This area of law is, by its nature, fact-specific. Until there are more cases it will remain difficult to advise clients as to their prospects of success.

Drafting mishaps

Duncan v Glasa LLP[1] provides helpful authority on drafting mishaps. Two afflicted a deed of servitude in that case. One was a muddle about benefited and burdened owners. The servitude began, unpromisingly, in this way:

DEED OF SERVITUDE

By

IAN ALEXANDER DUNCAN residing [address] (who and whose successors as proprietors of the Benefited Property (after defined) are hereinafter referred to as the 'Burdened Owner')

Alert readers will immediately spot something odd about the proprietor of the 'Benefited Property' being referred to as the 'Burdened Owner'. This was an obvious error; and, as was clear from other provisions in the deed, Mr Duncan, the 'Burdened Owner', was in fact the proprietor of the burdened (and not the benefited) property.

The other mishap concerned the following grant of servitude:

A servitude right to lay, construct, inspect, repair, maintain, renew and replace underground and overground water pipelines along Servitude Area 3, together with a servitude right of access, at all times, thereto.

The definition clause, however, made no mention of a 'Servitude Area 3'. Instead a definition was given of 'Servitude Area 2' as being 'those areas shown in dotted blue lines on Plan 5 annexed and signed as relative hereto'. No further mention was made of 'Servitude Area 2' in the deed. Furthermore, on Plan 5 the dotted blue lines were identified as being a pipeline. Again, therefore, the error was obvious enough: in granting a servitude over 'Servitude Area 3', what was really intended was a servitude over 'Servitude Area 2'.

What is the effect of mishaps of this kind? In *Hunter v Fox*, a decision of the House of Lords from 1964, Lord Reid set out his understanding of what was meant by a 'strict construction' of deeds of servitude:[2]

I can think of no stricter method of construction – and none was suggested in argument – than to ask whether a reasonable man with a competent knowledge of the English language could have any real doubt about the meaning of the provision read in its context in the disposition. If the words are self-contradictory, or so obscure that one has to grope for the meaning, then the provision is ineffective, and it is also ineffective if it is ambiguous or reasonably capable of having more than one meaning. There can be no benevolent construction in the sense of spelling a meaning out of

---

1 [2020] CSOH 26, 2020 SCLR 821.
2 *Hunter v Fox* 1964 SC (HL) 95 at 99. See also D J Cusine and R R M Paisley, *Servitudes and Rights of Way* (1998) para 15.18.

obscure phraseology or preferring one of two or more reasonably possible meanings. But if the meaning is clearly apparent, that is sufficient to satisfy the test of strict construction. I can find neither reason nor authority for holding that defective drafting which does not obscure the meaning of the provision is enough to invalidate it.

In *Hunter v Fox* the problem was two puzzling words ('at present') which, in the event, the House of Lords decided could simply be disregarded. But apart from *Hunter v Fox* itself, it is hard to find examples in the case law where defective drafting of a servitude has been cured by means of common-sense interpretation. *Duncan v Glasa LLP* is such a case. The drafting mishaps could be overlooked, said the Lord Ordinary,[1] because, in the light of the deed as a whole, the intended meaning was obvious:[2]

> It is apparent to the reader that there has been a mistake. In these circumstances the Deed should be construed so as to give effect to the parties' intention.

Even if that had not been the case, it would have been possible to have recourse to s 8 of the Law Reform (Miscellaneous Provisions) (Scotland) Act 1985, which empowers the court to rectify errors in expression. That is how drafting blunders are usually corrected.[3] But in *Duncan v Glasa LLP* the errors were sufficiently obvious to be cured by interpretation alone.

Extrinsic evidence

To what extent can the terms of a servitude be supplemented by extrinsic evidence? The rule for real burdens is strict: the full terms of the burden must be set out within the four corners of the deed.[4] With servitudes, by contrast, there is acknowledged to be greater flexibility. The limits of that flexibility, however, are unclear.[5] Two new cases provide examples of where extrinsic evidence was or was not allowed, but no general rule was laid down and the law remains less settled than one would wish. Indeed the approaches taken in the two cases seem impossible to reconcile.

'Information which is publicly available in the Registers'

The circumstances of the first case, *Duncan v Glasa LLP*,[6] were these. One of the conditions in a deed of servitude was that 'the Benefited Owner will make payment according to the Table of Crop Compensation per Schedule 4'. But there was no 'Schedule 4' in the deed, nor was there, anywhere in the deed, a 'Table of

---

1 Lord Ericht.
2 [2020] CSOH 26, 2020 SCLR 821 at para 92. See also para 100: 'It is open to the court to correct this mistake as a matter of construction'.
3 For correction by judicial rectification, see G L Gretton and K G C Reid, *Conveyancing* (5th edn, 2018) ch 21. There were two new cases on that topic in 2020, both of some significance: see pp 49–54 above.
4 See eg *Conveyancing 2019* pp 128–31, discussing *Scottish Woodlands Ltd v Majekodunmi* [2019] SAC (Civ) 38, 2020 Hous LR 23.
5 For a brief discussion, see D J Cusine and R R M Paisley, *Servitudes and Rights of Way* (1998) para 15.10.
6 [2020] CSOH 26, 2020 SCLR 821.

Crop Compensation'. It was true that such a table could be found in an agreement entered into between the parties for the purposes of the joint venture for which the deed of servitude had been granted, though it was not in Schedule 4 of that agreement. But not only was the agreement an entirely separate document, it was not registered in the Land Register, unlike the deed of servitude. In refusing to allow recourse to the agreement, the Lord Ordinary[1] gave particular weight to the absence of registration:[2]

> A servitude condition is binding not only on the parties to the deed of servitude but also on their singular successors. It is therefore important that full information about the servitude condition is contained in the Deed of Servitude. The Deed of Servitude is a public document available from the Registers of Scotland. Singular successors are entitled to rely on the information which is publicly available in the Registers. They are not bound by information contained in private contracts which are not publicly available. The principle that parties may rely on the faith of the record is a long established one.[3]

In the absence of recourse to the agreement, there was no information as to the Table of Crop Compensation, and in the absence of such information, the servitude condition could not take effect.[4] The Lord Ordinary's reasoning, however, leaves open the possibility that the result would have been different if the missing information had been contained in a publicly available document, such as a grant of planning permission or a document registered in the Land Register or Books of Council and Session. But it would be unwise to rely on that. The practical message for drafting servitudes, as for drafting real burdens, is to include everything within the four corners of the deed.

Anything goes

The approach taken in the second case, *Johnston v Davidson*,[5] could hardly be more different. By a disposition recorded in 1998 a servitude right of access was granted over (i) a driveway and (ii) a path. The former was suitable for vehicles, the latter was not. The disposition being silent on the matter, a question before the Sheriff Appeal Court was whether the servitude in respect of the driveway extended to vehicles. Since the land in question was a driveway, and since it

---

1 Lord Ericht.
2 Paragraph 94.
3 In support of the last sentence, the Lord Ordinary quoted from Lord Reid in *Hunter v Fox* 1964 SC (HL) 95 at 99: 'This provision appears in the Register of Sasines, which is open for all to see, and a purchaser is entitled to rely on the faith of the record. He is not concerned with the intention of the person who created the burden: he is concerned with the words which appear in the Register of Sasines.'
4 By contrast, the Lord Ordinary upheld the identical provision in a second servitude, on the basis (i) that, as the original parties were in place, the deed bound the parties as a matter of contract; and (ii) that in an ordinary contract, it was permissible to look at an extrinsic document, especially where, as here, the deed of servitude contained a provision that, 'in the event of any difference of opinion on the terms of this clause it shall be interpreted in accordance with' the extrinsic document (ie the agreement): see paras 101–104.
5 [2020] SAC (Civ) 22, 2021 SCLR 17. The Opinion of the court was delivered by Sheriff Principal D L Murray.

had actually been used for cars without complaint for the first 10 years of the servitude, the court's conclusion that vehicles were allowed was not unexpected.[1] But in reaching that conclusion the court gave weight to evidence of what had been intended by those who, in 1998, had granted the disposition and created the servitude.[2] One of the granters, David Soutar, had given evidence in person at the proof. 'Importantly', said the Sheriff Appeal Court, 'the evidence of Mr Soutar was that it was intended that the proprietors of number 16 had a right to park on the disputed area.'

It is hard to see how evidence like this can ever be of relevance to the interpretation of a real right, such as servitude. The question to be determined is, not what parties intended to do, but what they actually did. And, in deciding that question, the court must use only such evidence as is readily and reasonably available to third parties lacking in knowledge of the circumstances of the original grant. Mainly, and often exclusively, that will mean that only the words in the deed are of relevance. Both combatants in *Johnston v Davidson* were successors of the original parties to the deed. Their rights should not be determined, even to a limited extent, by reference to the intentions of the original granters. 'Singular successors', as the Lord Ordinary said in *Duncan v Glasa LLP*,[3] 'are entitled to rely on the information which is publicly available in the Registers. They are not bound by information contained in private contracts which are not publicly available.'

DONATIONS AND SPECIAL DESTINATIONS

Jack owns a house. He enters into a relationship with Jill. They live together in the house, and perhaps they marry. They agree that the property should be in joint names. They see a solicitor. A disposition by Jack in favour of himself and Jill equally between them is executed and registered. Should the solicitor have proffered advice about the possible use of a survivorship destination?

The issue arose in *Ford v W & A S Bruce*.[4] Mr Ford was the sole owner of a house. He became engaged, and in 2000 he gratuitously disponed a half share in the house to his fiancée, soon to be his wife. In 2013 his wife died. Her will bequeathed her half share in liferent to Mr Ford and in fee to her children from a previous relationship. Mr Ford was unhappy. He sued the law firm that had acted in the conveyancing for damages. He averred that 'he made the defenders

---

1 See eg *Parkin v Kennedy*, 23 March 2010, Lands Tribunal, discussed in *Conveyancing 2010* pp 178–79.
2 The granters were David and John Soutar. Following a proof, the sheriff's finding-in-fact 32 had been: 'They [the Soutars] considered that off street parking facilities would make the redeveloped properties more desirable to prospective purchasers. Prior to the sale of number 16 [the dominant tenement in the servitude], David Soutar made Mr Duncan and Ms Brown [the purchasers] aware of that intention. Prior to the sale of number 14 [the servient tenement], he similarly advised Mr Christie and Ms Howell [the purchasers].' See *Johnston v Davidson*, 29 August 2019, Forfar Sheriff Court.
3 [2020] CSOH 26, 2020 SCLR 821 at para 94 (quoted above).
4 [2020] SC KIR 9, 2020 Rep LR 56.

aware that he was transferring a one-half *pro indiviso* share of the property to his soon-to-be spouse for love, favour and affection on the basis that he anticipated that in the event of her pre-deceasing him, her share of the property would revert to him ... '.[1] He further averred:[2]

> The defenders negligently failed to advise him as to the possibility of a survivorship destination being inserted into the title to the property. He avers that the defenders did not advise him of the advantages and disadvantages of incorporating a survivorship destination into the disposition putting the title into joint names which he claims was standard practice at the time ... *Esto* it was not standard practice, he claims that, if he had been given advice about the possibility of such a survivorship destination, he would have instructed that it be incorporated into the Disposition ... He claims that the defenders' failure to so advise him was negligent *et separatim* in breach of their contract with him ...

The action presupposes that, had there been a survivorship destination, Mrs Ford's will could not have validly evacuated it. Rather oddly, this vital step in the pursuer's argument does not emerge in the case as reported. The presupposition is, we think, correct.[3]

The defenders denied fault, and also pled that any claim that might have existed must have been extinguished by prescription, since the writ had been served on them in 2018 (just under five years from the date of the wife's death) whereas the prescriptive clock had begun to tick in 2000 when the original conveyancing had been done. The question of fault was never determined, because the sheriff[4] sustained the defence of prescription. On that point one would perhaps have liked to have seen more discussion of the possible relevance of s 11(3) of the Prescription and Limitation (Scotland) Act 1973.

Gratuitous dispositions between family members (and cohabitants) are fairly common. The pursuer averred that it was 'standard practice' to include a special destination back to the granter – a 'clause of return' as it is called, of which, more below. We do not know what the basis for that assertion would be. A survivorship destination is common when two people *buy* property. But that is a different matter.

The situation in which Mr Ford found himself gives rise to a conveyancing situation as to which we are not aware of a precedent, namely what would happen were he to seek a division and sale. As a co-owner he would be entitled to insist on this. He would receive, by virtue of his *pro indiviso* share, one half of the net proceeds of sale. What would happen to the other half? Would he receive part of it, as compensation for the loss of his liferent? We incline to think that he would, the exact amount falling to be determined, through actuarial means, by his life expectancy.

In this case what was being gifted was a half share. But the same issues may arise where the donation is of a whole property, for instance where a spouse

---

1 Paragraph 2.
2 Paragraph 3.
3 G L Gretton and K G C Reid, *Conveyancing* (5th edn, 2018) p 473 overlooks this type of case.
4 Sheriff Alistair Thornton.

donates a whole property to the other spouse, or a parent donates a whole property to a child, or two children, and so on. Whilst the commonest special destination in modern practice is the survivorship destination as between co-owners, special destinations are not limited to that type of case. If Jill dispones a whole property to Jack, it is perfectly possible to have a special destination back to Jill, the destination applying to the whole title.[1] Does the pursuer's case suggest that that would be 'standard practice' and that in such a situation there would be a duty to advise about such a destination? We offer no view, except to note that this line of argument would mean that in every case of donation, the law firm is under a duty to advise the donor about special destinations. We suspect that that is not generally done.

There is a difference, as to any duty to advise about destinations, between dispositions by reason of sale, and dispositions by reason of donation. In the former, any duty to advise would be owed to the disponees, whereas in the latter it would be owed to the disponer.

It would have been possible for the disposition in the *Ford* case to have had a special destination attached to just one half of the title: for instance: 'do hereby dispone a one-half *pro indiviso* share to myself and a one-half *pro indiviso* share to [my fiancée] whom failing to myself ...'. That could also be done when property is being purchased. For instance Jane and Kate buy a house, the shares being 10% to Jane and 90% to Kate. The disposition could dispone a 10% share to Jane whom failing to Kate, and 90% to Kate. Thus Jane's share would be subject to a destination, but not Kate's. Vanilla-flavour survivorship destinations are not the only types that the law allows.

A destination back to the granter is called a clause of return. Thus if in the *Ford* case the disposition had contained a survivorship destination, then, as far as Mrs Ford's share was concerned, the destination would have involved a clause of return. Likewise if, to take the example above, Jill dispones a property to her son Jack, whom failing back to herself, that is a clause of return for the whole property. A destination in the form of a clause of return cannot be evacuated *mortis causa*.[2] Could it be defeated by an *inter vivos* deed? In general, special destinations can be defeated in that way. But there exists old authority that the same is not true of special destinations by way of clauses of return. Whether this old law is still good law is a matter that would call for modern scholarly investigation.

RENT ABATEMENT

The doctrine of abatement of rent does not often come before the courts and so a new case on the topic, *Fern Trustee 1 Ltd v Scott Wilson Railways Ltd*,[3] is notable,

---

1 For instance: '... do hereby dispone to my said son Jack Armstrong whom failing to myself the said Jill Fairbairn or Armstrong ...'.
2 Unless the deed otherwise provides. In our view it is wise, whenever a special destination is used, to specify in the deed whether or not there is power to evacuate, rather than leaving the matter to the implication of law.
3 [2020] SC GLA 45, 2021 SLT (Sh Ct) 7.

and the practical importance for the parties is evidenced by the fact that both sides were represented by senior counsel.

The doctrine is that if a tenant is for a time partly or wholly deprived of the use of the let property, for a reason that is the fault neither of the tenant nor of the landlord, the rent falls to be reduced, potentially to zero, during the period of deprivation. If the problem is the tenant's fault, obviously there will be no abatement, while if it is the landlord's fault, that is breach of contract, which may also have effect on the rent, but that is a separate branch of the law (though the term 'abatement' is sometimes used in this context as well). Abatement, in its technical sense, applies where the problem is the fault of neither party, for instance where there has been a *damnum fatale*. A typical case, and indeed arguably the leading case, is *Muir v McIntyre*[1] where an accidental fire destroyed several farm buildings. As Lord President Inglis said in that case, 'where, through no fault of his own, a tenant loses part of the subject let to him, he is entitled to an abatement of his rent, that is to say, he ceases to be the debtor of his landlord to the extent to which he is entitled to an abatement'.[2]

Fern Trustee 1 Ltd v Scott Wilson Railways Ltd involved a 14-year lease (2005 to 2019) of the sixth floor of Buchanan House, 58 Port Dundas Road, Glasgow. The landlords (Jersey companies, Fern Trustee 1 Ltd and Fern Trustee 2 Ltd holding the property in trust) sued for unpaid rent. But, pled the tenant, it had been deprived of possession for a substantial period. Accordingly (i) no rent was, for the deprivation period, payable (doctrine of abatement), and (ii) such payments as had already been made should be returned by the landlord (doctrine of abatement combined with the doctrine of unjustified enrichment).

The facts of the case are not known in detail. But in broad terms the 'curtain walling' of the building proved to be defective. There seems to have been litigation against the company that had done the work, and eventually that company agreed, it seems, to carry out remedial work without charge. A Remedial Works Agreement (RWA) was signed by that company, by the various tenants, and by the owners. The details are not known, but the tenants all agreed that the contractor could have access.[3] The contractor was required to use 'reasonable endeavours' to complete the work within 93 working weeks,[4] which meant, it seems, by 1 July 2018 Although the work was eventually completed, it took longer than 93 working weeks – how much longer is unclear. The tenant continued paying the rent until May 2019, when it stopped. The lease itself came to an end in November 2019. So in this action the landlords seem to have been suing for the rent for the period May–November 2019, while the defender was

---

1 (1887) 14 R 470.

2 (1887) 14 R 470 at 492–93.

3 Access to 'their respective demises', evidently drafted by someone who thought that Glasgow is in England. But even in English law access to a demise makes no sense, since a demise is intangible.

4 According to *Scottish Legal News* (www.scottishlegal.com/article/tenant-of-glasgow-office-building-with-defective-curtain-walling-entitled-to-abate-rent/) the period was not 93 weeks but 93 days.

counterclaiming for repayment of the rent for the period July 2018 to May 2019. We do not know the amount claimed by the landlords, but the amount of which the tenant sought repayment was £310,621.51.

The tenant averred that while the remedial work was going on it had been deprived of the use of the property. Its counterclaim seems to have been based on rent paid for the period *after* the expiry of the 93-week period. If that is right then one wonders why it did not also seek repayment of the rent paid *during* the 93-week period, when it had also, perhaps, been deprived of the use of the property.[1] One also wonders what sort of latitude was conferred by the 'reasonable endeavours' provision. But these issues are not raised in the case as reported.

The central questions in the case were: (i) was the doctrine of abatement in principle applicable? (ii) if so, was it nevertheless excluded by the terms of the lease? As to the first, the landlords had two arguments.[2] One was that the language of previous case law about 'accidents' and 'unforeseen' and 'unanticipated' events was inapplicable because the problem was simply one of disrepair:[3]

> The giving of possession to the contractor was no accident. The event (there is no accident) which underlies that giving of possession is disrepair of the common parts which … is a repair the cost of which is a liability of the defender as Tenant. The provisions of the Lease provide in Schedule IV paragraph 1 that the Common Parts are to be repaired 'irrespective of the cause of the damage, destruction or deterioration necessitating such repairs' … The parties have anticipated repairs to the Common Parts and reserved rights for the Landlords to carry out those repairs and made provision for the payment of the costs of those repairs. Thus there is no accident. The event which causes the repairs is not a matter which has been unanticipated.

The other argument was that any deprivation resulted from the voluntary act of the tenant in agreeing to the RWA:[4]

> If a tenant for his own purposes wishes to carry out internal upgrading works and for that purpose allows contractors possession of the subjects to carry out works he has no ordinary use of the premises. There is no 'fault' on his part. He has however not lost the premises. He has in reality used them for his own purposes. He has allowed their use to the contractors to achieve his purposes. In the present case the defender has allowed access to MCLH [the contractor] to achieve their (the defender's) purposes. It is necessary for the remedy to be available that the Tenant is *deprived* of possession.

---

1 'The defender narrates that the works under the RWA were not completed by the estimated date of 1 July 2018. It argues that after that date it has been denied occupation and quiet enjoyment of the premises.' This is from the pursuers' note of argument, numbered 'P11' in the judgment. Perhaps the defender's position was that it could not complain of deprivation in the 93-week period but could complain of deprivation thereafter. In this connection much may turn on the wording of the RWA.

2 The pleadings of the pursuers are complex and interlocking, and what follows is only one way of summarising them.

3 Paragraph 45 of the pursuers' note of argument.

4 Paragraph 39 of the pursuers' note of argument. Emphasis as in the original.

These arguments did not persuade the sheriff.[1] As to the first, he said, referring to one of the significant earlier cases, *Renfrew District Council v Gray:*[2] 'Lord Caplan does not suggest that abatement applies solely to unforeseen accidents. On the contrary he opines that abatement is based on the fact that the tenant should not pay for rights he never enjoyed.'[3]

As to the second argument, the sheriff said:[4]

Analogies to situations where a tenant allows contractors access for, for example, refitting or improvements, are not apt. There a tenant has a choice. Here the choice available to the defender was to agree to the works or to have the works carried out in the teeth of refusal. In relation to the equitable principle of abatement of rent the choice was illusory.

Given that abatement was in principle applicable, the next question was whether the right to abate had been waived in the lease. Clause 4.1 of the lease said that 'the tenant shall not be entitled to exercise or seek to exercise any right to withhold the rent or any other charges payable under this lease or right of compensation or set off'. The sheriff held that that provision was irrelevant, because it was about the rent. If abatement was applicable, no rent was due.[5]

So abatement was applicable, and proof was allowed as to its extent. There remained one important question. Whilst abatement was applicable to the period in which no rent had yet been paid, could the tenant go further and claim back rent already paid, on the basis that no rent had in fact been due (abatement), and that money paid in error can be reclaimed under the law of unjustified enrichment? The landlords sought to deny this, but their position was evidently weak. Money paid without a valid basis constitutes an unjustified enrichment of the payee, and must be returned. If no rent was due, but was paid, the landlords were clearly obliged to return it (subject to questions of quantum, to be determined by proof). The payment is classifiable as *indebiti solutio* (payment of what is not due), and thus returnable under the *condictio indebiti*.

The case is an important one. No doubt law agents acting for landlords will be examining their house styles to see whether abatement is excluded or not. Given that the predominant practice since the 1960s has been for commercial leases to be drafted in a pro-landlord manner, it may be that styles will mutate in an anti-abatement direction. However, we understand that the Property Standardisation Group[6] has decided not to make any changes to their styles, leaving the matter for individual negotiation.[7]

---

1 Sheriff John McCormick.
2 1978 SLT 70.
3 Paragraph 13.
4 Paragraph 24.
5 Paragraph 26. The sheriff does not comment on clause 5 of the lease which provided: 'The rent payable hereunder and the tenancy hereunder shall both continue in full force and effect notwithstanding any damage to or the destruction of the Premises or the Development or any part thereof by fire or any of the insured risks or by any other cause whatsoever.' It may be that the problem did not arise from any 'damage' or 'destruction'.
6 www.psglegal.co.uk/.
7 A decision communicated to us by Ann Stewart.

The question of rate abatement has again come into prominence because of Covid-19. Whether the doctrine could be invoked by Covid-affected tenants seems to us unclear: a stateable case could be made either way. The reported cases, which go back many centuries, tend to be favourable to tenants, and the courts have been very willing in practice to apply the doctrine.[1] As against that, all the cases that we have noted (admittedly in less than exhaustive research) have involved *physical* problems with the property, such as fire damage or disrepair for which the tenant is not responsible. Finally, we may remark that English case law is often relevant to the law of leases in Scotland, but, we think, not here. English law in this area is different from Scots law, and questions of rent abatement will have to be determined by Scottish authorities.

OVERLAPPING TITLES ON THE LAND REGISTER
The nature of the problem

Introduction

Potentially overlapping Sasine titles have long been a fact of life. With the introduction of registration of title in 1981[2] there then came the new peril of conflicts between a title on the Land Register and a neighbour's title still on the Register of Sasines. Something was said about that in a previous volume in this series.[3] But there is also a third possibility which has attracted less attention: competing titles on the Land Register itself. In theory such a thing cannot happen; indeed the Land Registration etc (Scotland) Act 2012 says that it *must* not happen.[4] So if an area of land is included in the title sheet for property A then that same area of land cannot be included in the title sheet for property B.[5] Yet for first registrations under the Land Registration (Scotland) Act 1979, at least, such things did sometimes happen.[6] The new case of *BAM TCP Atlantic Square Ltd v British Telecommunications plc* is an example.[7]

The new case

The essential facts of *BAM TCP Atlantic Square Ltd* are straightforward, but also puzzling. Back in the 1990s, Pardev (Broomielaw) Ltd owned a development site in Glasgow, lying between James Watt Street and York Street. Pardev's title was registered in the Land Register under title number GLA161133. The development took place in two phases, with the southern half of the site forming the 'Phase I Land' and the northern half the 'Phase II Land'. In the middle of the site, and

---

1 It may be mentioned that the doctrine is not restricted to commercial leases.
2 The Land Registration (Scotland) Act 1979 came into force on 6 April 1981.
3 *Conveyancing 2018* pp 148–55.
4 Land Registration etc (Scotland) Act 2012 s 12(2).
5 To this there are some qualifications, such as where there is a lease title sheet. For the co-ownership case, see below.
6 A well-known example is *Safeway Stores plc v Tesco Stores Ltd* 2004 SC 239; see *Conveyancing 2003* pp 91–96.
7 [2020] CSOH 57, 2020 GWD 25-334.

separating the Phase I and Phase II Land, were two vehicular ramps, each with an accompanying turning circle, leading to the basement level from, respectively, York Street and James Watt Street. In terms of a deed of conditions registered by Pardev on 10 June 1997, the ramps and turning circles comprised 'Vehicular Access', and 'Vehicular Access' in turn was part of the 'Common Parts' of the proposed development. As clause 13 of the deed went on to make clear, the 'Common Parts' were to be the common property of the Phase I and Phase II proprietors.[1]

A deed of conditions cannot, of itself, have dispositive effect, as the court accepted.[2] But when the Phase I Land came to be sold to British Telecommunications plc ('BT'), the disposition followed the standard practice of conveying the land together with 'the whole rights, common, mutual and exclusive pertaining thereto as specified in the Deed of Conditions'. Those words were mirrored in the title sheet issued, following registration of the disposition on 2 July 1997, for the Phase I Land:[3] in the A (property) section, the property was said to include 'the rights specified in the Deed of Declaration of Conditions in Entry 3 of the Burdens Section'. Although an attempt was made to argue otherwise, it was clear, and accepted as such by the Lord Ordinary, Lady Wolffe, that on 2 July 1997 there was vested in BT as the new owner of the Phase I Lands a right of common property in the 'Common Parts', including the two ramps. And as clause 13 of the deed of conditions envisaged ownership being divided between the Phase I and Phase II proprietors, it may be taken that BT received a one-half *pro indiviso* share. No further transfer had taken place by the time of the litigation, so that BT remained the owner of the Phase I Land.[4] So far, then, so unremarkable.

A gap of two years elapsed before the Phase II Land was sold in turn by Pardev. It was to be expected that, in relation to the 'Common Parts', the disposition in favour of the purchaser – who is unnamed in Lady Wolffe's judgment and who is referred to here as 'A' – would be in identical terms to the earlier disposition in favour of BT. Whether this was so we do not know because, unexpectedly, the contents of that disposition do not seem to have been founded on by any of the parties to the litigation. What we do know, however, are the terms of the title sheet which was issued following the registration of the disposition in October 1999.[5] This showed both ramps within the area edged red on the title plan. The clear implication was that A was sole owner not only of the Phase II Land but of the two ramps as well.

After October 1999 the Phase II Lands passed through three further sets of hands (whom, not knowing the names, we may call B, C and D) before, in April 2002, being conveyed by D to BAM TCP Atlantic Square Ltd ('BAM'), the pursuer

---

1   The Common Parts 'will be owned in common by the Phase I Proprietor and the Phase II Proprietor'.
2   Paragraph 70.
3   Title number GLA157916.
4   The Phase I Land had, however, been leased by BT to Firleigh Ltd under a 175-year lease, and BT had then taken a sublease from Firleigh.
5   Under title number GLA161133.

in the present action.[1] In this action BAM sought a declarator (i) that it was the sole and exclusive heritable proprietor of one of the ramps (the one leading from York Street), and accordingly (ii) that the ramp was not common property.

Last in time, first in right

How was the title dispute to be resolved? The same area of land – the disputed ramp – was (a) included in the BT title sheet of 1997 as common property and also (b) included in the BAM title sheet of 2002 as the sole property of BAM. The title sheets could not both be right. Either the disputed ramp was the common property of BT and BAM, as the 1997 title sheet indicated, or it was the sole property of BAM, as stated in the 2002 title sheet. It could not be both. Where title sheets conflict in this way, which title sheet is to be preferred?

A conventional property law analysis would go like this. (i) BT acquired a one-half *pro indiviso* share in the ramp in 1997. (ii) When, in 1999, the disposition by Pardev to A purported to convey 100% of the ramp,[2] it was *a non domino* to the extent of the half share which had previously been disponed to BT. (iii) Hence, whatever A's title sheet actually said, following registration of the disposition, A became owner of, at most, the half share in the ramp which had still belonged to Pardev. (iv) As A owned only a half share in the ramp, A could only transfer that half share to B. (v) The same was true of the subsequent transfers by B, C and D (the last being the transfer to BAM). (vi) Hence, despite the terms of BAM's title sheet, BAM had no more than a half share in the ramp. The rule, in other words, is 'first in time, first in right'. BT registered before A, and of course before A's remote successor, BAM. Hence BT's acquisition of the half share could not be disturbed by later conveyancing carried out by Pardev. In a conflict between title sheets, it is the *first* title sheet which is to be preferred.

The rule just described is the rule of ordinary property law. For that very reason it is also the rule which applies for registrations under the Land Registration etc (Scotland) Act 2012, because one of the important merits of that Act is that it works with, and not against, the rules of property law.[3] But it was not the rule under the 1979 Act. For registrations under the 1979 Act the Keeper had a 'Midas touch'.[4] Defects in dispositions did not matter. Whatever entry was made on the Register was, as a matter of law, true. So if X was registered as owner of Blackmains, then X *was* the owner of Blackmains even if the disposition in X's favour was void. This conferral of title, however, was not future-proof. X became owner on the date of registration. But X would cease to be owner in the event that a competing title in favour of someone else (Y) came subsequently to be registered;[5] for Y would then benefit from the Midas touch in turn, and if Y

---

1 Although not relevant for the outcome of the litigation, it may be noted that BAM disponed the southern part of the Phase II Lands to Legal & General Pensions Ltd in 2018 but no title sheet had been issued by the time of the litigation. The disposition evidently did not include the ramps.
2 Assuming that it did. As mentioned earlier, we do not know the terms of the disposition.
3 See K G C Reid and G L Gretton, *Land Registration* (2017) para 9.20.
4 Land Registration (Scotland) Act 1979. See further, Reid and Gretton, *Land Registration* para 2.7.
5 In that case X would be entitled to indemnity from the Keeper in respect of the loss: see Land Registration (Scotland) Act 1979 s 12(1)(b).

thus became owner by virtue of Midas, then necessarily X ceased to be owner. None of this makes much sense. That is one reason why the Midas touch was discarded by the 2012 Act.[1] But for all title sheets registered under the 1979 Act, the effect of the Midas touch continues to apply.

Now, apply the Midas touch to the present facts. Steps (i) and (ii) remain the same: BT acquired a half share in the ramp in 1997, and the subsequent disposition by Pardev to A was *a non domino* in respect of that half share. But thereafter everything is different. Because of the Midas touch, the infirmity in the Pardev-A disposition did not matter. On registration in October 1999, A acquired all of the property indicated in A's title sheet, including 100% of the ramp. The same was true of the subsequent registrations of B, C, D and, finally, BAM. Although therefore BT had acquired a half share in the ramp in 1997, that half share had been lost to the Midas touch in 1999.

As will be obvious, the Midas touch turns conventional property law on its head. Instead of the rule being 'first in time, first in right', it becomes '*last* in time, first in right'. He who registers *last* prevails. Losing the race means winning the prize. And in a conflict between title sheets, it is thus the later title sheet which is to be preferred.

With this analysis done, it is now possible to settle the conflict in the present case. BT's title was registered in 1997. BAM's title was registered in 2002. Hence, necessarily, it was BAM's title that must prevail. As Lady Wolffe put it,[2] 'In the event of any conflict between two (or more) titles registered under the 1979 Act, the last-registered title prevails.' In 2002, therefore, BAM became the sole owner of the ramp.[3]

The random nature – some would say the absurdity – of the Midas touch is shown by considering the position if, subsequent to 2002 but prior to 8 December 2014 (when the 2012 Act replaced the 1979 Act), BT had disponed the Phase I Land to someone else. On registration of the disposition, BT's disponee would immediately have reclaimed the one-half share in the ramp, due to the Midas touch, and BAM's title would in consequence have been reduced to a half share.[4] Title ping-pong of this kind could have continued indefinitely.[5] But it did not even get going. As BT did not dispone the Phase I Land, BAM's title to the ramp remained unimpaired.

---

1 For a critique, see Reid and Gretton, *Land Registration* paras 2.11–2.16; K G C Reid, 'De-throning King Midas: the new law of land registration in Scotland', in A Goymour, S Watterson and M Dixon (eds), *New Perspectives on Land Registration: Contemporary Problems and Solutions* (2018) 157.

2 At para 73, under reference to K G C Reid, *The Law of Property in Scotland* (1996) para 685.

3 BT had actually lost its half share earlier, in 1999, when A's title was registered in the Land Register.

4 See *Conveyancing 2003* pp 95–96.

5 Here it might be objected that the ping-pong would have been stopped, or prevented altogether, by a refusal on the Keeper's part to register the new and competing disposition. That might sometimes be true. But where, as here, the overlaps were created on first registration of each of the titles in question, and where all subsequent transfers were dealings with whole, there would be no reason for the Keeper to question the extent of the property as shown on the title sheets. And indeed no questions appear to have been raised in respect of the sequence of dispositions of the Phase II Land.

The miracle of 8 December 2014

That, however, is not quite the end of the matter. In conflicts involving 1979 Act titles, the miracle of 8 December 2014[1] must always be taken into account; and this is true of conflicts of any kind and not just those concerning overlapping titles. At this point some background may be helpful.

The shoogliness of pegs

Where, under the 1979 Act, ownership was acquired not under the ordinary principles of property law but only with the help of the Midas touch, the entry in the Register was viewed as an 'inaccuracy'.[2] A title by Midas was thus an inaccurate title. The registered proprietor was owner, but shouldn't be. In principle, inaccurate entries could be rectified, and the shouldn't-be owner stripped of his or her title in favour of the person who should be owner.[3] But, with some exceptions, rectification was not possible where this prejudiced a proprietor in possession.[4] So a shouldn't-be owner in possession of the property had, in practice, a title that could not be challenged. Conversely, a shouldn't-be owner not in possession was on a shoogly peg, vulnerable to future rectification.

In moving from the 1979 Act to the 2012 Act, the transitional provisions in the latter sought to replicate, so far as possible, the respective shooglinesses, or not, of the 1979 Act pegs.[5] This was done by judging matters immediately before the 'designated day' of 8 December 2014, which was the day on which the 2012 Act replaced the 1979 Act. If, immediately before that day, a title was subject to an inaccuracy which could have been rectified by the Keeper, if anyone had troubled to ask, then on the designated day itself, the title was reallocated as if rectification had actually taken place.[6] So a shouldn't-be owner would lose title in favour of the person who should (under normal rules of property law) be the owner. This change occurred automatically by force of law and without any alteration taking place on the Register itself (though there could later be rectification to bring the Register into line with the legal position).[7] Conversely, if a title was subject to an inaccuracy which could not have been rectified by the Keeper immediately before the designated day – usually because the shouldn't-be owner was in possession – then the inaccuracy was extinguished.[8] The shouldn't-be owner, in other words, became the should-be owner, and hence no longer subject to

---

1 The expression, described as 'colourful' by Lady Wolffe at para 78, comes from Reid and Gretton, *Land Registration* para 11.9.
2 There was, however, no definition of 'inaccuracy' in the 1979 Act and it was some time after its passing before there was agreement as to its meaning: see Reid and Gretton, *Land Registration* para 2.8. An inaccuracy caused by Midas came to be known as a 'bijural' inaccuracy.
3 Land Registration (Scotland) Act 1979 s 9(1).
4 LR(S)A 1979 s 9(3)(a).
5 In paras 77 and 78 of her judgment, Lady Wolffe provides a sure guide to provisions which she describes (in para 84) as 'less than straightforward'.
6 Land Registration etc (Scotland) Act 2012 sch 4 para 17.
7 For rectification, see LR(S)A 2012 ss 65 and 80.
8 LR(S)A 2012 sch 4 para 22. In both cases compensation would then be due, at least in principle, to the disappointed party.

the peril of future rectification. Taken together, these changes constituted the miracle of 8 December 2014.

Two questions

How, then, did the miracle of 8 December 2014 map on to the facts in *BAM TCP Atlantic Square Ltd v British Telecommunications plc*? That depended on the answer to two further questions. Was BAM's title, immediately before the designated day, inaccurate and hence vulnerable in principle to rectification? And if so, could the Keeper have rectified the title – which in practice boiled down to asking whether BAM was or was not in possession of the ramp?

The first question: a continuing inaccuracy?

BAM, immediately before the designated day, was the sole owner of the ramp. But was BAM's title sheet inaccurate in showing such ownership? Was BAM, in other words, a shouldn't-be owner? Or, to put it another way, was BAM owner *only by virtue of Midas*?

That is a harder question than might at first seem to be the case. Certainly, there could be no doubt (as already seen) that when A, the first disponee of the Phase II Lands, acquired a registered title in 1999, A's title to the ramp depended on Midas; for without Midas, the disponer, Pardev, could not have conveyed to A more than the half share Pardev still held following the earlier disposition to BT. But BAM was not the first disponee. On the contrary, the Phase II Lands had passed through four different sets of hands (A, B, C and D) before finally, in 2002, they were conveyed by D to BAM. Did that make any difference as to the accuracy or otherwise of BAM's title to the ramp? Was the inaccuracy which affected A's title somehow washed out in the subsequent transfers to B, C, D and BAM? Or, conversely, was a successor still tainted by the inaccuracy in the title of an author?

This important question has not previously been the subject of decision.[1] Nor is there anything in the 1979 Act which, directly at least, points to an answer. In doctrinal terms a perfectly good case can be made for saying both (a) that successors are affected and the title continues to be inaccurate, and also the very opposite, namely (b) that successors, at least if in good faith, are not affected, so that the inaccuracy flies off. Either approach accepts the crucial question as being whether the successor has had recourse to Midas.[2]

On the first approach the answer is – yes, successors remain tainted by the inaccuracy of an author's title. This is on the basis that if A became owner only due to Midas, the same must be true of anyone deriving a title from A. To put the matter another way, if the successive transactions are judged by the ordinary rules of property law, B could no more acquire a title from A than A could acquire a title from Pardev. The same would then be true of C, D and finally BAM. In

---

1 For brief discussion, see K G C Reid, 'De-throning King Midas: the new law of land registration in Scotland', in A Goymour, S Watterson and M Dixon (eds), *New Perspectives on Land Registration: Contemporary Problems and Solutions* (2018) 157 at 171–72.

2 It is having recourse to Midas that produces a 'bijural' inaccuracy.

each case their title to the ramp, denied by ordinary property law, could only be achieved by recourse to the Midas touch.

On the second approach, however, the answer is no. Although the ordinary rules of property law are to be applied, they are to accept as their starting-point that A really did become owner by registration (albeit with the assistance of Midas). And as A became owner, so, under ordinary rules of property law, A could transfer a good title to B, and so on right down the line to BAM. On this view, only A has needed the help of Midas and, that help having been received, A's successors took a good title as a matter of course.

The existence of the first of these approaches seems not to have been considered in *BAM TCP Atlantic Square Ltd v British Telecommunications plc*. Instead, on the basis of submissions by BT, Lady Wolffe adopted what may be described as a refined version of the second approach.[1] In 1999 A became owner of the ramp only with the aid of Midas. Hence A was owner on a title that could be set aside by rectification. Such a title was thus a voidable title.[2] On ordinary rules of property law, A's successors would take a title free from this voidability if they were in good faith. But there could be no good faith in the present case because the deed of conditions was incorporated as part of the title sheet and it was obvious from that deed that the ramp was intended to be common property. Hence the title, even in BAM's hands, remained 'voidable', ie inaccurate and vulnerable to rectification.

While, however, there is nothing to choose between the two approaches when viewed doctrinally, there is a sharp difference between their respective merits on policy grounds. On the first approach, a successor's title will always remain inaccurate;[3] on the second (at least in the version adopted by Lady Wolffe), it will remain inaccurate only if the successor acquired in bad faith. At first sight, legal policy might seem to fall on the side of the second approach, for there is much to be said for protecting good-faith acquirers, especially those acquiring in reliance on the Land Register. But such an approach meets a serious policy objection. If good-faith acquisition wipes out the inaccuracy, the original 'true' owner (BT in the present case) is thereby deprived of the opportunity to claim indemnity from the Keeper. This is because, under the 1979 Act, indemnity was available only for loss suffered in consequence of an inaccuracy.[4] Removing the inaccuracy removes, also, the possibility of indemnity. In giving the good-faith acquirer an unassailable title, such an approach at the same time expropriates

---

1 Paragraphs 85–88.

2 As para 85 makes clear, this idea was taken from para 3.5 of the Scottish Law Commission's *Discussion Paper No 125 on Land Registration: Void and Voidable Titles* (2004). It should be said that, despite obvious functional similarity, a title vulnerable to rectification is not precisely the same as a title which is voidable on some ground of the common law such as fraud. Apart from anything else, the remedy is different, being rectification rather than reduction. There might, therefore, be a question as to whether the role of good and bad faith is the same in a question with acquirers.

3 Subject, however, to the possibility of the 'should-be' owner losing the right to challenge the title due to the long negative prescription.

4 Land Registration (Scotland) Act 1979 s 12(1)(a), (b); see Scottish Law Commission, *Discussion Paper No 128 on Land Registration: Registration, Rectification and Indemnity* (2005) paras 7.6 and 7.7.

the property of the 'true' owner without compensation. It seems improbable that that can be the law.

As it happens, it made no difference, on the facts of *BAM TCP Atlantic Square Ltd*, which of the two approaches was selected. On the first approach, BAM's title on the eve of the designated day would remain inaccurate. But that was also true on the second approach, adopted by the court, because BAM's bad faith prevented the inaccuracy from being washed out.[1] Bad faith, however, will be unusual in cases involving successors, and so on other sets of facts the difference between the approaches is likely to be important.

The second question: the Keeper's power to rectify?

On 7 December 2014, therefore – on the very eve of the designated day – BAM owned the ramp, but the fact of its ownership (beyond 50%) was an inaccuracy. But was it an inaccuracy which, on that day, was capable of being rectified by the Keeper, had the Keeper been asked to do so? That depended on whether BAM was in possession of the ramp, and hence eligible for the protection against rectification conferred by the 1979 Act on proprietors in possession.[2] A proof was therefore ordered on the issue of possession.[3] The Lord Ordinary's decision has, however, been reclaimed.

In any proof of possession, matters are normally assisted by a statutory (though rebuttable) presumption that the person registered as proprietor was in possession immediately before the designated day.[4] But as in the present case *both* competing parties (ie both BAM and BT) were registered as proprietor of the ramp, the presumption must be regarded as self-cancelling.

If the eventual proof (assuming it goes ahead) shows possession to have been with BT and not at all with BAM, then the miracle of 8 December 2014 will have operated to return to BT the half share in the ramp which was first lost, back in 1999, to A. Formal rectification of BAM's title sheet would then follow as a matter of course. Conversely, if BAM was in possession just before the designated day, then BAM's 100% title to the ramp, originally conferred by the Midas touch, will remain undisturbed, and become unassailable for the future.

---

1 Paragraph 88: 'I therefore find that there is a relevant, ie bijural, inaccuracy in the pursuer's title and that it is susceptible to rectification, subject to the satisfaction of the other elements governing the Keeper's powers of rectification.' It might perhaps be added that the definition of 'inaccuracy' set out, for the purposes of the 2012 Act, in s 65 of that Act, which was given some weight in para 79 of Lady Wolffe's judgment, is not relevant for the meaning of 'inaccuracy' under the 1979 Act. The definition in s 65 is of an 'actual' inaccuracy, whereas 'inaccuracy' under the 1979 Act means, usually, a 'bijural' inaccuracy. For the difference between these concepts, see Reid and Gretton, *Land Registration* para 2.8.
2 Land Registration (Scotland) Act 1979 s 9(3)(a).
3 Possession was also relevant for BT's second-string argument, which was that it had acquired ownership in common of the ramp by positive prescription.
4 Land Registration etc (Scotland) Act 2012 sch 4 para 18.

THE DECLINE AND FALL OF THE *A NON DOMINO* DISPOSITION[1]

Introduction

Conveyancers understand the *a non domino* disposition, and they understand its value. Politicians, or at any rate most politicians, do not. They see it as black magic, a piece of abracadabra whereby lawyers can – no doubt for the sort of hefty fees that explain why all lawyers drive brand-new top-of-the-range Mercedes-Benz GLA SUVs – call up the spirits of the underworld so that their clients can snaffle property that is not rightfully theirs. The reason why the politicians do not understand is, probably, that they are looking in the wrong direction. Positive prescription requires two things: ostensible title plus 10 years of possession, and of these it is the latter that is the key. The reason for positive prescription is that if there is a difference between the paper title (to use an American expression) and the social reality – the facts on the ground – then that situation should not be allowed to continue indefinitely, both for reasons of fairness to the parties involved, and for reasons of social utility. So there should eventually come a time when the paper title should, if its holder never asserts it, eventually yield to the facts on the ground. To the paper owner there is no unfairness: the prescribing claimant has published his claim both by long possession and by registration. The *a non domino* disposition looks as if it is about a magic deed. In reality it is about long-term possession. Indeed, it is arguable that the requirement of a registered deed should be made unnecessary, possession being the central issue.[2]

Until the Land Registration etc (Scotland) Act 2012 there was no legislative regulation as to when the Keeper should accept or reject such a deed. The rule should perhaps have been that, as far as the Register of Sasines was concerned, such deeds were acceptable, while for the Land Register, as regulated by the Land Registration (Scotland) Act 1979, such deeds should have been rejected in all cases,[3] mainly because registration in that register conferred title, even if indemnity was excluded.[4] Nevertheless, initially the Keeper would accept *a non domino* deeds for registration in the Land Register.

In the mid-1990s the Keeper's policy changed, and became more restrictive for both registers.[5] Then came the 2012 Act. For the first time, statutory regulation

---

1 A full account of the law can be found in K G C Reid and G L Gretton, *Land Registration* (2017) ch 17.

2 This has been argued by one of the authors: see G L Gretton, 'Reforming the Law of Prescriptive Title to Land', in D Bain, R Paisley, A Simpson and N Tait (eds), *Northern Lights: Essays in Private Law in Memory of Professor David Carey Miller* (2018) 66.

3 The Register of Sasines is a repository of deeds, and it is not the Keeper's role to pronounce on their validity in terms of substantive law. (Of course the Keeper is always able to reject deeds in respect of the Register of Sasines if they are not validly executed, or do not identify the property etc.) The Land Register operates on quite different principles, and the Keeper has an active duty to reject deeds that are invalid, not only formally, but also substantively.

4 Land Registration (Scotland) Act 1979 s 3(1)(a). This was the so-called 'Midas touch'. It does not exist under the Land Registration etc (Scotland) Act 2012. This is implicit in the whole structure of the statute, and is explicit in s 49(4).

5 See A M Falconer and R Rennie, 'The Sasine Register and dispositions *a non domino*' (1997) 42 JLSS 72. See also I Davis and A Rennie (eds), *Registration of Title Practice Book* (2nd edn, 2000) para 6.4.

of *a non domino* dispositions was put in place. It was restrictive, and, no less importantly, in practice it has been applied by the Keeper with rigour.[1] No hero in a fairytale needs more perseverance to win the hand of the fair princess than the *a non domino* applicant must display to persuade the Keeper to accept his suit. Few try; fewer succeed. And of course, even in the event of success, applicants still need 10 more years of possession before a prescriptive title is finally attained. It is no surprise that the number of *a non domino* registrations has, since the 2012 Act came into force, become a mere trickle.[2]

The process

Pre-application possession

In the first place, the applicant under the 2012 Act must 'satisfy' the Keeper that the property has been possessed by the disponer, or disponee, or both successively, for at least a year before the application.[3] The Act does not say how the Keeper is to be satisfied, nor does the subordinate legislation. The Keeper's practice is spelt out in her *General Guidance: Prescriptive Claimants*.[4] The Keeper requires affidavit evidence, and this is likely to mean *several* affidavits, including neighbours. The affidavits should typically include, and we quote:

- A sworn statement by the relevant party that the land has been possessed openly, peaceably and without judicial interruption;
- The duration of the applicant's and/or disponer's possession. Where possession extends back further than the required one year period, and an accurate duration cannot be given, an approximate start date may be acceptable provided the required one year period is covered;
- Details of the type of land it is, e.g. garden ground, parking place, grazing land, overgrown space, etc;
- A detailed statement as to the specific nature of the possession, i.e. not a bald statement. For instance, that the land has been used as garden ground for a house, and that a shed has been constructed on it;
- A plan that clearly identifies the extent of the land possessed, unless relating to the whole of a registered title;
- Confirmation of who has access to the land, who uses the land, and who maintains the land;
- Confirmation of the apparent age and nature of the boundary features surrounding the ground, e.g. stone walls, wire fencing etc, and details of any maintenance provisions in place for these boundaries.

---

1 *General Guidance: Prescriptive Claimants* (https://kb.ros.gov.uk/land-and-property-registration/inaccuracies-and-compensation/prescriptive-claimants/). We refer to the most recent version, dated 31 May 2018. Quotations in this section are from this source unless otherwise indicated.
2 In the first three years of the 2012 Act, only 17 applications were accepted: Scottish Parliament, *Official Report: Economy, Jobs and Fair Work Committee*, 21 November 2017, col 32.
3 Land Registration etc (Scotland) Act 2012 s 43(3). The possession must have been enjoyed 'openly, peaceably and without judicial interruption' – the same requirement as for prescription itself, as set out in the Prescription and Limitation (Scotland) Act 1973 s 1.
4 See n 1 above.

In the normal case each affidavit should contain a plan, of the scale and standard appropriate to registered conveyancing. Even such affidavits may not be enough to satisfy the Keeper. For instance, 'the Keeper may require photographic evidence showing the age and nature of boundaries or the use of the land in question. Evidence from local authority records or utility providers may also be useful in certain circumstances.'

Notification and the three cases – (a), (b) and (c)

In the second place, s 43(4) of the 2012 Act says that the applicant must satisfy the Keeper:

> that the following person has been notified of the application –
>
> (a) the proprietor,
> (b) if there is no proprietor (or none can be identified), any person who appears to be able to take steps to complete title as proprietor, or
> (c) if there is no proprietor and no such person (or, in either case, none can be identified), the Crown.

This is a major change from the previous law, where *a non domino* dispositions could slip on to the register undetected by the owner of the target property.[1] From the applicant's point of view, it will often destroy any prospects of success.

The 2012 Act does not spell out how notification is to be done. Some detail is provided by subordinate legislation, which says that the notification must be at least 60 days before the application is made[2] and which prescribes a form that must be used.[3] As with evidence of possession, much of the practical detail is to be found neither in the primary legislation nor in the subordinate legislation but in the Keeper's *General Guidance: Prescriptive Claimants*. The applicant must satisfy the Keeper that the notification was sent to the right person. If, as is commonly the position in such cases, the property is not in the Land Register then:

> [T]he Keeper will require evidence as to how the applicant has traced the owner in the General Register of Sasines. Such evidence may include copies of the relevant search sheets and perhaps copy deeds. Where the applicant has instructed searches from a private searching company then details of those instructions, and records of the results, should be submitted to the Keeper.

There is the possibility that the person identified might in fact be dead, or, if a company, might have been dissolved. The *Guidance* covers these cases:

> The Keeper will also require evidence … that the person identified is still alive or that the company identified has not been dissolved. In the latter case it is likely that a check with Companies House will be sufficient … [I]n the former case the Keeper may require evidence such as the results of searches of the electoral roll or searches of other local authority registers, evidence of contact with local solicitors (eg the last solicitor to act), and even local newspaper advertisements.

---

1 There was an exception for the foreshore: Land Registration (Scotland) Act 1979 s 14.
2 Land Register Rules etc (Scotland) Regulations 2014, SSI 2014/150, r 18(1).
3 Land Register Rules sch 2.

There is more. So far we have discussed only the first case, where the applicant is notifying the person thought to be the owner: case (a) mentioned in s 43(4) of the 2012 Act. What if the applicant cannot identify the owner, so that it becomes case (b), namely 'any person who appears to be able to take steps to complete title as proprietor'? The Keeper will not take the applicant's word that this has become a (b) case:

> In order for notification to be acceptable under this paragraph the Keeper must be satisfied that notification under paragraph (a) has not been possible. Therefore, the applicant must demonstrate that it has not been possible to identify or trace a proprietor. Evidence of failed searches would be required or, where appropriate, evidence showing a proprietor was traced but has died, including a death certificate.

So: if the applicant says that he has identified the owner, he must satisfy the Keeper that that person is indeed the owner, and is still alive etc; if the applicant says that, despite best endeavours, he has been unable to identify the owner, he must satisfy the Keeper of that fact. If the applicant can satisfy the Keeper that this is *not* an (a) case, he must then meet the evidential burden for a (b) case, and needless to say, this burden is not light:

> It is likely that in some cases the person will be a beneficiary of the person who has died, who can potentially complete title because they hold a confirmation with docket transferring title to them, but they have never done so. The evidence required in those circumstances would be the confirmation and docket. It may be that in certain circumstances a person may be able to complete title by relying on a will that is sufficient in its terms. In order to be satisfactory for this purpose the will must contain a clear conveyance to the beneficiary in person. The Keeper would also require the death certificate of the former proprietor and confirmation that the will is the last will and testament of the former proprietor.

If no one can be found to whom notification is to be made under cases (a) or (b), notification has to be made to the Crown, ie case (c). At this stage too the applicant has a negative evidential burden:

> The applicant must demonstrate that all steps, which might have identified potential persons under paragraphs (a) and (b), have been taken but have failed to reveal anyone. … The evidence required will include details of failed searches, evidence showing that a proprietor was traced but they have died, and evidence of attempts to trace individuals able to complete title, such as letters to last known addresses, contact with local solicitors or advertisements in local newspapers.

'The Crown' does not mean Her Majesty Elizabeth Windsor, Holyroodhouse, Edinburgh EH8 8DX. We quote the *Guidance* again: 'The Crown is represented by the Crown Estate Commissioners[1] … in respect of property falling within the *regalia minora* (foreshore, seabed, salmon fishings, etc) and the Queen's and Lord

---

1 Here the *Guidance* is no longer up to date: Crown Estate in Scotland is now administered not by the Crown Estate Commissioners but by Crown Estate Scotland *(Oighreachd a' Chrùin Alba)*: see Scottish Crown Estate Act 2019.

Treasurer's Remembrancer … for *bona vacantia* and *ultimus haeres* cases.'[1] The distinction is not free from difficulty. For instance, if a section of the foreshore was owned by Euphemia Macdonald who died 50 years ago without traceable beneficiaries, it is thought that it is the QLTR, rather than Crown Estate Scotland, who is the person to be notified.

Whilst the thought is of limited practical significance, it may perhaps be doubted whether (c) is needed at all. If property falls to the Crown, via the QLTR, that could be argued to be merely a type of (b) case, whilst if something forms part of the Crown Estate, that would seem to be an (a) case.

Notification by the Keeper

Notification must be effected by the applicant, to the Keeper's satisfaction. It might be thought that that would suffice. Not so. The notification requirements outlined in s 43 of the 2012 Act, and described above, are repeated in s 45, this time the notifier being the Keeper. So it has to be done all over again, perhaps to the puzzlement of the person notified.

Objection

If the person notified objects within 60 days, the Keeper must reject the application.[2] It may be assumed that an objection will usually be made, for why should a person agree to a procedure which is designed to deprive him of his property?

Registration

Registration of an *a non domino* disposition is rare, because of all the foregoing hurdles. In those few cases where it happens, the entry in the Land Register is marked 'provisional' and, as such, has no real effect, because prescription has not yet run – on the contrary, it is only now, on the making of the provisional entry, that prescription can begin to run. It will require a further 10 years for the title to be validated by prescription, and then only if there is possession that satisfies the requirements for a prescriptive title, namely that it be enjoyed 'openly, peaceably and without any judicial interruption'.[3] Section 44 of the 2012 Act sets matters out fairly clearly and concisely:

---

1 The QLTR website (www.qltr.gov.uk/sites/default/files/QLTR%20-%20policies%20-%20%20 13%20June%202019.pdf) has some material. Among other points, 'the QLTR will expect to be approached in advance of any notification under s 43 of the 2012 Act' (p 10).
2 Land Registration etc (Scotland) Act 2012 s 45(4), (5).
3 Prescription and Limitation (Scotland) Act 1973 s 1. Note that the total period of possession must be not less than 11 years, because as well as the 10 years of post-registration possession there must be the one year (at least) of pre-application possession. Indeed, to be strictly accurate the total period will be somewhat longer than 11 years because the one-year period must have been completed *before* the application is made, and the 10-year period does not begin until *after* the provisional registration has been effected, and between these two dates there will always be a gap.

44 Provisional entries on title sheet

(1) Where the Keeper accepts an application ... the Keeper is to mark any resulting entry in the title sheet as provisional.
(2) The Keeper is to remove the provisional marking from an entry if and when the real right to which the entry relates becomes, under s 1 of the Prescription and Limitation (Scotland) Act 1973 ... exempt from challenge.
(3) While an entry remains provisional –
    (a) it does not affect any right held by any person in the land to which the entry relates, and
    (b) rights set out in the register are not to be altered or deleted by virtue only of the entry.

And the next 10 years ...

The third subsection of s 44 spells out the point that a title that is still in the course of prescriptive possession is still not a valid title, and thus leaves existing rights in the land unaffected, for the time being. If Alan is the owner of Blackmains and Beth achieves a provisional registration, Alan is still the owner, not Beth. Likewise, any deeds Beth may grant – a standard security for example – will be invalid in terms of real rights.[1] Her title as 'prescriptive claimant' is not warranted by the Keeper.[2] Only after positive prescription has run its course will she become owner (and conversely Alan will cease to be owner) and any deeds she may have granted will be validated.[3]

The Keeper will delete the 'provisional' marking, and thus register Beth as owner, only if satisfied as to the fact that Beth has been in possession for the 10 years. For this she will have to present to the Keeper the same sort of evidence that she presented earlier in respect of her possession for one year – affidavits etc.[4] Once, however, Beth meets the requirements of the 1973 Act she becomes owner automatically on the expiration of the 10-year period. The Keeper's consequent change to the Land Register is a recognition of something that has already taken place. Finally, as and when the Keeper does delete the 'provisional' marking, warranty is granted.[5] And Beth lives happily ever after.

Pre-2012 Act registrations

What has been described above is the procedure required under the 2012 Act for new *a non domino* cases. The 2012 Act is prospective in its effect: existing *a non domino* dispositions already in the system are not affected. That means (i) *a non domino* dispositions recorded in the Register of Sasines, and (ii) *a non domino* dispositions registered in the Land Register before the 2012 Act came into force on 8 December 2014.

---

1 Nevertheless the Keeper will accept them: LR(S)A 2012 s 43(5).
2 LR(S)A 2012 s 73(5).
3 If Beth has granted a disposition to Cheryl, the effect will be that Cheryl becomes owner, of course, not Beth.
4 If the Keeper is not satisfied, Beth can always consider litigating.
5 LR(S)A 2012 s 75(4).

Cheating

The post-2012 Act system described above presupposes the honest applicant. There is an alternative: dishonesty. Why should the applicant, Beth, not simply *keep quiet*? She submits a disposition in her favour granted by her friend Amy, and simply ignores all the procedures for *a non domino* deeds. With a bit of luck the Keeper will not notice that there is anything wrong. Admittedly the title will not be valid for 10 years, but then, assuming that there has been possession, prescription will have operated. It might be argued that Beth was not in good faith – but good faith has never been a prerequisite for prescription. It would be like the Good Old Days. Does this happen in practice? We do not know. Is there any downside to doing it this way? Yes. The solicitor who is tempted to help his client by this manoeuvre should read ss 111 and 112 of the 2012 Act.

The A-to-A (self-granted) disposition

What form should an *a non domino* disposition take? Until 2005 practice varied. If Beth wished to register an *a non domino* disposition in her favour, some conveyancers would draft the deed so that she was herself the disponer as well as disponee: this was the so-called 'A-to-A' or 'self-granted' disposition. Other conveyancers thought that someone else should be the disponer, and that Beth should appear in the deed solely as disponee. Who that person – the disponer – was did not matter: it could be the conveyancer himself, or an office clerk, or indeed anyone. But whilst some conveyancers preferred the latter style, not many went as far as to say that the A-to-A, or self-granted, disposition was ineffective as a foundation writ for prescription. Then, in 2005, came the Outer House case of *Board of Management of Aberdeen College v Youngson*.[1] That case held that a self-granted disposition cannot be a good foundation writ on which prescription can run. The Lord Ordinary's view was that:[2]

> the disposition by William Phillip Youngson and others in favour of William Phillip Youngson and others recorded 23 July 1993 does not amount to a deed which is sufficient in respect of its terms to constitute in favour of the defenders a title to the interest in the subjects which they claim. I am also of the view that this disposition was a deed which is invalid *ex facie* for the purposes of s 1(1A) of the Prescription and Limitation (Scotland) Act 1973.

Substantially the same facts arose in a new case, *Ardnamurchan Estates Ltd v Macgregor*.[3] This was a dispute about the ownership of about an acre of ground at Glenborrodale, Acharacle, Ardnamurchan, Argyll. The defenders had bought their property in 1992, the disposition in their favour being recorded in the Register of Sasines. In 1994 they disponed the disputed area to themselves, this disposition too being recorded in the Register of Sasines. They had enjoyed possession of the disputed area, they asserted, since 1992. In the present phase of

---

1 [2005] CSOH 31, 2005 1 SC 335, discussed in *Conveyancing 2005* pp 62–65.
2 Paragraph 14. The Lord Ordinary was Lord Menzies.
3 [2020] SAC (Civ) 2, 2020 SC (SAC) 1, 2020 SLT (Sh Ct) 49, 2020 SCLR 408. The opinion of the court was delivered by Sheriff Principal C D Turnbull.

the litigation they claimed that the 1994 self-granted disposition had given them a good prescriptive title to the disputed ground. They also claimed that, even if that was not accepted, the 1992 disposition was capable of being interpreted as including the disputed area and that accordingly, even if prescription had not run on the 1994 deed, it had run on the 1992 deed. That fall-back position was not tested in the present phase of the litigation. They also had a further fall-back position also not tested at this stage, that *esto* they did not own the disputed area, they held a servitude of way over it.

The pursuer had bought its property early in 2014 (and thus before the 2012 Act came into force, though the significance of this is not great), and its title was, of course, registered in the Land Register. The registered title included the disputed area, but in respect of that area there was an exclusion of indemnity.[1]

The pursuer raised an action to reduce the 1994 disposition, and for declarator that it was the owner of the disputed area. The defenders counterclaimed for declarator that they had a good prescriptive title by virtue of more than 10 years of possession following the 1994 deed.

So the question was: can an *a non domino* disposition in the 'A-to-A' or 'self-granted' form constitute a good foundation writ for the purposes of positive prescription? At first instance the sheriff answered that question in the affirmative.[2] The pursuer appealed, and the Sheriff Appeal Court has now reversed, following *Aberdeen College v Youngson* (which, as an Outer House case, was only of persuasive, not binding, authority).[3] The SAC decision does not come as a surprise. *Aberdeen College v Youngson* made waves at the time, and if it had been appealed (reclaimed) it is not impossible that a different result might have been arrived at. But in the course of 15 years it has come to be accepted, and the SAC would have required strong arguments to depart from it. No such strong arguments could be deployed.[4]

Two provisions of s 1 of the Prescription and Limitation (Scotland) Act 1973 were invoked by the pursuer, as also happened in *Aberdeen College*. One was

---

1   There is a technical aspect in the shape of paras 17 ff of sch 4 to the Land Registration etc (Scotland) Act 2012, which seems not to have been discussed in the case. The disposition to the pursuer was registered under the Land Registration (Scotland) Act 1979. That meant that the pursuer became heritable proprietor of the disputed area, even if the defenders had, before 2014, held a valid GRS title – because of the 1979 Act's 'Midas touch' (see s 3(1)(a)). If that was the situation, paras 17 ff of sch 4 to the 2012 Act would have operated, automatically, on 8 December 2014, so as to reverse the Midas touch, removing the pursuer's right to the disputed area. At that point the pursuer's title sheet, in showing the pursuer as owner of the disputed area, would have been simply inaccurate. (See further p 157 above.) All this is irrelevant if the defenders never had a good GRS title to the disputed area, as indeed the court has now held, at least under the 1994 deed. But the possibility remains that they might have had such a title under the 1992 deed.

2   The decision at first instance, given on 14 June 2019 in Fort William Sheriff Court, has not been reported, but it is summarised in *Conveyancing 2019* pp 69–70.

3   Indeed, not only the Sheriff Appeal Court but even the ordinary sheriff court is, strictly, not bound by Outer House decisions.

4   The court was given a somewhat broader citation of authority than was given to the court in *Aberdeen College v Youngson*. No mention in the decision is made of academic literature, such as D Brand, A Steven and S Wortley (eds), *Professor McDonald's Conveyancing Manual* (7th edn, 2004) pp 163–64, and Ken Swinton, 'Self-granted *a non domino* dispositions' (2005) 73 *Scottish Law Gazette* 52.

that s 1 says that a deed cannot be a valid foundation writ, for the purposes of prescription, if it is 'invalid *ex facie*'. The other is that the deed must be 'sufficient in respect of its terms to constitute in favour of that person a real right' in the property in question. These two rules to some extent overlap, and in both cases it was held that a self-granted disposition fails the test. As to the first, the Sheriff Appeal Court said:[1]

> The 1994 Disposition is invalid *ex facie*. It is unnecessary to look beyond the 1994 Disposition to reach such a conclusion. It affords complete and exclusive proof of its nullity – it purports to dispone the subjects from the respondents to the respondents in exactly the same capacity. The defect is intrinsic.

As to the second, the court said:[2]

> The requirements for the transfer of ownership of land are described thus at paragraph 613 of volume 18 of the *Stair Memorial Encyclopaedia*: 'As a general rule, two things are required for the transfer of ownership, namely (1) some positive act, the nature of which varies with the type of property, for example … the granting and registration of a disposition … , accompanied by (2) the intention of both parties, the intention of the transferor to be divested and the intention of the transferee to be invested.' The respondents cannot, at the same time, intend (i) to be divested of property; and (ii) to be invested in the same property. There is no transfer of ownership in such circumstances. A disposition, such as the 1994 disposition, in which the same party is both disponer and disponee is not sufficient in respect of its terms to constitute in favour of the disponee a real right in the land in question.

The SAC said that 'the question for this court is whether the 1994 disposition is or is not a fundamental nullity'.[3] Ken Swinton has pointed out that this is not strictly accurate.[4] A deed that is a fundamental nullity can still be a good foundation writ: the issue is whether its nullity is intrinsic or extrinsic, ie whether, to ascertain its nullity, it is necessary to go beyond the deed itself. However, this seems to be an error more of expression than of substance.

Policy

As suggested above, the underlying policy reason for prescription, both positive and negative, is that if the position in law and the position in reality differ, then that state of affairs should not be allowed to persist for ever, and that there should come a time when the position in law should come to reflect the position in reality. Whilst our law recognises prescription, and rightly so, it has become too restrictive as to positive prescription. Suppose that Angus has farmed a field, as owner, since the reign of Alexander III of happy memory, and is still alive, though now, no doubt, rather stiff in his joints, but of course enjoying the company of his very numerous descendants, all of whose birthdays he can remember. Notwithstanding the passage of more than 700 years he cannot assert

---

1 Paragraph 18.
2 Paragraph 24.
3 Paragraph 11.
4 K Swinton, 'Yet another *a non domino* case' (2020) 88 *Scottish Law Gazette* 14.

a prescriptive title to the field, unless there is some ostensibly valid recorded/registered deed in his favour. Some may feel that the law is unfair to Angus. Unfairness to Angus is a matter of *aequitas*; there is also the question of *utilitas*: some may feel that the current law is against the public interest.[1]

HIGH HEDGES

Rizza v Scottish Ministers[2] appears to be the first reported case on the High Hedges (Scotland) Act 2013.[3] It concerns rather a fundamental question. The Act is about high hedges – *but what is a hedge*? Mr Rizza was ordered to cut down his hedge, because it was too high, but he said that he had no *hedge*: what he had was *woodland*.

The dispute concerned two properties in suburban Inverness, one being 'Blair Lomond' in Drummond Crescent, and the other being 24 Drummond Circus. Though on separate streets, the two properties adjoined each other at the rear. Each consisted of a detached house and garden, of the general type familiar in suburban developments. The owners of 24 Drummond Circus were unhappy with the trees near the boundary on the 'Blair Lomond' side, and eventually requested Highland Council to issue to the owner of 'Blair Lomond' – Mr Rizza – a high hedge notice.

The legislation says that the complainer must first have taken 'all reasonable steps to resolve ... matters'[4] so by the time the local authority becomes involved in such cases there is typically already a history of conflict.

After investigating, Highland Council agreed with the complainers and issued a high hedge notice to Mr Rizza. He lodged an appeal to the Scottish Ministers.[5] A reporter was appointed and, following a site visit, she upheld, in essentials, the Council's decision. But the long dispute was not over. Mr Rizza raised the present action for judicial review of the reporter's decision. The nub of his case was that the trees in question did not form a hedge, but woodland.

Near the boundary were 17 trees,[6] one an ash, and the others Leyland cypress, the well-known garden evergreen. The distribution of these trees is shown in a plan appended to the judgment.[7] They did not line up on the boundary, and, indeed, it was possible to walk among them. With some imagination one might consider them as arranged in a number of rows, and that was how the reporter saw them. Was this a hedge? The Act does not define 'hedge': s 1 defines 'high hedge' but that definition is not of a hedge but of a *type* of hedge.

1 For the view of one of the authors, see G Gretton, 'Reforming the Law of Prescriptive Title to Land', in D Bain, R Paisley, A Simpson and N Tait (eds), *Northern Lights: Essays in Private Law in Memory of Professor David Carey Miller* (2018) 66.
2 [2020] CSOH 22, 2020 SLT 388.
3 As to which see *Conveyancing 2013* pp 163–67.
4 High Hedges (Scotland) Act 2013 s 3(1).
5 High Hedges (Scotland) Act 2013 ss 12–17.
6 In the case there is also mention of some 'deciduous specimens' that were 'self-seeded' but these seem to be separate from the 17.
7 It is not reproduced in the SLT report, but can be found in the judgment on the Scottish Courts website.

1 Meaning of 'high hedge'

(1) This Act applies in relation to a hedge (referred to in this Act as a 'high hedge') which –

    (a) is formed wholly or mainly by a row of 2 or more trees or shrubs,

    (b) rises to a height of more than 2 metres above ground level, and

    (c) forms a barrier to light.

(2) For the purposes of subsection (1)(c) a hedge is not to be regarded as forming a barrier to light if it has gaps which significantly reduce its overall effect as a barrier at heights of more than 2 metres.

(3) In applying this Act in relation to a high hedge no account is to be taken of the roots of a high hedge.

The situation in the *Rizza* case would seem to fall within the general policy objectives of the legislation: a mass of Leyland cypresses blocking out the light to a neighbouring property. The effect of these trees was the same as the effect of a hedge in the ordinary sense. But there lay the rub: *was* this a hedge, understood in an extended sense? The Lord Ordinary (Lady Carmichael) was prepared to accept that it was. 'Whether trees and or/shrubs are a hedge is a qualitative assessment which may involve a number of different considerations. If that assessment is carried out in a way that is reasonably open to a decision maker, there should be no real risk that a wood or a forest is found to be a hedge.'[1] She continued:[2]

> While the overall planting at Blair Lomond could be considered woodland, the part of the planting in respect of which she [the reporter] issued a revised high hedge notice differed from the remainder of the planting. She explained that she took this view because it had a higher concentration of leylandii, the trees were planted in discernible rows, and the deciduous trees were self-seeded. She referred to the letter quoted above as to the original purpose of the planting.
>
> The considerations on which she founded are ones which she was entitled to take into account. None of them is conclusive as to the question she required to address, and they may have explanations other than the presence of a hedge. They are, however, relevant to the question of whether the trees were a hedge as opposed to woodland. It is a matter of public notoriety that leylandii are used to form hedges. While the circumstance that leylandii are planted will not be conclusive as to whether there is a hedge, it is a relevant consideration. It may well be, as the petitioner submitted, that woodland is sometimes planted in discernible rows. The pattern of the planting in rows was nonetheless a relevant consideration in discerning whether the trees were a hedge. Hedges are generally planted in a line of some sort. It was, further, relevant to whether they were a high hedge, as the word 'row' forms part of the definition of a high hedge.

The last sentence in this passage refers to s 1(1) of the 2013 Act, which says that the statute applies to 'a hedge ... which (a) is formed wholly or mainly by a row of 2 or more trees or shrubs, (b) rises to a height of more than 2 metres above

---

1 Paragraph 33.
2 Paragraphs 50 and 51.

ground level, and (c) forms a barrier to light'. Requirements (b) and (c) were met, but was (a)? The petitioner argued that it was not, because the section uses the word 'row' in the singular, and the reporter had identified more than one row. This argument was additional to – though linked with – his basic argument that no hedge existed, only woodland. The argument was rejected. As a matter of statutory interpretation the singular can include the plural: Interpretation and Legislative Reform (Scotland) Act 2010 s 22. And: 'It would … be perverse and absurd if the owner of a hedge were able to avoid a finding that it was a high hedge because he had planted more than one row of trees or shrubs so as to achieve a more dense and effective screen.'[1]

So, after a long battle, Mr Rizza lost. The case is important for holding that the word 'hedge' can be taken in an extended sense. Whether in a particular case a collection of trees is a hedge for the purposes of the Act is largely a question for the judgement of the council, or, on appeal to the Scottish Ministers, of the reporter.

One question that remains open is whether the result would have been different if the trees, instead of being – rather vaguely – in rows had been more higgledy-piggledy, but of the same number etc, and having the same detrimental effect on the neighbouring property. Would that still be a hedge for the purposes of the Act? Another is whether it would have made a difference if the trees had been native species, rather than Leyland cypress. Another would be whether the distinction between planted trees and self-sown trees is significant. Yet another would be the role of subjective intention. The reporter had evidence from the previous owner who had planted the trees. This said:

> I can confirm that my wife and I resided there from 1978 until 1993. … With reference to your question relating to the trees on the boundary between Blair Lomond and 24 Drummond Circus, I have discussed the matter with my wife, and we can confirm that when we planted the Leylandii they were planted as a hedge.

The reporter considered this relevant, even though it was evidence (i) of subjective intention and (ii) of the intention of the *previous* owner. The Lord Ordinary offered no comment on this point.

The Leyland cypress, a hybrid of *Cupressus macrocarpa* and *C nootkatensis*, is seldom mentioned without reference to its speed of growth, to the fact that it is evergreen, and coniferous,[2] and that it is a non-native species.[3] The 2013 Act is particularly associated with Leyland cypress, and generally with trees that are alien, coniferous, evergreen and fast-growing. For instance, para 27 of the *Rizza* case says: 'The situation which Parliament sought to address involved fast growing conifers.'[4] But the Act is not limited to fast-growing species, or to non-

---

1 Paragraph 34.
2 Not the same thing, for there are deciduous conifers and there are evergreens that are non-coniferous.
3 John Wyndham missed a trick by not having written an even better-seller, *The Day of the Leyland Cypresses*.
4 See also para 23 and para 41, the latter citing the policy memorandum that supported the Bill leading to the 2013 Act.

native species, or to conifers, or to evergreens. And in policy terms it is hard to see why these qualities should make the Leyland cypress more of a nuisance than other species. Deciduous trees may also be a problem, as may slower-growing species. So may native species. The looming holly or beech hedge that darkens the gladsome August noontide does so equally, whether it has taken 10 years or 15 to achieve that dismal effect.

ADJUSTMENTS TO COMMON PARTS FOR THE DISABLED

The problem

In a tenement, maintenance of common parts – or, to use the language of the Tenement Management Scheme ('TMS'), 'maintenance to scheme property'[1] – can be carried out with the agreement of the owners of a majority of the flats.[2] But 'maintenance' does not include alteration or improvement.[3] A person who wishes to *alter* the common parts in a tenement receives no help from the TMS or indeed from the Tenements (Scotland) Act 2004 as a whole. Instead, the matter is governed by the common law, and the common law says that where property is owned in common, any alterations to the property require the consent of all of the owners.[4] That rule, not unreasonable in itself, works poorly for alterations which are needed because of the disability of one of the owners or tenants. For example, to access a tenement building with comfort, or perhaps even at all, a disabled owner might need a chair lift, or a push-button front door, or even just a ramp or hand rail. At common law all the other owners would have to agree to this. One refusal and the change could not be made.

Since 2010 Scottish Ministers have had power, under s 37 of the Equality Act 2010, to deal with this problem by regulations. They have not rushed to do so.[5] But finally, in 2020, regulations were promulgated. The Relevant Adjustments to Common Parts (Disabled Persons) (Scotland) Regulations 2020[6] came into force on 21 February 2020. Although not perhaps prepared to the highest standard, they are nonetheless of some importance.

---

1 Tenement Management Scheme ('TMS') r 3.1(a). The TMS is set out in sch 1 of the Tenements (Scotland) Act 2004.
2 TMS r 2.5. It should be added, however, that problems concerning shelter and support may not need such a majority: see below p 215.
3 TMS r 1.5.
4 See eg K G C Reid, *The Law of Property in Scotland* (1996) para 25.
5 At first they moved quickly, publishing a consultation on possible regulations on 10 January 2011: see *The Right to Adapt Common Parts in Scotland*, available at/www.scotland.gov.uk/ Publications/2011/01/10092726/4. The proposals were modelled on s 52 of the Housing (Scotland) Act 2006, which allows a disabled person to make alterations to privately rented housing. For discussion, see *Conveyancing 2010* pp 102–03. The new Regulations differ in some significant respects from the consultation proposals.
6 SSI 2020/52. Guides to the Regulations for flat-owners are available at www.gov.scot/ publications/guide-adapting-common-parts/ and www.gov.scot/publications/change-common-areas-property-easy-read/.

The scope

The 2020 Regulations confer entitlement to carry out appropriate alterations. Unlike the Tenement Management Scheme,[1] however, they do not provide for a sharing of costs. On the contrary, any alterations carried out by a disabled person are at the expense of that person alone. More than that, the disabled person must pay for future maintenance and, where this is insisted upon, for reinstatement when the alteration is no longer needed – typically when the disabled person leaves the tenement.[2]

The entitlement is framed in some detail. With the agreement of a majority of owners, a disabled person 'is entitled to make *relevant adjustments* to *common parts* in relation to *premises* in Scotland'.[3] Each of the italicised terms is itself defined.

'Premises' are the private dwelling lived in by the disabled person,[4] who may be the owner or tenant, or simply someone who lives there by permission of the owner or tenant.[5] The premises must be the person's only or main home.[6] 'Premises', in the Regulations, are generally seen as being part of a larger 'building'; in other words, although this is not said expressly, the Regulations are concerned mainly with tenements, in which context 'premises' means a tenement flat.

What may be altered under the Regulations are the 'common parts' of the building. These are defined by function rather than by ownership.[7] They comprise:[8]

- the structure of the building;
- the exterior of the building;
- any common facilities within the building (eg the entrance passage and stair);
- any common facilities used in connection with the building (eg a path or garden ground).

The alterations themselves must take the form of 'relevant adjustments', which are defined broadly to mean, 'in relation to a disabled person, alterations or additions which are likely to avoid a substantial disadvantage to which the disabled person is put in using the common parts in comparison with persons who are not disabled'.[9] Specifically mentioned in an ancillary definition are alterations to the means of access to the premises as well as alterations to the

---

1 TMS r 4.
2 Relevant Adjustments to Common Parts (Disabled Persons) (Scotland) Regulations 2020 reg 9.
3 2020 Regulations reg 3(1).
4 2020 Regulations reg 2(1). Premises are not disqualified merely because they are used in part as a shop or office or for business.
5 2020 Regulations reg 3(2).
6 2020 Regulations reg 3(2).
7 Although they cannot be owned solely by the person (whether the disabled person or someone else) who owns the premises in question.
8 Equality Act 2010 s 37(5).
9 Equality Act 2010 s 37(5).

common parts 'to make the premises suitable for the accommodation or welfare of a disabled person'.[1] A key safe would be an example of the latter.

The procedure

Normally, under the Regulations, a majority of the owners of the common parts must agree to the alterations, although it is possible to appeal to the sheriff against a refusal.[2] The procedure for obtaining majority consent is unrealistically cumbersome, and compares unfavourably with the studied informality of the equivalent procedure for repairs under the Tenement Management Scheme.[3] There are three distinct stages, each initiated by a formal written notice in prescribed form (reproduced below).

First, the disabled person must send an application for consent to all the owners of the common parts affected by the proposed works.[4] This gives details of the works and sets out a timetable for their completion. The application may be sent (i) by personal delivery (eg through the letter-box of the flat), (ii) by registered or recorded post to the person's last known address (or registered office in the case of a company), or (iii), if the recipient had previously agreed in writing, by email or other electronic means.[5]

Next, and in response to the application, each owner of a share in the common parts must send a formal written reply within a month.[6] Where a share in the common parts has itself two or more owners – as for example where a flat is owned by a married couple and a single *pro indiviso* share of the common parts attaches to the flat – any one of the owners can reply, unless there is disagreement between them.[7] In replying, the owner must indicate consent or refusal. A person who fails to reply in time or in the proper way is taken to have refused the application, which means, rather bizarrely, that a person who agrees to the alterations but cannot be bothered completing the form, or is a day late in replying, must be counted amongst the noes.[8] This in itself may be enough to sink many requests. Consent must not be unreasonably withheld, and in considering an application an owner:[9]

> is entitled to have regard to –
>   (a) the health, safety, welfare and convenience of those occupying any part of the premises and other persons using the common parts,
>   (b) the costs which the owner is likely to incur, directly or indirectly, as a result of the proposed works,

---

1 2020 Regulations reg 4.
2 2020 Regulations reg 3(3).
3 TMS r 2.
4 2020 Regulations reg 5(1).
5 Interpretation and Legislative Reform (Scotland) Act 2010 s 26. We are grateful to Scott Wortley for drawing this provision to our attention.
6 2020 Regulations reg 5(4).
7 2020 Regulations reg 5(6). In the event of disagreement, they will be taken to have withheld consent, except that a person or persons holding a majority stake in the share can decide against the wishes of the others.
8 2020 Regulations reg 5(5).
9 2020 Regulations regs 5(3)(c) and 6(1).

(c) whether the proposed works are likely –
    (i) to reduce the value of their property, the common parts or of any other part of the premises, or
    (ii) to make their property, the common parts or any other part of such premises less suitable for letting or sale,
(d) whether, if the proposed works were to be carried out, the common parts could be re-instated,
(e) any code of practice issued by the Equality and Human Rights Commission in relation to the Equality Act 2010 which relates to reasonable adjustments made to premises for disabled persons.

It is unclear if this list is supposed to be exhaustive, or indeed how it is to be determined whether an owner took matters not on it into account. The form does, however, require an owner who refuses consent to give the reason for that refusal, and in appropriate cases this might presumably form a ground of appeal on the part of the disabled person.

More usually, one imagines, owners will agree to the proposals. But acceptance can be made subject to 'reasonable conditions',[1] and a list of possible conditions is given in the Regulations,[2] although again it is unclear whether the list is exhaustive. According to the list, a condition may –

(a) specify the standard to which the proposed works must be carried out, having regard to the age, condition and appearance of the premises, and the likely cost of complying with this condition,
(b) require the disabled person to –
    (i) reinstate the common parts, when the disabled person is no longer the tenant, owner, or otherwise entitled to occupy the premises, to the condition they were in before the work was carried out,
    (ii) provide a plan for the maintenance of the adjustments once made.

Any condition imposed must be stipulated in the form sent by the owner. It can be rejected by the disabled person, but in that case the owner's response counts as a rejection.[3]

The final stage – the last of the three – is for the disabled person to count the votes and send out a notice to all of the owners giving the result. Anyone, including the disabled person, is at liberty to appeal against the result to the sheriff by way of summary application.[4]

Assuming the result was to allow the alterations to go ahead, the disabled person is required to delay beginning the work until 'the deadline set by regulation 10(1) has passed [for making an appeal] without an appeal having been made under that regulation'.[5] Unhappily, no deadline is prescribed in reg 10(1), giving rise to the logical inference that the work can never begin. It is assumed that this slip in the Regulations will be corrected.

---

1   2020 Regulations reg 5(3)b).
2   2020 Regulations reg 6(2).
3   2020 Regulations reg 8.
4   2020 Regulations reg 10.
5   2020 Regulations reg 3(4)(a).

Apart from on this last point, the Regulations aim to produce certainty, both as to the fact of consent (if consent there is) and also as to any conditions to which the consent is subject. In addition, the mandatory use of writing contributes to the ease of any appeal as well as providing evidence should an incoming flat-owner query the changes that have been made. Yet, well meaning as these Regulations are, it is hard not to be sceptical as to whether they will actually be complied with. Disabled persons, in the future as in the past, will often carry out work without permission, especially if the changes are small. Even if consent is sought, it is hard to imagine that they will often fill in the necessary forms, assuming they happen to know about them. And even if they do fill in the forms, what are the chances of persuading each of the owners in the tenement, in responding, to fill them in as well (though a good start would be to include a blank copy of the relevant form with the initial application for consent)?

The forms

The three forms prescribed by the Regulations are reproduced below, with the numerous 'notes for completion' being given in the footnotes.[1]

Form 1
Application for consent to relevant adjustments

This application for consent is given by a disabled owner, tenant or occupier who is or will be living in the premises and who proposes to alter or add to common parts of the premises for the purpose of avoiding a substantial disadvantage which would otherwise arise in using the common parts. The costs of the alteration or addition are to be met by the applicant.

Alteration or addition being proposed:
(*see note for completion 1*)[2]

To the owner(s) of the other properties with a share in the common parts of the premises affected by the proposed works:
(*see note for completion 2*)[3]

Name and address of the owner, tenant or occupier making the application:
(*see note for completion 3*)[4]

Property to which the application relates (if different from above):
(*see note for completion 4*)[5]

---

1 The forms and notes are found in the schedule to the 2020 Regulations.
2 Provide as much information as possible concerning the nature of the alteration or addition.
3 This application must be sent to each owner of the other properties with a share in the common parts of the premises whose share of the common parts will be affected by the proposed works. You must insert the full name and address of the owner, if known.
4 You must insert your full name and address.
5 This is only applicable if you do not currently reside at the above address eg you may be the guardian of a disabled person requiring the proposed alteration or addition. Otherwise put 'not applicable'.

The timetable for carrying out the work, including proposed dates of commencement and completion:
(*see note for completion 5*)[1]

Consent or any objections or other representations relating to the relevant adjustments must be sent using the prescribed form by not later than one month after this application is received by an owner of the common parts to:
(*see note for completion 6*)[2]

Date:
(*see note for completion 7*)[3]

Form 2
Notice of decision of owner of a property with a share in the common parts of the premises

Alteration or addition being proposed:
(*see note for completion 1*)[4]

To the owner, tenant or occupier making the application:
(*see note for completion 2*)[5]

From the owner of a property with a share in the common parts of the premises:
(*see note for completion 3*)[6]

Address of owner if different from above:
(*see note for completion 4*)[7]

Consent, consent subject to conditions, or withhold consent:
(*see note for completion 5*)[8]

Reason for withholding consent:
(*see note for completion 6*)[9]

Description of conditions to which consent is subject:
(*see note for completion 7*)[10]

---

1 Provide a proposed timetable for the duration of the work.
2 Specify the address to which any objections or other representations are to be sent. The deadline for such objections or representations is not later than one month after this application is received by an owner of a share in the common parts.
3 Provide the date on which you are posting the application; or if you are transmitting it by electronic means, the date of transmission. [Oddly, nothing is said about what might be regarded as a normal means of delivery, namely putting the notice through each letter box.]
4 Repeat the description of the alteration or addition as detailed on the Application for Consent to Relevant Adjustments.
5 Insert the full name and address of the owner, tenant or occupier applying for consent for the relevant adjustments.
6 Insert your full name and address.
7 This only applies if you do not reside at the address above eg you may be the landlord of the property. Otherwise put 'not applicable'.
8 State whether you consent, consent subject to conditions, or withhold consent to the application.
9 Provide the reasons for why you are withholding consent, giving as much detail as possible. Consent cannot be unreasonably withheld. If you have not withheld consent, put 'not applicable'.
10 Detail the nature of the condition(s) to be applied and the reasons why you consider them necessary. If you do not request conditions to be applied, put 'not applicable'.

Date:
(*see note for completion 8*)[1]

The majority decision may be appealed by the disabled person by way of summary application in the sheriff court.

Form 3
Notice of majority decision

Total number of responses received:
(*see note for completion 1*)[2]

Total number of respondents consenting to the proposal:
(*see note for completion 2*)[3]

Total number of respondents withholding consent:
(*see note for completion 3*)[4]

Total number of respondents consenting with conditions:
(*see note for completion 4*)[5]

Statement of outcome:
(*see note for completion 5*)[6]

Reasons given for withholding consent:
(*see note for completion 6*)[7]

Details of conditions to be applied:
(*see note for completion 7*)[8]

The majority decision may be appealed by the owner by way of summary application in the sheriff court.

FAMILY PROPERTY LAW

Property where there is a marriage (or civil partnership)

Many countries have a system in which matrimonial property[9] is automatically co-owned, this rule overriding what is said in the property registers (but of

---

1 Provide the date on which you are posting your decision, or if you are replying by electronic means, the date of transmission.
2 Include in the total number of responses received the owners who have not sent a notice of their decision. [This is an extraordinary note. It says that the total number of responses received is to include the responses *not* received. It is true that this total is needed for the purposes of working out the necessary majority. But that could have been accommodated by using a different heading. As it is, many applicants, rubbing their eyes with incredulity, are likely to fill this in incorrectly.]
3 Include only those consenting without conditions.
4 Include those who have failed to respond by the deadline in the total number of respondents withholding consent.
5 Include only those consenting with conditions [!].
6 Insert a statement of the majority decision.
7 Insert any reasons given for why consent is being withheld.
8 Provide details of the conditions to be applied to the decision.
9 For brevity, in what follows no separate treatment is given to civil partnership.

course with protection for third parties acting in good faith).[1] That is not Scots law, of course, though a case could be made that it should be.[2] Section 24 of the Family Law (Scotland) Act 1985 says:

> Subject to the provisions of any enactment (including this Act), marriage or civil partnership shall not of itself affect the respective rights of the parties to the marriage, or as the case may be the partners in the civil partnership, in relation to their property.

So the starting-point, for marriage, is that the spouses' property is just as separate as if they were unmarried. But as the first 10 words indicate, there are qualifications. The most important of these[3] is where the marriage ends in divorce, when the law provides a well-developed system for dealing with the property issues. The basic idea is that such property as is regarded as 'matrimonial', which will typically be most property of both parties,[4] is notionally placed in a single pot, regardless of whether title is in the name of H or in the name of W or in joint names. Then the contents of that pot are divided, the presumption being for equal division, though of course there are various qualifications and exceptions. So although the starting-point is separation of property, where there is a divorce the 'matrimonial property' of the parties is treated *as if* there were a system of community property: title location does not matter, at least in substance. (It will matter procedurally.)

Outside the context of divorce, however, separation of property applies, and so title location is important. Among other things, it is important where the marriage is dissolved not by divorce but by death. The property separation principle is also important if one of the parties becomes insolvent.

The divorce system seems to work reasonably well – at least in theory, albeit not always in practice: but whatever does work perfectly in practice? It provides a unitary framework for resolving the property issues when a relationship has broken down. It is only occasionally that the question of resolving property issues outside the divorce process arises, though by chance there was one such case this year, *Malak v Inglis*[5] discussed below.

---

1 It is sometimes supposed that this is the position in the Civil Law countries but not in the Common Law countries. In fact it is more complicated than that. For instance nine US states (Arizona, California, Idaho, Louisiana, Nevada, New Mexico, Texas and Washington) have community property systems.

2 The possibility was considered, but eventually rejected, by the Scottish Law Commission: see *Consultative Memorandum No 57 on Matrimonial Property* (1983) and *Report No 86 on Matrimonial Property* (1984). The former contains, in an Appendix (pp 136 ff of vol 2), an outline scheme for statutory co-ownership of the matrimonial home, based on a draft prepared by one of us.

3 The Matrimonial Homes (Family Protection) (Scotland) Act 1981 constitutes another significant qualification to the general principle set out in s 24.

4 The definition is in s 10(4) of the Family Law (Scotland) Act 1985: 'all the property belonging to the parties or either of them … which was acquired by them or him (otherwise than by way of gift or succession from a third party) – (a) before the marriage for use by them as a family home or as furniture or plenishings for such home; or (b) during the marriage …'.

5 [2019] SC HAM 100, 2020 Fam LR 47.

Property where there is no marriage (or civil partnership)

In order to obtain the blessings of divorce it is first necessary to undergo the torments of marriage. For those who have never tied the unhappy knot, the divorce regime is unavailable.[1] Until 2006, the law had nothing to offer tailored to them. If they had a dispute, it had to be resolved by general law, such as invoking the law of promise, or contract, or unjustified enrichment and so on. These claims might be fought out in the context of an action of division and sale or in the context of a standalone action. More of this is said below. In 2006 a statutory right appeared.

Weapons of choice (i): the 2006 Act

In 2006 came the Family Law (Scotland) Act 2006[2] which set up a system for a financial award between separating unmarried couples. Any claim for financial provision has to be made within 12 months of the date when cohabitation ceases,[3] and in practice that deadline is often missed. Does the statutory regime oust the common law rights that the parties may have against each other? That issue becomes particularly relevant where the 12-month deadline has been missed, though it is also possible that a common law claim is made even before the expiry of the deadline. Clearly, a common law claim based on promise or contract remains possible. But what about a claim in unjustified enrichment? In *Courtney's Executors v Campbell*,[4] decided in 2016, it was held that, as a matter of general law, an enrichment claim can be made only where no other claim is available, so that the introduction of the new rules in 2006 meant that enrichment claims as between separating cohabitants were no longer available. The decision was controversial, and the matter has been reviewed in 2020 by the Inner House in *Pert v McCaffrey*,[5] discussed below.

Although a claim under the 2006 Act may have property at its centre, in itself it is a financial claim. And, as already stressed, it has to be made within 12 months of the separation.

Weapons of choice (ii): constructive or implied trust

The most popular weapon south of the border is the constructive or implied trust. It is seldom claimed here. Such trusts can in theory exist but it is exceedingly hard to persuade judges. No more will be said about them here.[6]

---

1 This includes couples who entered a religious marriage but not a marriage recognised by law. Practitioners must always bear in mind that parties may say and believe that they are married but may not be. Divorce lawyers are generally aware of this issue, but it is not only divorce lawyers who need to be aware of it. In this context the old doctrine of marriage constituted by cohabitation with habit and repute, a doctrine which converted many religious-only marriages into legally-recognised marriages, is now defunct: see Family Law (Scotland) Act 2006 s 3.
2 Family Law (Scotland) Act 1985 s 28.
3 There is a minor exception in s 29A.
4 [2016] CSOH 136, 2017 SCLR 387, discussed briefly in *Conveyancing 2016* p 56.
5 [2020] CSIH 5, 2020 SC 259, 2020 SLT 225.
6 Cases in which trust has been averred include *Barbour v Marriott* 2012 GWD 18-358 and *Johnston's Tr v Baird* [2012] CSOH 117, 2012 GWD 25-514, both discussed in *Conveyancing 2012* pp 51–55. For an odd case, involving spouses rather than cohabitants, with the husband arguing that the wife owned property under implied or constructive trust not directly for him but for a company, see *Chemcem Scotland Ltd v Beaton* 2018 SLT (Sh Ct) 371 (*Conveyancing 2018* Case (45)).

Weapons of choice (iii): agreement to dispone

Sometimes it is claimed that there was some sort of agreement that one party would dispone heritable property to the other. This could be a (bilateral) contract or a (unilateral) promise. If the agreement is in formal writing, then well and good, but that is unusual. Without formal writing the claimant has a major problem, because obligations to dispone must be constituted in that manner.[1] This problem can be overcome if 'statutory personal bar' can be established[2] but this is seldom easy. The claimant must climb two high fences: (a) proof that there was such an agreement, albeit informally constituted, and (b) proof of actings in reliance. In one of the cases from 2020, *Brenchley v Whyte*,[3] it was argued that formal writing is not required anyway, but that argument was rightly rejected. The pursuer still had the possibility of establishing 'statutory personal bar' and the case went to proof on that matter. Another case from 2020 in which an obligation to dispone was averred was *Pert v McCaffrey*.[4] That case is discussed below.

Weapons of choice (iv): unjustified enrichment

The other common – indeed commoner – weapon of choice is unjustified enrichment, usually pled in the context of an action of division and sale. Though in principle it had always been possible, the breakthrough case was relatively recent, namely *Shilliday v Smith*.[5] Here an unmarried couple broke up, and one party sued the other to recover the money that she had expended on repair and improvements to his house. Her argument was that she had expended this money in expectation of marriage, and since marriage had not taken place, she could recover it under the branch of enrichment law known as the *condictio causa data causa non secuta*. She was successful.

Since then the enrichment route has been tried quite often.[6] It is sometimes used as a stand-alone claim, as in *Pert v McCaffrey*,[7] but is also often used in actions of division and sale, where one of the parties claims that the net proceeds of sale should not be distributed in accordance with the share of title. Another such case cropped up in 2020, *Malak v Inglis*.[8] A married couple co-owned the matrimonial home in Motherwell. Later they divorced. The divorce did not deal with the property. Later the former husband raised an action of division and sale. The basic issue was whether the defender, the former wife, was entitled to insist on receiving the whole of the net proceeds even though her title share was one-half. The pursuer argued that if the defender wished to make a financial

---

1   Requirements of Writing (Scotland) Act 1995 s 1(2).
2   Requirements of Writing (Scotland) Act 1995 s 1(3).
3   [2020] SC FOR 08, 2020 GWD 5-74. For fuller details, see p 200 below.
4   [2020] CSIH 5, 2020 SC 259, 2020 SLT 225, discussed below.
5   1998 SC 725.
6   For a valuable account, see H L MacQueen, 'Cohabitants in the Scottish Law of Unjustified Enrichment' 2019 *Acta Juridica* 419.
7   Discussed below.
8   [2019] SC HAM 100, 2020 Fam LR 47. For valuable discussion, see Derek Francis, 'The missing co-owner and jurisdiction' 2020 SLT (News) 57 and 63.

claim against him then she should have done so in the divorce action, and it was too late to do it now. The court rejected that argument. Then there was the substantive case that the defender advanced. The financial details are not wholly clear, but it seems that the couple had bought the property from the defender's father and that the price had been below market value, so that there had been a donative element in the transaction. Her case was that this was in her favour alone, rather than to both of them. We do not know the basis for that. The amount that they had paid to her father had been financed by a loan, and the defender asserted that she had repaid the loan. Accordingly, she said, her ex-husband had contributed nothing to the purchase of the property, and that it followed that he should receive nothing from the proceeds of sale. This argument seems to have been accepted by the court, which ordered a proof to take place as to factual details.

It has long been settled that in a division and sale the net proceeds may not be divided according to title share. But one needs to discern what is happening here. In such cases what is *in form* a single action is *in substance* a double action. In the first, the parties are entitled to the net proceeds of sale according to title share. The court cannot change that: it cannot override the title.[1] If there is unequal division, that is because one party can establish a separate financial claim against the other. It could be asserted in a separate action for payment, but for convenience, to avoid multiplicity of actions, it is combined with the division and sale action. That claim will often be a claim based on unjustified enrichment. But if so then, to state the obvious, it must be shown that there has been (a) enrichment that was (b) unjustified. In many of these cases, it is far from clear that that has been so.

Take *McKenzie v Nutter*, decided in 2006.[2] Here Mr Nutter and Ms McKenzie bought a house together for £105,000. Mr Nutter contributed £73,000 from his own resources. The balance of £29,000 they borrowed jointly. Title was taken in both names equally between them. They split up even before Ms McKenzie moved in and there was an action of division and sale. The question for the court was how the proceeds of sale should be divided. It was held that the whole net proceeds should go to Mr Nutter. The court took the view that Ms McKenzie had contributed nothing and so the 50% of the title she had acquired had constituted an unjustified enrichment. Obviously the case is similar to *Malak*. Now, if one party pays the whole of a joint debt, such as a mortgage, then in principle recovery ('relief') against the non-paying co-debtor is competent.[3] But the decision went beyond that, saying that the fact the deposit on the property had been wholly paid

---

1   In a leading English case, *Stack v Dowden* [2007] UKHL 17, [2007] 2 AC 432 at paras 6–10, that most distinguished judge Lord Hope made some *obiter* remarks about Scots law, among which were that: 'Where the title to a dwelling house is taken in one name only, the presumption is that there is sole ownership in the named proprietor. Where it is taken in joint names those named are common owners and, if the grant does not indicate otherwise, there is a presumption of equality of shares.' This is, with respect, not the right approach. One must not conflate the title share with the possibility that the value of that share may be changed by the existence of a personal claim.

2   2007 SLT (Sh Ct) 17. For a discussion, see *Conveyancing 2006* pp 117–21. See also *Conveyancing 2010* pp 168–77.

3   Though the facts and circumstances of the case may disclose donative intent.

by Mr Nutter amounted to an enrichment that was unjustified. An enrichment it certainly was: Ms McKenzie obtained a half share of a property without paying for it. But it is hard to see how it was unjustified. There was no error. Placing the title in joint names was a deliberate action. If it constituted unjustified enrichment then *any* donation is an unjustified enrichment: if Tom gives Selena a book as a Christmas present, then on Boxing Day he can sue her for its return, or for the payment of its value. That is not the law. She has been enriched, but not without justification. The justification was *donatio*.

So in these cases payment of the mortgage may be relevant for the second aspect of the action (settling of debts between the parties), as may other matters such as paying for repairs. But the original decision as to how title was to be divided cannot normally be regarded as a matter that can give rise to a claim in unjustified enrichment. The claim that 'I paid for everything so I should get everything' seems to appeal to some judges but it does not stand up, any more than the claim that 'I paid for the present so I should get it back'. To what has just been said there may be qualifications, but the general principle is surely as stated.

Pert v McCaffrey

In the new case of *Pert v McCaffrey*[1] an Inner House bench of five judges overruled *Courtney's Executors v Campbell*,[2] mentioned earlier, which had held that the passing of s 28 of the Family Law (Scotland) Act 2006 had the effect of barring ex-cohabitants from pursuing claims against each other in unjustified enrichment. (Claims not based on enrichment were unaffected by *Courtney's Executors*.) This is important because so many claims between separating cohabitants are enrichment-based. Whilst that overruling has been generally welcomed, there are aspects of the case that have caused some concern.[3] We will not seek to cover the full range of possible arguments, but will look at just one or two points.

Mr McCaffrey and Ms Pert cohabited from 2004 but never married. In 2008 they bought a house in Trident Way, Renfrew, the whole price being, seemingly, provided by Ms Pert.[4] (The seller was Ms Pert's mother.[5]) Title was taken in joint names. They parted in 2012. In 2015 Ms Pert was sequestrated, and her trustee

---

1 [2020] CSIH 5, 2020 SC 259, 2020 SLT 225.
2 [2016] CSOH 136, 2017 SCLR 387.
3 See eg H MacQueen, 'Cohabitants, unjustified enrichment, contract and subsidiarity: *Pert v McCaffrey*' (2020) 165 *Family Law Bulletin* 4; M Campbell, 'Unjustified Enrichment and Statute: *Pert v McCaffrey*' (2020) 24 *Edinburgh Law Review* 400. These authors prefer the opinion delivered by Lord Brodie to the majority decision delivered by the Lord President and concurred with by the other three judges. But it should be stressed that all five judges agreed in overruling *Courtney's Executors*.
4 We are not quite clear whether this was merely an averment by Ms Pert or whether it was admitted by Mr McCaffrey.
5 Cf *Malak v Inglis* [2019] SC HAM 100, 2020 Fam LR 47, where the seller was the father of one of the parties. But in *Pert* the mother/daughter sale seems to have been at full value, whereas in *Malak* the father/daughter sale was at a price far below value, so that there was a large donative element.

sold the house.[1] Half of the proceeds went to pay her creditors. The other half was remitted to Mr McCaffrey.

Following her discharge from her sequestration Ms Pert sued Mr McCaffrey for the money that he had been paid by the trustee from the sale of the property. The legal basis of her claim is obscure, but in broad terms seems to be (i) that he had been unjustifiably enriched because all the money for the purchase of the property had come from her, and also (ii) that he had agreed, at the time of purchase, that 'in the event the relationship ended he would walk away with nothing in view of the source of funds that facilitated the purchase of the property'.[2]

Whilst *Courtney's Executors* was overruled, Ms Pert's claim nevertheless was rejected, for two reasons. The first was that it had prescribed. The second was that she had averred (see above) that he had agreed to 'walk away with nothing'. We quote from para 25:

> Since the property was already in joint names, this must be taken to mean that the parties had agreed that, in the event of the breakdown of the relationship, the defender would convey his share to the pursuer. On the basis of these averments (ie assuming that they can be proved), the pursuer's most obvious remedy, albeit not one which forms a basis for the action, was to seek specific implement of the agreement or, given that the house had been sold by her trustee, to seek damages as a consequence of the defender's breach of the agreement. It may be that the pursuer would have run into difficulties of proof (Requirements of Writing (Scotland) Act 1995, s 1(2)), but that was not advanced as a reason for not pursuing that remedy. It is this alternative remedy that is fatal to the pursuer's claim.

So: Ms Pert had averred contract, or promise, and, that being the case, her claim based on unjustified enrichment was not stateable. Perhaps, one wonders, it would have been different if she had pled her case in an *esto* form, ie 'he agreed, but *esto* he did not agree, I have an enrichment claim'. Her claim based on agreement was shaky, given that there was nothing in writing. The court's view that s 1 of the 1995 Act is about proof looks like a slip of the pen. In fact, s 1 is about the more fundamental issue of the *constitution* of obligations to convey. Ms Pert's averment as to agreement on the part of Mr McCaffrey could, conceivably, have been set up by 'statutory personal bar'.[3] But her pleadings do not seem to have mentioned that possibility. So it may be that, absent pleading to support 'statutory personal bar', her case as based on agreement was self-destructive. But in any case, had the case gone to proof, one suspects that her prospects of proving any such agreement would have been thin. Be that as it may, the court's argument that 'she is claiming that there was an agreement so an unjustified enrichment claim is excluded' is not wholly convincing. *Shilliday* itself shows that some sort of shared understanding, falling short of an enforceable agreement, may form a basis for an enrichment claim.

---

1 Presumably Mr McCaffrey consented to the sale, for there is no mention of the trustee forcing matters through an action of division and sale.
2 Paragraph 3.
3 Requirements of Writing (Scotland) Act 1995 s 1(3).

Perhaps the oddest feature of the case is that, even if Ms Pert could have established the existence of a valid claim against Mr McCaffrey, it would have availed her nothing, because any such claim had vested in her trustee when she was sequestrated. She had, of course, been discharged, but a person's discharge from sequestration does not – subject to some minor ifs and buts – reinvest the estate. So if Mr McCaffrey had received money that was not due to him, the person he was bound by law to repay was not Ms Pert but her trustee. This rather obvious point does not appear in the case as reported. We do not know why.

PRE-EMPTIONS AND SECTION 84

Two parallel regimes

Many pre-emption clauses still shown on the Land or Sasine Register are extinct (a point to which we will return). But assuming a pre-emption clause is still alive, then the property must be offered back to the pre-emption holder before it can be sold and disponed to someone else. Halliday's style of pre-emption is typical of the sort of thing that titles contain, although variants are possible and indeed not unusual:[1]

> It shall not be in the power of the said CD or his assignees or successors to sell, alienate or dispose of the said subjects or any part thereof to any person until he has first offered the same in writing to me or my successors as proprietors of [*specified lands*] at such price and on such other conditions as any other person shall have offered for the same, and I or my foresaids shall be bound to intimate in writing acceptance or refusal of the offer within 21 days after the offer shall have been received.

Faced with such a clause, the task for sellers is irksome but also straightforward. In principle, they must await receipt of an offer which they feel inclined to accept.[2] Then, but only then, are they in a position to offer back to the pre-emption holder 'the same in writing ... at such price and on such conditions as any other person shall have offered for the same'. The pre-emption holder then has 21 days to accept or refuse the offer. In the event of a refusal (or silence which, after 21 days, comes to the same thing), then the sale can go ahead.

But there is also a different way of proceeding. Section 84 of the Title Conditions (Scotland) Act 2003 – re-enacting in modified form s 9 of the Conveyancing Amendment (Scotland) Act 1938 (now repealed) – makes separate provision for an offer-back. For historical reasons, however, the s 84 procedure is restricted to pre-emptions contained in feu dispositions and other grants in feu, or in ordinary dispositions executed after 1 September 1974. Section 84 is not therefore available for pre-1974 dispositions.[3]

---

1   J M Halliday, *Conveyancing Law and Practice* (2nd edn, 1997) vol II para 32-80. The style has been lightly adapted.
2   The wait can be avoided if it has been possible to persuade the pre-emption holder to enter into a pre-sale undertaking not to exercise the pre-emption, as provided for by s 83 of the Title Conditions (Scotland) Act 2003. So far as we are aware, this facility is little used; perhaps it should be.
3   Title Conditions (Scotland) Act 2003 s 82.

The rules in s 84, when it applies, are quite precise. First, the offer-back must be in formal writing, ie signed by or on behalf of the sellers in conformity with ss 2 (paper documents) or 9B (electronic documents) of the Requirements of Writing (Scotland) Act 1995. Secondly, the offer is to be open for acceptance for 21 days, or for the period set out in the clause of pre-emption if that is shorter. Thirdly, the offer must be made on terms that are 'reasonable' – in effect on terms which could be met with an unqualified (ie *de plano*) acceptance. More precisely, it is provided in s 84(4) that:[1]

> An offer shall be made on such terms as may be *set out*, or *provided for*, in the constitutive deed; but so far as no terms are set out, an offer shall be made on such terms (including any terms so provided for) as are reasonable in the circumstances.

This provision needs some unpacking. A distinction is made between those terms that are 'set out' in the clause of pre-emption and those that are merely 'provided for'. 'Set out' speaks for itself. A term is 'provided for' where, although the term is not set out as such, the place where the term can be found is identified. So where the pre-emption clause provides (as in the Halliday style above) that the offer is to be made 'at such price and on such other conditions as any other person shall have offered for the same', these are terms which are 'provided for'.

With that initial distinction established, s 84(4) goes on to provide, in effect, that the offer-back is to comprise (i) such terms (if any) as are actually 'set out' in the pre-emption clause; (ii) such further terms as are 'provided for' in the clause, which typically means the terms of the offer made by the potential purchaser; and (iii) if desired, some further terms. Importantly, any terms included under (ii) and (iii) must be 'reasonable in the circumstances'. Some care is needed here. Not all terms in the offer by the potential purchaser may be 'reasonable' in this sense,[2] although to the extent that the offer follows the Scottish Standard Clauses the terms may presumably be taken to be 'reasonable'. If, on receiving the offer-back, the pre-emption holder considers any of the terms to be unreasonable, then it is necessary to say so at once; for, unless the pre-emption holder objects in writing within the 21 days (or shorter period) allowed for acceptance of the offer, all the terms are deemed by s 84(5) to be reasonable. On the other hand, if the pre-emption holder does object, and the objections are well founded, a new offer-back will need to be made, shorn of the objectionable terms.

So far we have presented matters as if there were two different ways of proceeding. But of course an offer-back which follows strictly the terms of the clause of pre-emption (the first way) may also be an offer-back which conforms to s 84 (the second way). In that case the two alternatives come to the same thing. But offers-back quite often fall short of the s 84 requirements. This is particularly the case where the sellers, wishing to avoid (or delay) the trouble involved in making a formal offer-back, simply write to or email the pre-emption holder

---

1 Our emphases.
2 See Scottish Law Commission, *Report No 181 on Real Burdens* (2000) para 10.39.

asking whether the holder wishes to exercise the pre-emption. Sometimes even, whether through neglect or rashness, the sellers may proceed with the sale without making contact with the pre-emption holder at all. There are thus three possibilities altogether:

    (i) the sellers send a s 84 offer to the pre-emption holder;

    (ii) the sellers send a non-s 84 offer, ie they write to the pre-emption holder but in a manner that falls short of s 84; or

    (iii) the sellers fail to make contact with the pre-emption holder at all.

The third possibility breaches the pre-emption and can lead to trouble further down the line. The pre-emption holder could, for example, prevent the sale by interdict, or if the sale is completed, procure the reduction of the purchaser's disposition.[1]

Each of the first and second possibilities satisfies the terms of the pre-emption. So far as the *current* sale is concerned, their effect is identical, namely that, if the pre-emption holder fails to accept the offer, the sale can safely go ahead. But a s 84 offer has the important further effect of bringing the pre-emption to an end for *future* sales.[2] It is a matter of one strike and you are out. Faced with a s 84 offer, the pre-emption holder must either accept it or give up forever the chance to buy the property back.

For sellers, it will normally be good practice to ensure that the offer-back conforms to s 84 (where it is available) on the basis that, while it makes little difference to the sellers (the pre-emption being live in respect of the current sale), it is of great assistance to the purchasers (because the pre-emption is then extinguished and so will not apply when the purchasers come to sell in turn). Indeed a vigilant purchaser should insist that a s 84 offer is used.

All of this is important in itself. But it is also by way of background to two new cases on pre-emptions.

Is the pre-emption still alive?

Just because a pre-emption appears in the titles (and on the Land or Sasine Register), it should not be assumed that it is still alive and runs with the land as a real burden. Many, probably most, pre-emptions are not and do not. There are two different types of reason why a pre-emption may no longer be alive.

The first reason is intrinsic to the pre-emption itself. Thus any pre-emption created in a grant in feu was extinguished, with the feudal system itself, on 28 November 2004, except where, most unusually, it was preserved by registration of an appropriate notice before that date.[3] Such pre-emptions may safely be ignored, and indeed should be removed from the title sheet at the first opportunity. Pre-emptions in dispositions are more likely still to be enforceable, but only if the

---

1 On the latter, see *Matheson v Tinney* 1989 SLT 535; *Roebuck v Edmunds* 1992 SLT 1055.

2 Title Conditions (Scotland) Act 2003 s 84(1). There is, however, an exception for rural housing burdens (as to which see s 43 of the Act).

3 Abolition of Feudal Tenure etc (Scotland) Act 2000 ss 17, 18 and 18A.

benefited property in the pre-emption is sufficiently identified in the deed.[1] Older dispositions quite often fail that test.

Of course, even where a pre-emption is extinguished as a real burden, it might still bind the original parties to the deed as a matter of contract (for a disposition or feu disposition is itself a type of contract). But this is only possible where the original grantee (or a universal successor of the grantee such as the grantee's executors) continues to own the property in question.[2] Once the property has passed into the hands of a singular successor, the successor takes free of any contractual pre-emption which was binding on his author. Furthermore, pre-emptions created or after 28 November 2004 cannot usually be contractual.[3]

The second reason is due to subsequent events. That was the focus of the decision in *Toomey v Smith*.[4] As already explained, a pre-emption which is otherwise valid as a real burden will be extinguished as to future sales if an offer-back is made under s 84 of the Title Conditions (Scotland) Act 2003. Negative prescription, furthermore, provides a second possible ground of extinction. The relevant provision is s 18(2) of the Title Conditions Act. Where a pre-emption is breached – where, in other words, property is sold without first being offered back to the pre-emption holder – the pre-emption is extinguished after five years unless, during that period, either the holder seeks to enforce the pre-emption or the defaulting owner acknowledges the breach. Importantly, negative prescription does not just excuse the particular breach; it extinguishes the pre-emption for ever.

These are handy provisions. The possible effect of subsequent events should not, therefore, be overlooked when evaluating the enforceability of a pre-emption clause in a title. But there is an evidential difficulty. Section 84 requires the property to have been offered back in a way which satisfies the conditions set out in that provision. Section 18(2) requires the property not to have been offered back at all. Evidence may exist as to the first of these: indeed it is important to preserve a copy of any offer which is made under s 84. Evidence as to the second – proof that something did *not* happen – is likely to be harder to come by.

Toomey v Smith is a case in which sufficient evidence was found to exist. The owners of land applied to the Lands Tribunal for the discharge of certain real burdens which had been imposed by a disposition in 1995. One of the burdens was a pre-emption. The first sale after 1995 had taken place in 2006. According to the applicants, who had been the purchasers in 2006, the property was not offered back to the pre-emption holder. Accepting this evidence, the Tribunal found that the pre-emption had been extinguished by negative prescription five years after the breach took place:[5]

---

1 For pre-emptions created on or after 28 November 2004, that is the result of s 4(2)(c) of the Title Conditions (Scotland) Act 2003. For older pre-emptions, the rule derives from *Braes v Keeper of the Registers of Scotland* [2009] CSOH 176, 2010 SLT 689.
2 *West Lothian Council v Clark's Exrs* [2020] SC LIV 30, 2020 SLT (Sh Ct) 269, discussed below, is an example of universal succession.
3 Title Conditions (Scotland) Act 2003 s 61.
4 2020 GWD 10-146. The Tribunal comprised R A Smith QC and C C Marwick FRICS.
5 Paragraph 20.

The papers indicate, on the face of it, that an event specified in s 84 and the deed had occurred, namely an arm's length sale at a time when the clause was in effect. That would normally trigger the s 84 mechanism leading to a sale to the benefited proprietor, failing which extinction of the burden. The applicants buying the land in 2006 do not suggest that the s 84 procedures were carried out, but rather that any right of the benefited proprietor to challenge the sale would have prescribed in terms of s 18(2) within five years of an assumed breach from that time. There has been no relevant claim. The result of s 18(2) is that the burden is extinguished altogether.

This passage might possibly be read as suggesting that there are only two possibilities to be considered.[1] On the occasion of a previous sale the property was either offered back under s 84 or it was not offered back. Either way the pre-emption is at an end. In the first case the pre-emption was extinguished at once by the mere fact of making the offer. In the second case it was extinguished five years later due to negative prescription. If that were correct it would solve the evidential problem completely because, after five years, it would not matter whether an offer-back had been made under s 84 or not. Either way the pre-emption would have gone. There would be no need to inquire further.

Unfortunately, however, matters are not quite so simple. As was seen earlier, there is also a third possibility, namely that the property was offered back but with an offer which did not comply with s 84. Such an offer would attract neither s 84 nor s 18(2). The pre-emption would therefore remain. In assessing the continued enforceability of a pre-emption, this possibility, at least, will always require to be considered.

Whether the law is satisfactory is another matter. There is something odd about a rule that extinguishes a pre-emption if the owner ignores the pre-emption but preserves it if the owner complies and offers the property back, albeit in a manner which does not satisfy s 84. But this result is inherent in the idea of negative prescription, which can only be triggered by a breach. In the second case there is no breach.

Contractual pre-emptions

The facts

The other case, *West Lothian Council v Clark's Exrs*,[2] concerned a pre-emption which had once been a real burden but which was now enforceable only as a matter of contract. The facts were unusual. By a feu disposition recorded GRS Midlothian on 7 November 1985, Lothian Regional Council feued West Muir Farm in West Calder to a Mr George Clark. Among the real burdens in the deed was a right of pre-emption. Various events then occurred which had a potential bearing on the enforceability of this pre-emption. First, Lothian Regional Council was abolished in 1996 and replaced, so far as West Muir Farm was concerned, by West Lothian Council. Then the feudal system was abolished in 2004. Finally, Mr Clark died, with the farm passing to his executors by virtue of confirmation.

---

1 In saying this we should not be taken as questioning the decision that was reached in the case.
2 [2020] SC LIV 30, 2020 SLT (Sh Ct) 269.

The effect of these events was as follows. As the superior (West Lothian Council) had not, apparently, registered a notice to preserve the pre-emption, the pre-emption ceased to be enforceable as a real burden with the abolition of the feudal system in 2004. Nonetheless, it remained enforceable as a contract. This was because (i) a feu disposition is a type of contract,[1] (ii) the terms of that contract remained enforceable against the grantee for as long as the grantee (or the grantee's universal successor) still owned the property, and (iii) this contractual effect was expressly preserved by s 75 of the Abolition of Feudal Tenure etc (Scotland) Act 2000. In 2004 the pre-emption would have been enforceable by West Lothian Council against Mr Clark. Following Mr Clark's death it was enforceable against his executors on the basis that they were universal (as opposed to singular) successors. Unlike singular successors (such as a purchaser of the property), a universal successor takes on the liabilities as well as the rights of his author.[2] So far as Mr Clark's executors were concerned, the obligations under the pre-emption were among Mr Clark's liabilities. Thus the executors were as much subject to the pre-emption as Mr Clark had been before them.

The validity of the notice

Mr Clark's executors proposed to sell part of West Muir Farm. As the pre-emption still bound the executors as a matter of contract, such a sale would potentially trigger the pre-emption. Hence it was necessary for the executors to comply with the procedure which the clause of pre-emption set out. Accordingly, on 17 December 2015 solicitors acting for the executors wrote to West Lothian Council in the following terms:

> We act on behalf of the Executors of the late George Anderson Aitken Clark ('the Executors'). Following the death of Mr Clark, the Executors are the uninfeft proprietors of the above mentioned subjects ('the Feu'). The late Mr Clark was the original feuar by virtue of a Feu Disposition granted by the Lothian Regional Council in his favour dated 7th November 1985 and recorded in the Division of the General Register of Sasines applicable to the County of Midlothian on 30th May 1986 ('the Feu Disposition'). We understand that West Lothian Council is the successor to any interest which Lothian Regional Council had under the Feu Disposition.
>
> As required in terms of the Feu Disposition, we hereby give you notice, on behalf of the Executors, that the Executors desire to dispose of that part of the Feu shown coloured red and brown on the plan annexed, by way of a sale.

This was not an offer-back as such. But this particular clause of pre-emption required no more than a notice in writing of a desire to sell. This was such a notice. There was, however, a problem. While the plan annexed to the letter

---

1 That view of things was strenuously disputed by the defenders, but the law is clear and the defenders' arguments were rejected.

2 For the distinction, see K G C Reid, *The Law of Property in Scotland* (1996) para 598; Jan Peter Schmidt, 'Transfer of Property on Death and Creditor Protection: The Meaning and Role of "Universal Succession"', in A J M Steven, R G Anderson and J MacLeod (eds), *Nothing so Practical as a Good Theory: Festschrift for George L Gretton* (2017) 323.

showed an area coloured red, it did not – or so it was averred – show any area coloured brown. It was thus unclear which precise area was to be sold by the executors, and hence which precise area the Council would have to offer for if it wished to exercise the right of pre-emption.[1]

This uncertainty prompted the following reply from the Council, sent just before Christmas, on 23 December 2015:

> I refer to your letter dated 17 December 2015 indicating that your clients wish to sell the land shown coloured red and brown on the plan annexed to your letter. The area coloured brown is not clearly visible on plan. Please confirm where this is located.
>
> As you are aware, the Council has a right of pre-emption in terms of clause (SIXTH) of the feu disposition recorded on 30 May 1986. The Council may be interested in exercising its right of pre-emption but will require to seek authority to do so. To allow the Council to consider its position, please issue an offer to sell in terms of section 84 of the Title Conditions (Scotland) Act 2003. This should include price and such other terms as would reasonably allow the Council to consider the offer.
>
> The offer should be open for acceptance for a period of twenty one days. I look forward to hearing from you.

Over the Christmas period there was silence, but early in the New Year, on 25 January 2016, the solicitors for the executors sent a bombshell letter:

> We thank you for your letter of 23 December 2015. That letter does not give the requisite notice in terms of the relevant Feu Disposition. The time limit within which you had to give the relevant notice has now expired. Your interest in the subjects of our letter of 17th December 2015 is at an end and our clients do not have to make an offer to you.

It was this letter which prompted the litigation. The executors said they were free of the pre-emption. The Council said that they were not. The Council raised an action of declarator coupled with an interdict to prevent the sale of the property.[2] Following a proof it has now been found by the sheriff,[3] on the basis both of his own observations[4] and of the evidence of witnesses, that the plan did not identify an area coloured brown. Hence the subjects to be sold had not been properly identified. Hence the notice was invalid:[5]

> I therefore come to the conclusion, without any real difficulty, that the purported notice sent by the solicitors for the executors by letter dated 17 December 2015 to West Lothian Council did not give West Lothian Council sufficient information

---

1 The issue of a plan which is, or is said to be, unsatisfactory crops up quite often. Such problems are varied, and include missing north signs, north signs that do not point north, incorrect scales, floating shapes, boundaries marked with a broad brush, and so on. Colours are often problematic, for instance plans that are said to be in colour but in fact are monochrome, plans that are in colour but the colouring does not tie in with the accompanying documents, and so on.

2 An interim interdict was duly granted: see *West Lothian Council v Clark's Exrs* [2019] SC LIV 58, 2019 GWD 24-378, discussed in *Conveyancing 2019* pp 174–78.

3 Sheriff Douglas A Kinloch.

4 Paragraphs 48–49: 'I will start by saying that it seems to me that I must, at least to some extent, be able to use the evidence of my own eyes as to whether or not there was any brown area visible on the plan. It would, in my view, offend against common sense if I was not able to do so ... Having examined the plan myself, there is in my view simply no brown area visible to the naked eye.'

5 Paragraphs 65–67.

to allow them to identify the brown area referred to on the plan. As only part of the farm was being offered back to West Lothian Council they had no way of knowing what area of land was included in the brown area referred to. They could not tell whether the brown area had been omitted by mistake from the plan sent with the letter, and how extensive the brown area was. They needed to know precisely what land was being offered back to them before they could decide whether or not to purchase it.

It is accordingly clear to me that the purported notice given by the executors was not a valid notice at all, and I am made even more certain in that conclusion by the fact that in law strict compliance with the terms of the pre-emption notice was required. The matter was potentially of great importance to West Lothian Council and it was therefore of crucial importance that the executors made it entirely clear just which area of land they were considering selling: see eg, *HOE International Limited v Andersen* 2017 SC 313; *Batt Cables plc v Spencer Business Parks Limited* 2010 SLT 860.

The pre-emption clause required notice to be given to West Lothian Council in the event that the executors wished to 'dispose of the feu or a specified part thereof'. The notice did not specify properly which part of the farm they wished to sell, and it was essential that it did. It was not a valid notice.

An appeal has since been refused by the Sheriff Appeal Court: [2021] SAC (Civ) 11, and we will cover the appeal in next year's volume.

Applicability of s 84

Some of the interest of the sheriff's judgment lies in a quite different point, which takes us back to the opening of the present section. Even if the notice sent by the executors had been valid – even if, in other words, the brown area had been properly identified – the sheriff would still have found for the Council. In reaching this view, the sheriff accepted the following argument on behalf of the Council. (i) The pre-emption was subject to s 84 of the Title Conditions (Scotland) Act 2003 (ie to the provision which provides for the extinction of pre-emptions for all time where an offer-back is made in conformity with s 84). (ii) The notice given by the executors was such an offer-back. (iii) In pointing out the muddle as to the colouring, the Council was making an objection to the reasonableness of the terms of the offer-back. (iv) Hence the Council's failure to accept the offer did not extinguish the pre-emption, as would be the normal consequence of a s 84 offer, but on the contrary left it open for future acceptance.

The foundation of the argument was the proposition that s 84 applied to the pre-emption. That proposition was supported by the sheriff only 'with some diffidence'.[1] His caution was well judged. The only purpose of s 84 is to extinguish, for the future, pre-emptions which, being real burdens, would otherwise continue to run with the land.[2] But a contractual pre-emption, such as that under consideration in *West Lothian Council v Clark's Exrs*, does not run with the land in any event. It has no need of s 84. To apply s 84 to contractual pre-emptions would be pointless. The sheriff thought that one result of so

---

1 Paragraph 71.
2 Scottish Law Commission, *Report No 181 on Real Burdens* (2000) paras 10.35–10.40.

doing might be to provide 'a uniform system for the operation of all rights of pre-emption',[1] but all pre-emptions are prisoners of the clause by which they are created, and these clauses, as we have seen, are far from uniform. The most that can be said is that, employing an expansive view of the relevant definition, it is *possible* to conclude that s 84 applies to contractual pre-emptions, at least where they were formerly real burdens.[2] What would be gained by adopting this view is unclear.

There are problems with other parts of the Council's argument as well. Even if s 84 could have applied in principle, it could not have applied to the notice given by the executors. Highly prescriptive in matters of detail (as we have seen), s 84 requires a formal 'offer to sell' the property to the pre-emption holder. The mere 'notice ... that the Executors desire to dispose of' the property which was given on 17 December 2015 falls far short of an offer to sell. Indeed this point was taken by the Council itself when, in its reply of 23 December 2015, it asked the executors to 'issue an offer to sell in terms of section 84 of the Title Conditions (Scotland) Act 2003'. Finally, even if the notice had been an offer-back, it seems improbable that the Council's complaint about the failure to identify the brown area – a complaint which in any event was not relevant on the hypothesis that the notice was clearly expressed – could be viewed as an objection to the *reasonableness* of the terms of the offer.[3]

The truth is that the notice given by the executors was no more, and no less, than what was required under the clause of pre-emption. It did not comply with s 84 because it did not need to. As soon as the notice was received, the Council had 21 days to accept it. No acceptance was issued within this period. If, therefore, the notice had been valid (which on the sheriff's view it was not), the Council would have lost the opportunity to buy back the land.

COMMON GOOD

'Common good' property[4] is a perennial source of litigation. Local authorities wish to do this, that or the other with some building, or a park, or whatever it may be, and some local residents are unhappy, and may litigate. Not only do the cases keep coming, but the legislation too does not stand still. The most recent changes were made by the Community Empowerment (Scotland) Act 2015,[5] and we would not be in the least surprised if more legislation were to be in the womb of time.

---

1 Paragraph 73.
2 By Title Conditions (Scotland) Act 2003 s 82, s 84 of the Act applies to 'any [A] subsisting right of pre-emption [B] constituted as a title condition [C] which was originally created in favour of a feudal superior' (our lettering). In a sense all three requirements are satisfied. But while the pre-emption in *West Lothian Council v Clark's Exrs* was 'subsisting' and had indeed originally been 'constituted as a title condition ... in favour of a feudal superior', it did not, now, subsist *as a title condition*.
3 As is required by TC(S)A 2003 s 84(5).
4 For which the indispensable guide is A C Ferguson, *Common Good Law* (2nd edn, 2019).
5 See Community Empowerment (Scotland) Act 2015 ss 102–106.

Common good property existed only in burghs. When the old system of local government was swept away, and the burgh system with it,[1] by the Local Government (Scotland) Act 1973, common good nevertheless survived, so that today in a local authority area there will be common good property, but only in the areas of the former burghs, not landward of them.[2] Many authorities say that common good is the property of the inhabitants of the burgh (or today former burgh) but this is not, in the eyes of a property lawyer, strictly correct. Common good property belongs to the burgh, or, today, the local authority, and thus common good land will appear in the Land Register showing the local authority as the heritable proprietor in the B section of the title sheet. But the inhabitants of the former burgh have certain rights in relation to common good property.

It is not always easy to know precisely what property held by a local authority is common good property. Matters have, however, improved as a result of s 102(1) of the Community Empowerment (Scotland) Act 2015, which says that 'each local authority must establish and maintain a register of property which is held by the authority as part of the common good'.[3] It is a statutory requirement that the register should be available on a website, and the registers (or in some cases draft registers) are now becoming available for consultation.[4]

2020 brought with it yet another common good case. *Guild v Angus Council*[5] concerned a leisure centre in Forfar, called Lochside Leisure Centre, built in architecture's Golden Age, the 1970s. It was now disused. It was situated within Forfar Country Park, also known as Forfar Loch Country Park. Angus Council decided to demolish it and restore the site to parkland. Two Forfar residents raised the present action for reduction of that decision and for interdict against demolition. Their case was that 'disposal' and 'change of use' of common good property both require a consultation process to be conducted, in terms of s 104 of the Community Empowerment (Scotland) Act 2015, and Angus Council had not conducted such a process.

At first instance[6] the Lord Ordinary (Lady Carmichael) held that demolition would be neither a disposal nor a change of use. It would not be a disposal because no rights were being granted to anyone else: the site was not being disponed or leased. It would not be a change of use because its use for leisure purposes would continue, albeit in a different form. In addition Lady Carmichael held that 'the common good property in this case was the land, and not the building' so that what was to be demolished was not itself common good property.[7] Accordingly the petition failed. The petitioners reclaimed.

---

1 Not everyone thinks that the change was wise.
2 We refer here to land. But moveables can also be part of the common good.
3 The provision came into force on 27 June 2018, at which time statutory guidance was issued by the Scottish Government: see *Conveyancing 2018* pp 113–14.
4 See eg the registers for Glasgow (https://glasgow.gov.uk/24074), and Edinburgh (www.edinburgh.gov.uk/commercial-property-sale-let/common-good-register/1).
5 [2020] CSIH 50, 2020 SLT 939, 2020 SCLR 685.
6 [2020] CSOH 16, 2020 SCLR 685. This contains a fuller account of the facts and circumstances of the case than can be found in the Inner House case.
7 Paragraph 45.

The Inner House, by a majority (the Lord President and Lord Menzies, with Lord Malcolm dissenting) reversed the Lord Ordinary's decision. As to the idea that the building was not part of the common good even though the land on which it was built was part of the common good, the majority took the view that that would be inconsistent with the principle, familiar to all conveyancers, that what is attached to land becomes part of the land – an aspect of the law of *accessio* which, like so much else in property law, has been inherited from Roman law. Further, they held that the proposed demolition would be both a 'disposal' and a 'change of use'. Hence, they said, s 104 was engaged.

Lord Malcolm's dissent was as learned and well argued as the opinion of the majority. Agreeing with the Lord Ordinary, he took the view that the demolition would be neither a disposal nor a change of use. Moreover (though this was only *obiter*) he opined that, whilst from the standpoint of property law the leisure centre was part of the land, it did not necessarily follow that the same was true for the purposes of classifying assets as common good: 'I consider it more in line with the law and the facts to say that the common good is the park, and does not include the bricks and mortar of the centre.'[1]

The decision does not mean that demolition will not take place. It merely means that everything is reset. If the council still wishes to proceed, it must now undertake a s 104 consultation.

Two final thoughts. One is that if four Court of Session judges – one in the Outer House and three in the Inner House – were equally divided as to the meaning of 'disposal' and 'change of use' then it would perhaps be desirable that there should be some legislative clarification. Indeed, much of common good law is somewhat fuzzy, so that one might be looking at an overall law reform project here. The topic is currently being reviewed by the Scottish Land Commission, although the focus is not primarily a legal one.[2] The other thought is that one of the petitioners was seeking to buy the leisure centre: if that were to happen the result would be … that it would no longer be part of the common good.

AIRBNB AND REAL BURDENS

Introduction

Rightly or wrongly, properties on short-term – often weekend – lets are seen as an unwelcome source of parties, excessive alcohol, drugs and other forms of anti-social behaviour. For those seeking to curb short-term lets, the solution has usually been thought to lie in public law, and the significant steps taken during 2020 towards regulation by licensing and by planning consent were described earlier in this volume.[3] But private law too may have a part to play. In particular, real burdens often impose use restrictions which may touch, at least indirectly, on short-term letting. So far as we know, this issue has yet to be tested in the

---

1 Paragraph 58.
2 See *Conveyancing 2019* pp 113–15.
3 See p 76 above.

Scottish courts, but there has been litigation in England.[1] The most recent case there, *Triplerose Ltd v Beattie*,[2] is worthy of attention, not least because the clause which was litigated is one frequently found in the titles of Scottish properties.

Triplerose

Triplerose concerned a flat in Newcastle held on a 125-year lease. Following a change in job, the tenants moved away from Newcastle and, pending a possible sale, employed an agency to let the flat out on Airbnb and Booking.com. The landlord objected on the basis of a covenant in the lease by which the tenant undertook:

> Not at any time to carry on or permit to be carried on upon the Property any trade or business whatsoever nor to use or permit the same to be used for any purpose other than as a private dwelling house for occupation by one family at any one time.

Both parts of the covenant, said the landlord, had been breached.

The case in respect of the first part of the covenant was not especially strong. It was true, certainly, that in letting out the flat on Airbnb the tenants were carrying on a business. But they were not carrying it on 'upon the Property'. On the contrary, the property was being used for residential purposes. Thus there was, concluded the Upper Tribunal, no breach of this aspect of the covenant.

The second part, however, was a different matter. This required the flat to be used for no other purpose 'than as a private dwelling house for occupation by one family at any one time'. Were those enjoying weekends in Newcastle using the flat 'as a private dwelling house'? The answer, said the Upper Tribunal, was no. On the contrary:[3]

> [Sh]ort-term occupation by paying strangers is the antithesis of occupation as a private dwellinghouse. It is neither private, being available to all comers, nor use as a dwellinghouse, since it lacks the degree of permanence implicit in that designation.

In English law, this position was well established by previous case law.[4]

The position in Scotland

It is plausible that in Scotland, too, a court would regard short-term letting as a breach of a real burden requiring use as a private dwellinghouse.[5] But that would only be half the story, for a neighbour seeking to enforce such a burden would

---

1 See most notably *Nemcova v Fairfield Rents Ltd* [2016] UKUT 303 (LC), [2017] 1 P & CR 4.
2 [2020] UKUT 180 (LC), [2020] HLR 37, [2021] 1 P & CR 4.
3 Paragraph 20.
4 In this connection the Upper Tribunal, at para 20, cited Lord Justice Lewison (ed), *Woodfall's Law of Landlord and Tenant* para 11.206.
5 On this topic, see Malcolm M Combe, 'Land law responses to the sharing economy: short-term lets and title conditions' 2017 *Juridical Review* 219; Andrew Todd and Hannah Leslie, 'Short-term lets and title conditions: a house builder's perspective' 2018 *Juridical Review* 197.

also have to show interest to enforce.[1] In terms of s 8(3)(a) of the Title Conditions (Scotland) Act 2003 a person has interest to enforce a real burden if and only if:

> in the circumstances of any case, failure to comply with the real burdens is resulting in, or will result in, material detriment to the value or enjoyment of the person's ownership of, or right in, the benefited property.

So there are, under s 8(3)(a), two possible ways of showing interest to enforce. One is by demonstrating a material fall in the *value* of the enforcer's property due to the breach of the burden. Whether a key safe and the prospect of weekend parties would have this effect is a matter of valuation evidence. In some cases a decline in value could doubtless be shown. Of the existing decisions on this aspect of interest to enforce, the most helpful is *Kettlewell v Turning Point Scotland*,[2] in which the Lands Tribunal accepted evidence that house values would fall by between 10% and 15% in the event that a neighbouring house were used (as was intended) as care accommodation for up to six adults with learning difficulties.

Alternatively, interest to enforce is established by showing 'material detriment' to the *enjoyment* of the enforcer's property. This has proved to be a less straightforward ground. The very first case to be decided under this head, *Barker v Lewis*,[3] is discouraging for those seeking to use real burdens to prevent short-term lets. In that case the defender was using her house for a bed-and-breakfast business, contrary to a real burden. Detailed evidence was amassed of the disruption and inconvenience to neighbours caused thereby. But no interest to enforce was established on the part of the neighbours. No doubt there had been 'detriment' to the neighbours, but the detriment had not been 'material'.

Since the decision in *Barker* there have been signs of a lowering of the threshold for interest to enforce. In the most recent significant case, *Franklin v Lawson*,[4] it was said that '[w]here an adverse element of detriment can be identified as something more than fanciful or insignificant it can properly be described as material'. The law, however, remains in flux, and the uncertainty is increased by the fact that all decisions so far have been at the level of the sheriff court or Lands Tribunal.

In whatever way material detriment to enjoyment is defined, however, it is likely that some instances of short-term letting will satisfy the test. But, often, the use of neighbouring property as an Airbnb or similar may be mildly annoying rather than seriously disruptive. In *Triplerose* itself there was found to be 'no evidence that occupiers of the flat had caused nuisance or annoyance to others'.[5] In English law that does not matter; in Scots law it would prevent enforcement of the real burden.

---

1 For a full discussion of interest to enforce, see W M Gordon and S Wortley, *Scottish Land Law*, 3rd edn, vol II (2020) paras 24–90 to 24–102 (Craig Anderson). In *Triplerose* and other leasehold cases in England, enforcement is by the landlord, who is the functional equivalent of the former feudal superior in Scotland; in the case of superiors, interest to enforce was presumed.

2 2011 SLT (Sh Ct) 143; see *Conveyancing 2011* pp 87–90.

3 2008 SLT (Sh Ct) 17; see *Conveyancing 2008* pp 92–95.

4 2013 SLT (Lands Tr) 81; see *Conveyancing 2013* pp 122–23.

5 Paragraph 11.

Enforceable or not, of course, a real burden might still have a deterrent effect.[1] On being told that short-term letting is contrary to the titles, the neighbour might be persuaded to desist. But if not, it will be necessary to give careful consideration to interest to enforce before incurring the expense of a court action.

OBLIGATIONS TO DISPONE: IS FORMAL WRITING ALWAYS NEEDED?

A contract, or a promise, to dispone heritable property must be in formal writing, subject to the rules about personal bar.[2] Or is that right? In recent years there have been two decisions, *McFarlane v McFarlane*[3] and *DWS v RMS*,[4] holding that in some types of case a written agreement is not needed. Which type of case? At least three (probably more) possible *rationes* can be extracted, which we set out in ascending order of remarkability. One is that an agreement to settle litigation (a compromise agreement) is valid without writing, even though part of the settlement is that there will be a disposition of heritable property. The second possible *ratio* is that, if an agreement includes other matters as well, then writing is not required so that, for instance, a sale of a house and contents would not need writing in such a case. The third is that no obligation to dispone heritable property requires writing. The requirement of writing applies to dispositions but not to missives. In other words, only documents granting real rights are covered by the requirement of writing, not documents granting personal rights, such as missives. We apologise to elderly readers with wobbly hearts: we should certainly have included a trigger warning at the beginning of this paragraph.

There is, of course, the doctrine that an agreement not in formal writing can become binding by a form of personal bar: this used to be a common law rule but is now to be found in s 1(3) of the Requirements of Writing (Scotland) Act 1995, and hence is sometimes called 'statutory personal bar'. But that is not what we are speaking about at present. Sometimes personal bar can be established, and sometimes it cannot: it is fact-specific. The cases just mentioned say that *regardless* of the possibility of personal bar, agreements to dispone do not need writing, in at least certain types of case.

Both the cases involved compromise agreements, or rather alleged agreements, in which one element of the settlement was to be that heritable property would be disposed by one party to the other. In both cases the agreement, or alleged agreement, was not in formal writing, and one party asserted that there had been a binding agreement and the other party denied it. In *McFarlane* Lord Menzies said that 'there is no requirement in our law for a particular formality or method of concluding a contract for the compromise of a court action'[5] and continued:[6]

---

1 Todd and Leslie, 'Short-term lets and title conditions: a house builder's perspective' 198.
2 That is the law as set out in s 1 of the Requirements of Writing (Scotland) Act 1995.
3 [2007] CSOH 75.
4 [2016] SC GRE 47, 2016 GWD 22-402 (*Conveyancing 2016* Case (18)).
5 Paragraph 41.
6 Paragraph 42.

> [I]t is important to bear in mind that what is being considered in the present case is not a contract for the transfer of title to heritable property, nor for the transmission of any real right; this is a contract for the compromise of a court action, conferring only personal rights.

And in *DWS* the sheriff said:[1]

> A compromise agreement ... confers only personal rights. It is therefore not a contract for the transfer of a real right in land.

All this makes no sense, of course. Contracts create personal rights. A contract for the transfer of a real right in land creates a personal right, regardless of whether it is in the context of a market sale or in the context of a settlement of a dispute. For an excellent discussion of these cases, one may refer to Craig Anderson's article, 'Compromise agreements and heritable property'.[2] Anderson's article was, happily, cited to the court in the latest case, *Brenchley v Whyte*,[3] in which Sheriff S G Collins QC, in an incisive and powerful judgment, declined to follow the earlier cases and pointed out that they were simply wrong.

Joan Brenchley and Douglas Whyte had been in a relationship but were not married. In 1999 they had a child. The relationship broke down in 2009 or 2010. In the latter year Mr Whyte bought a house, in Montrose, which he made available for his former cohabitant and their child to occupy. She provided none of the funding for the purchase. Some years later, after the child had become an adult, the parties came to be in dispute about the house. Ms Brenchley raised the present action for declarator and implement of an alleged agreement that Mr Whyte would dispone the house to her, without any payment.

There was nothing in writing. Naturally, Ms Brenchley argued that 'statutory personal bar' would validate the alleged agreement, but that was merely her backstop argument. Her first argument was that the alleged agreement to dispone did not need to be in writing anyway, and she cited *McFarlane v McFarlane* and *DWS v RMS* to support that position. Above we saw that at least three *rationes* can be extracted from these decisions, and in *Brenchley* the pursuer proposed what is perhaps a fourth. We quote the sheriff:[4]

> The principal submission for the pursuer was, in substance, that s 1(2)(a)(i) of the 1995 Act[5] should be understood as only applying to those contracts whose sole or primary purpose is the creation etc of a real right in land. Accordingly if the parties' agreement when considered as a whole is primarily directed to some other purpose or made for some other reason, and an agreement to create etc a real right in land is merely one aspect of it, then s 1(2)(a)(i) will not apply. In such a case the contract will not be 'for' the creation etc of a real right in land, but for some other purpose. On this approach the rule is therefore soft-edged, requiring a judgment on the circumstances of each case, as a matter of fact and degree. In the present case, the submission for the pursuer was that the primary purpose of the agreement was the global settlement of

---

1 Paragraph 29. The sheriff was Sheriff W M D Mercer.
2 2016 SLT (News) 169.
3 [2020] SC FOR 08, 2020 GWD 5-74.
4 Paragraph 18.
5 Ie the Requirements of Writing (Scotland) Act 1995.

all financial and other matters arising from the breakdown of the parties' relationship, and the transfer of title to the Montrose house was merely an aspect of this agreement. Accordingly the agreement was not one to which s 1(2)(a)(i) applied.

The sheriff was not persuaded:[1]

> As Ms Shewan[2] submitted, s 1(2)(a)(i) is not confined to contracts which are exclusively concerned with transfers etc of real rights in land. Had that been the intention, provision could have been made to this effect, but it was not. This is not surprising. Missives for the sale and purchase of heritable property will fall within section 1(2)(a)(i) even if, as they typically do, they also include agreement as to moveables or other ancillary matters.

As for the argument that compromise agreements do not require formal writing:[3]

> Even accepting that the contract argued for by the pursuer can properly be described as a compromise agreement, I do not accept that it follows that s 1(2)(a)(i) does not apply to it. The short answer is that s 1(2)(a)(i) applies to contracts generally, without relevant qualification. An agreement to compromise a claim is a contract by another name. If it is a contract for the creation etc of a real right in land it will fall within s 1(2)(a)(i), and therefore must be in writing. No exception is made in s 1(2)(a)(i) for compromise agreements. Nor is there any warrant to read in such an exception.

The sheriff's reasoning is cogent and persuasive.

REAL BURDENS: VOID FOR UNCERTAINTY?

Duffus v Malcolm Allan Housebuilders Ltd[4] offers a brainteaser. Which bit or bits of the following real burden are void for uncertainty?

> In respect that we may form certain portions of the Whole Area as public open spaces which may include amenity areas, bridle paths, visibility splays and play areas and being such portions as are not included in the Plots the same shall be formed, laid out and where necessary built upon and planted out by us and once completed by us shall remain open and unbuilt upon (except in so far as occupied by play equipment) in all time coming, each and every Plot being held under burden of the Proprietor of the dwellinghouse thereon maintaining as public open spaces and in neat and tidy condition, the said portions and any erections or equipment thereon, including footpaths traversing the same and any trees, shrubs, flowers and grass planted or to be planted therein and (so far as belonging to us and not exclusively conveyed to the owner of a Plot) the boundary walls and fences thereof, the expenses thereof being borne equally by all the Proprietors of dwellinghouses situated within the Whole Area and that until the said public open spaces are conveyed to or are taken over by any public authority for maintenance; declaring that no Proprietor of a dwellinghouse shall ever have a claim against the Superiors in respect of such maintenance.

---

1 Paragraph 20.
2 Rachel Shewan, advocate, for the defender.
3 Paragraph 24.
4 2020 GWD 16-236. In this decision of the Lands Tribunal the Tribunal comprised Lord Minginish and C C Marwick FRICS.

As may be surmised, the burden appeared in a deed of conditions of a housing estate. Its evident purpose was to impose maintenance obligations on each of the home-owners in respect of certain 'public open spaces'. Ownership of the open spaces themselves had been retained by the developer.

What is to be maintained?

But what were the 'public open spaces' that were to be maintained? Today their identity was, in a practical sense, clear because all the 'Plots' with the houses on them had long since been sold, and the 'public open spaces' were whatever was still left with the developer. But that was not the relevant test. The relevant test was whether the 'public open spaces' could be identified in the early 1990s when the deed of conditions was recorded and the houses were being sold. A real burden must make clear what is to be done or not be done. Unless, therefore, the identity of the subjects to be maintained was clear from the word go, the maintenance obligation would fail as a real burden, and so could not be enforced against someone like the applicant in *Duffus v Malcolm Allan Housebuilders Ltd*, who was a successor of the original purchaser of one of the houses.

The problem with the condition is immediately apparent. Only 'certain portions' of the 'Whole Area' were to be 'public open spaces', but what these 'portions' were to be was highly uncertain. They would be some or all of 'such portions as are not included in the Plots' but until all of the Plots had been sold and disponed away it was impossible to know with any degree of precision what land that would be. There was a plan attached to the deed of conditions, but this was of no assistance, being merely a crude outline of the Whole Area without showing the location of any Plots.

In these circumstances the Lands Tribunal had no hesitation in finding the description void from uncertainty:[1]

> The term the burden uses is 'public open spaces'. It is not defined. All that is said by way of description is that these spaces 'may include amenity areas, bridle paths, visibility splays and play areas' and that they shall be 'such portions as are not included in the Plots'. There is no plan to show where all the houses are, so it cannot be worked out where the public open spaces are. Nor is there reference to any other document from which the extent of the burden can be identified, not that such a reference would necessarily save it from falling foul of the four corners rule; *Marriott v Greenbelt*.[2] There is not even a firm commitment that public open spaces including amenity areas, bridle paths, visibility splays and play areas will be formed; condition 6 says only the that granters of the Deed *may* do so.

In an effort to save the description from the flames, the developers had sought to argue that, while matters were admittedly imprecise at the time of

---

1 Paragraph 45.
2 *Marriott v Greenbelt Group Ltd*, 2 December 2015, Lands Tribunal, discussed in *Conveyancing 2015* pp 138–51. A description which depends on something extrinsic to the deed (in the case of *Marriott*, planning consent) is fatal to the validity of the real burden.

the recording of the deed of conditions in 1990, the *maximum* amount of land involved, namely the 'Whole Area', had at least been identified. Identification of the precise part of the Whole Area had then followed in due course. To some extent this built on an argument which had been tentatively suggested by the Lands Tribunal itself in an earlier case.[1] That approach, however, had been rejected by the Sheriff Appeal Court in a case decided in 2019,[2] and it was rejected again now by the Lands Tribunal. 'That the public open spaces, if any should be created, must be within the Whole Area is certainly self-evident but it tells us nothing about the extent, location or nature of these spaces.'[3]

And so this is yet another case in which a condition providing for maintenance of common areas in a housing estate has failed as a real burden.[4] This is becoming practically an annual occurrence. One begins to wonder how many of these provisions in deeds of conditions are actually valid.

What is 'maintenance'?

There was another ground, too, for treating the maintenance condition in *Duffus v Malcolm Allan Housebuilders Ltd* as void for uncertainty. But this was an argument developed by the Tribunal on its own account, and was only a subsidiary ground of decision (the burden being void for the reason already discussed).[5] This second point of concern concerned the scope of the obligation of maintenance. Extracted from the rest of the clause (quoted above), the obligation was one of:

> maintaining as public open spaces and in neat and tidy condition, the said portions [ie the public open spaces] and any erections or equipment thereon, including footpaths traversing the same and any trees, shrubs, flowers and grass planted or to be planted therein and (so far as belonging to us and not exclusively conveyed to the owner of a Plot) the boundary walls and fences thereof ...

This, said the Tribunal, was fatally uncertain:[6]

> The burden says that the public open spaces are to be kept 'in neat and tidy condition' but to whose satisfaction and how does that relate to 'any erections of equipment thereon' and to 'the boundary walls and fences thereof'? Is there a duty to pay a share of the maintenance, repair and replacement of such equipment, walls and fences? Is there a duty to replace trees, shrubs and flowers as required? This lack of detail is in marked contrast to what is found in some of the other Deeds of Conditions in the recent tranche of cases on this subject, for instance in *Marriott v Greenbelt*[7] where

---

1 *Marriott v Greenbelt Group Ltd*, 2 December 2015, Lands Tribunal at para 177. This is the idea of 'overshooting' discussed in *Conveyancing 2019* pp 132–34.

2 *Scottish Woodlands Ltd v Majekodunmi* [2019] SAC (Civ) 38, [2020] Hous LR 23 at para 23.

3 Paragraph 47.

4 Last year's case was *Scottish Woodlands Ltd v Majekodunmi* [2019] SAC (Civ) 38, [2020] Hous LR 23; see *Conveyancing 2019* pp 128–31.

5 Paragraph 53, explaining why the Tribunal did not invite submissions on this point.

6 Paragraph 52.

7 *Marriott v Greenbelt Group Ltd*, 2 December 2015, Lands Tribunal. Deeds of conditions by Greenbelt and other land management companies typically go into a great deal of detail as to planting and so on.

there was a great deal of detail as to the standards to which the land in question had to be maintained. We do not say that such a level of detail is necessary but a great deal more than we have in this case is.

This is perhaps an unduly harsh view of things. No doubt the burden could have been better drafted. Even better organisation of the same words would have helped matters, as for example:

maintaining as public open spaces and in neat and tidy condition –
  (a) the said portions and any erections or equipment thereon
  (b) including footpaths traversing the same and
  (c) any trees, shrubs, flowers and grass planted or to be planted therein and
  (d) (so far as belonging to us and not exclusively conveyed to the owner of a Plot) the boundary walls and fences thereof

There can be no real objection to any of (a)–(d). What is listed is as clear as can reasonably be expected in relation to a long-term maintenance obligation. The main criticism of the Lands Tribunal seems to have been directed to the opening words – to the idea of maintenance 'in neat and tidy condition'. Yet this articulation of the standard to be met is actually fuller than is often found in title deeds, where a simple obligation to 'maintain' something (such as the roof of a tenement or a boundary wall) is commonplace, and is enforced every day.[1] 'To whose satisfaction', asks the Tribunal, is the maintenance to be carried out? The answer, surely, is that to maintain 'in neat and tidy condition' is an objective standard which, if necessary, could be interpreted by a court.

It is instructive to compare the wording of this clause with the wording used in the statutory Tenement Management Scheme[2] which applies, as a default set of rules, to all tenements. Rule 3.1(a) provides, simply, that the owners in a tenement may make a scheme (ie majority) decision 'to carry out maintenance to scheme property'. There is then a definition of 'maintenance' in rule 1.5 which, while setting out the *scope* of the term, rather as the clause in *Duffus* does at (a)–(d) above, does nothing to set the *standard* to be attained. In other words, the statutory Tenement Management Scheme, like many a real burden in many a set of titles, assumes that the standard implied in the single word 'maintain' is one which is generally understood.

That is not to say that disagreements might not occur among the owners as to what does and does not need to be done by way of maintenance. But that is catered for in a different way either by a decision-making rule in the titles,[3] failing which a statutory default rule – for both tenemental[4] and non-tenemental[5] property – that the decision of a majority of owners prevails.

1 K G C Reid, *The Law of Property in Scotland* (1996) para 418(4).
2 Tenements (Scotland) Act 2004 s 4 and sch 1.
3 We have not seen the deed of conditions in *Duffus* and so do not know whether a decision-making mechanism was provided (though we imagine it was).
4 Tenement Management Scheme r 2.5.
5 Title Conditions (Scotland) Act 2003 s 29.

BANKRUPTCY AND PATRIMONY

O'Boyle's Tr v Brennan[1] is a case about gratuitous alienations and, in itself, of only limited interest to conveyancers. But it contains interesting discussion by the Inner House about the conceptual structure of trust law, which conveyancers may wish to note.[2]

In September 2014 the defender, Karen Brennan, bought 16 Attlee Road, East Kilbride, taking title in her sole name. Her partner, John O'Boyle, provided her with the price, £190,960. So she acquired the property with his money. It seems that there was no documentation about this funding. Shortly thereafter, in February 2015, Mr O'Boyle was sequestrated. His trustee at first seems to have done nothing to query the transaction. In January 2017 the defender sold the house for £200,000, and immediately paid £197,462.20 to Mr O'Boyle, who by this time had been discharged from his sequestration. This figure, £197,462.20, was the whole price achieved on sale, less fees and outlays. For this payment too there seems to have been no documentation. 16 Attlee Road, East Kilbride, seems to have been a low-documentation zone.

The trustee in sequestration then raised the present action, seeking (i) declarator that the original payment (£190,960) by Mr O'Boyle to Ms Brennan had been a gratuitous alienation, and (ii) decree ordaining Ms Brennan to pay that sum to the pursuer.

Now, this is just the type of thing that the law of gratuitous alienations is intended to strike at. Donald is about to become bankrupt. He knows that what he has will be taken for the benefit of his unpaid creditors. The thought will strike him, as it strikes everyone in that situation: 'What if I could secrete some assets and pick them up later when the fuss is all over? The big bag of gold sovereigns under the floorboards? I could bury it at that spot in Glen Finglas and recover it in a year or two. Or maybe that would be too risky: some earnest hiker might notice the disturbed soil and start digging. Hmmm. Might be better to give it to

---

1 [2020] CSIH 3, 2020 SC 217, 2020 SLT 152, 2020 SCLR 470, affirming [2018] CSOH 90, 2019 SCLR 287 (*Conveyancing 2018* Case (83)). The Opinion of the court was delivered by Lord Drummond Young.

2 As to gratuitous alienations, we take the opportunity to mention a point drawn to our attention by Neil Webster of Messrs Walker & Sharpe, Dumfries. Suppose that Alan dispones to Benedict, and the disposition is voidable as a gratuitous alienation and can be reduced under subsection (5) of s 98 of the Bankruptcy (Scotland) Act 2016. Before it can be reduced, Benedict dispones to Callista (or grants some lesser right such as a servitude or a standard security etc). Callista is in good faith and gives value. Section 98(7) of the 2016 Act (like predecessor legislation) protects Callista, or is intended to protect her. But the subsection, instead of referring back to subsection (5) of s 98, refers back to subsection (6) which, in this context, is irrelevant. Does this mistake mean that Callista is unprotected? We think not. (i) The 2016 Act was a consolidation statute, and thus was intended to leave the substantive law unchanged. We think that as a matter of statutory interpretation a court would be prepared to disregard the error. (ii) It is a general principle of property law that a third party who transacts in good faith and for value (Callista in the example) is protected from the voidability of the preceding transaction, ie the Alan/Benedict transaction. (If the preceding transaction was void, the rules are different, but a gratuitous alienation is not void.) Thus the *statutory* protection is strictly speaking not necessary, since the common law rolls up its sleeves and does the job anyway. At all events, the error should be put right, and we have written to the Accountant in Bankruptcy, who has departmental responsibility for bankruptcy legislation.

Morag to keep safe for me – keep it safe from my trustee – and return it later. I can trust Morag. That's what I'll do.' This thinking has been around a long time: our law derives from the Roman law – the *actio Pauliana* – which was designed for precisely such shenanigans involving those shady Roman citizens Donaldus and Moragia. There are, of course, a thousand and one variations on this theme, involving various types of property, and various types of 'parking' assets, but all involve the same basic idea.

So the *O'Boyle* case involved the same old, old story. It should have been an easy case, yet it went all the way to the Inner House. The defender fought hard. She argued that the original payment had not been a gratuitous alienation because she had given adequate consideration. How? Because she had paid the money back. And she argued that it would be plain unfair if she had to pay the trustee, because she had already paid Mr O'Boyle, so that she would be paying twice. These arguments were rejected both in the Outer House and in the Inner House – unsurprisingly. Had they been sustained, the law of gratuitous alienations would have collapsed. Any dodgy Donaldus could cock the snoot at his unpaid creditors through the simple expedient of parking assets with Moragia.

But whilst it is odd that the case went all the way to the Inner House, there was a certain benefit to Scots law, because the Inner House took the opportunity to discuss the concept of *patrimony*. This concept, which has roots that are old and deep, has in recent years seen a revival, particularly in the context of trust law: a trust estate is an example of a patrimony.[1] We summarise it here. A patrimony (*patrimonium*) is a set of assets and liabilities.[2] A patrimonial right is an asset in the patrimony. Everyone has a patrimony – even a newborn, because a patrimony, so to speak, is a suitcase with two compartments, for assets and liabilities, so that a newborn has a patrimony even though, for the time being, both compartments are empty.[3]

In some cases a person may have more than one patrimony. Thus, as the Inner House put it in *O'Boyle's Tr*, a trust estate 'forms a distinct patrimony'.[4] As the diagram opposite shows, a trustee has both a general (ie private) patrimony and also a trust patrimony.[5]

In *O'Boyle's Tr*, Mr O'Boyle's pre-sequestration patrimony passed to his trustee, the latter holding it as a separate patrimony. Subsequently Mr O'Boyle acquired a new personal patrimony. As Lord Drummond Young explained:[6]

> [T]he two patrimonies that are relevant are, first, the estate of the debtor as it exists at the date of sequestration and, secondly, the estate acquired by the debtor following

1 For instance in 2015 the Inner House noted in passing: 'The theoretical nature of a trust is different, being based on the notion of legal estate and equitable interest in England, whereas in Scotland it is based on the notion of dual patrimonies of the trustee': see *Advocate General for Scotland v Murray Group Holdings Ltd* [2015] CSIH 77, 2016 SC 201 at para 50.
2 In the case of a company, its balance sheet sets out its patrimony.
3 The patrimony is the container, not the contained.
4 Paragraph 31.
5 If there are two or more trustees, the trust patrimony is shared between them.
6 Paragraph 35.

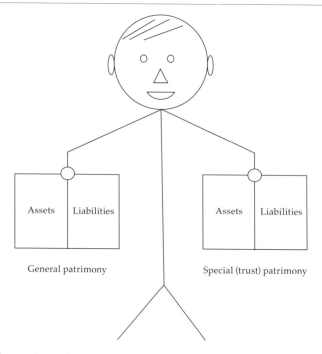

Assets | Liabilities

Assets | Liabilities

General patrimony   Special (trust) patrimony

his discharge from the sequestration. The first of these patrimonies, the estate at sequestration, is transferred to the trustee for the statutory purposes … Following sequestration, that estate must be applied by the trustee for those purposes, and in that way it forms a distinct patrimony. Following the discharge of the debtor from the sequestration, however, he is able to acquire further property, and in so far as he does so that property forms a distinct patrimony from the property that he held prior to sequestration which was transferred to the trustee. That result follows from s 55 of the 1985 Act,[1] which provides that on discharge and subject to certain exceptions the debtor is to be discharged of all debts and obligations contracted by him or for which he was liable at the date of sequestration. That necessarily implies that the debtor's estate after discharge is a distinct patrimony from his estate prior to sequestration; it cannot be used to meet debts incurred prior to sequestration, and conversely the estate held by the trustee (the pre-sequestration estate) cannot be used to meet debts incurred by the debtor after his discharge

Patrimony is, it might be said, just a matter of terminology. When a person dies, the person's assets and liabilities at death become the estate to be administered by the executor, and if one chooses to call the estate at death, and the estate in the hand of the executor, a 'patrimony', that is merely a matter of terminological taste. Likewise the estate of a debtor at the time of sequestration, and in the hand of the trustee. And so on. But new spectacles can lead to clearer vision, and the concept of patrimony does help in focusing certain matters, especially the basics of trust law, for in a trust there are (in this terminology) two

---

1 Ie the Bankruptcy (Scotland) Act 1985. The equivalent provision in the Bankruptcy (Scotland) Act 2016 (which has replaced the 1985 Act) is s 145.

patrimonies. The first is the general patrimony of the trustee – her assets and liabilities as an individual[1] – and the second is the separate trust patrimony. This so-called 'dual patrimony' way of seeing matters – always implicit in the Scots law of trusts, but not until recently made explicit – explains, among other things, the nature of the beneficiaries' rights against the trustee, without resorting to the bifurcation, which exists in a certain jurisdiction (that Must Not Be Named) between 'legal ownership' and 'equitable ownership'.

THE CONVEYANCING EXAM FROM HELL

Leafrealm Land Ltd v City of Edinburgh Council[2] posed, to counsel involved, and to the lucky, or unlucky, Lord Ordinary (Lady Wolffe), the conveyancing exam from hell. The case was fiercely, and no doubt expensively, fought, and many issues came into play, some of fact, some of law, and some of mixed law and fact. To her 30,000-word judgment we cannot do full justice here. Readers should swig a double espresso, turn on some white sound, and concentrate.

There was a dress rehearsal to the present case in the shape of a 2017 case, *Trustees of the Grange Trust v City of Edinburgh Council*.[3] But in that case the action had been dismissed because of lack of title to sue.

Setting the scene

The case concerned rights in the solum of a former boundary wall which, from 1912 until it fell down in 2014, had separated Comely Bank Road, in Edinburgh's Stockbridge area, from ground to the north. This long narrow strip was potentially worth a great deal of money. The pursuer, Leafrealm Land Ltd, claimed that this strip belonged to it and that no one else had any rights in respect of it. The City Council claimed that it was the owner, and that, even if it was not, the long narrow strip formed part of the road, so that the public right of passage would extend to it.

Comely Bank Road runs in an east–west direction. To the north are playing fields, both today and back in 1912, when the story begins. The road then was narrower than it is now. The City Corporation (as it then was) wished to widen it by taking in ground to the north. Some of that ground was part of the Raeburn Hotel, and with that part the present case was not concerned. Most of the ground that the Corporation wished to acquire was owned by the Trustees of the Grange Trust, who held that particular part of the land in trust for the Edinburgh Academical Club. The Corporation could have exercised statutory powers to acquire this strip of land, but in the event matters were settled by mutual agreement. What was called a 'minute of agreement' was signed between the Corporation, the Grange Trustees, and the Edinburgh Academical Club. Its general import was to transfer to the City Corporation a six-foot strip. No

---

1 The trustee may be a company, or other juristic person, but the same principles apply.
2 [2020] CSOH 34, 2020 GWD 15-219.
3 [2017] CSOH 102, 2017 GWD 23-387 (*Conveyancing 2017* Case (19)).

payment was made by the Corporation, but it undertook to erect, and maintain, at considerable expense, a new wall, which would henceforth be the boundary between the road (and pavement), on the one hand, and, on the other hand, the Edinburgh Academical Club playing fields. The road was widened accordingly. The new wall was erected.[1] The minute of agreement was recorded in the Register of Sasines. But there was an oddity about this document. It did not take the form of a disposition. Did it nevertheless have the effect of a disposition? Of this, more later.

The list of roads kept under s 1 of the Roads (Scotland) Act 1984 stated that the roadway included the wall.

In 1979 the Trustees of the Grange Trust disponed to the Edinburgh Academical Club that part of the land that was held in trust for the club. The disposition stated that the southern boundary of the area disponed was the *north* face of the wall. Thus whoever, after 1979, owned the solum of the wall, it was not the Club. So who did own it? If the 1912 minute of agreement was *not* a disposition, then the Grange Trustees still owned it,[2] at least until 2018. (For what happened in 2018 see below.) If it *was* a valid disposition, then there still remained a problem, namely whether the strip of ground disponed included the solum of the wall, or not. In other words, when, following the 1912 minute of agreement, the new wall was built, was it (i) built on the ground 'given up' to the City Corporation, or (ii) built on the ground retained by the trustees? It was a boundary wall, but boundary walls may stand on the one property or the other. (There was also the possibility that – like many boundary walls – it was a straddling wall, ie with the boundary running along its *medium filum*. But that possibility did not feature in the litigation.)[3]

In or about 2014 the wall collapsed, and it seems that the remains were removed. In 2018 the Trustees of the Grange Trust granted to Leafrealm Land Ltd (the pursuer in the present action) a disposition, purportedly of the solum of the ex-wall. It was on the basis of this disposition that Leafrealm raised the present action. However, the disposition was sitting in the Keeper's in-tray. It had not been rejected but it had not been accepted. No doubt the Keeper was considering the validity of the deed. What view the Lord Ordinary took of the deed's validity will be seen below.

Microcartography

A major issue in the litigation, which evidently took up much court time, was whether the wall erected in 1912 had been erected on the land retained by the Grange Trustees, or whether it was erected on the ground 'given up' by them in

---

1 And the old wall was demolished, its solum being subsumed into the widened roadway. This old wall features significantly in the litigation.
2 Subject to the complication that in the previous year, 1911, they had granted a bond and disposition in security to another party. To that point we will return, but – spoiler alert – it is in fact not relevant.
3 There exists a further possibility for boundary walls which is that they are co-owned from side to side, that co-ownership including the solum. This, while possible, is unusual, and clearly it was not a possibility here.

favour of the City Corporation. This question involved plenty of expert evidence from surveyors, plenty of scrutiny of old maps, and so on. The conclusion of the Lord Ordinary was that the wall had been erected on the ground taken over by the Council. That was contrary to Leafrealm's position. Leafrealm argued that the wall had stood on the land retained by the Grange Trustees, so that when in 1979 the Trustees had disponed the land to the Edinburgh Academical Club, the land being bounded to the south by the north face of the wall, the Trustees had kept title to the solum of the wall itself. This part of the decision was fatal to Leafrealm's case, because it would mean that the 2018 disposition would be invalid, since the granters had no title. However, nothing in this case was simple, and Leafrealm could still argue that the 1912 deed was not a valid disposition anyway, so that regardless of precisely what ground had been 'given up' by the deed, the Trustees had retained ownership, and therefore were in a position to grant a valid disposition in 2018. So now we move from the question of precisely what ground was made over by the 1912 deed, to whether that deed was a disposition.

The title issue

Was the 1912 deed a disposition?

The 1912 deed was called a 'minute of agreement'. It was tripartite, the parties being (i) the Grange Trustees, (ii) Edinburgh Academical Club, which had the beneficial right in the property, and (iii) Edinburgh Corporation. It provided that the Trustees 'hereby give up for the purpose of widening the street of Comely Bank Road ... a strip of ground six feet in width along the whole frontage'. The body of the deed had only that description of the property, but there was a plan attached. As already mentioned, the document was recorded in the Register of Sasines. However, in 1912 plans could not enter that register.[1] The word 'dispone' was not used in the document. That word is, indeed, not necessary to convey land. At common law it was necessary, but under s 27 of the Conveyancing (Scotland) Act 1874:

> It shall not be competent to object to the validity of any deed or writing as a conveyance of heritage coming into operation after the passing of this Act, on the ground that it does not contain the word 'dispone,' provided it contains any other word or words importing conveyance or transference, or present intention to convey or transfer.

Whilst, however, the word 'dispone' is not necessary, it has the benefit of clarity, which other words may lack, and its absence must cause enquiry, especially in what seems to have been a professionally-drawn deed, given that such deeds always use the word 'dispone' where the intention is that the deed is to make a transfer. Did the deed 'contain any other word or words importing conveyance or transference, or present intention to convey or transfer?' Maybe yes, maybe no. The deed is unclear: the words 'hereby give up' could be construed as

---

1 This became possible only with s 48 of the Conveyancing (Scotland) Act 1924.

meaning 'do hereby dispone'. But they do not compel that interpretation. When one reads the ensuing words 'for the purpose of widening the street' one might conclude that only use, not title, is in question. On the other hand the words 'for the purpose of widening the street' could be seen simply as narrative words, words recording the reason for the grant of the deed. Then again, if the deed is a disposition, why does it not identify a disponee? And then, as against that, it could be argued that the identity of the disponee is a matter of obvious implication. And so on, and so forth.

Why was it done in this strange way? We have no idea. We are baffled. If the intention was to convey the strip of land, why did the deed not take the form of a disposition? If the intention was to extend the public right of way to the strip, why was that not simply said? If the intention was that the Trustees were to retain title, why was that not made clear? If there is a solution to this riddle we are unable to guess it. Possibly one is looking at muddle, confusion and incompetence. Be that as it may, the Lord Ordinary had to go one way or the other. We think that either interpretation could be defended. In the event her decision was that the deed was a conveyance.

The 1911 bond

The year before, in 1911, the Trustees had granted a bond and disposition in security to a financial institution. There was a suggestion that this had divested the Trustees, thereby meaning that the 1912 deed had been granted by non-owners. The defenders cited *Campbell v Bertram*[1] for the view that a bond and disposition in security does not divest the granter. The Lord Ordinary seems to have made no express decision on this point, but by implication she must have accepted the defender's argument. There is no doubt that she was right to do so, the case just mentioned being decisive.[2]

Listing as a road not determinative of title

There is a tendency to suppose that the solum of a road must belong to the roads authority. Often indeed it does so belong, but not necessarily. As noted in the case, s 1(9) of the Roads (Scotland) Act 1984 says:

> Every road which is entered in the list of public roads kept by a local roads authority shall vest in the local authority for the purpose of their functions as roads authority: but such vesting shall not confer on an authority any heritable right in relation to a road.

It might be added that 'heritable' seems an odd word in this context. There is presumably no issue about whether the right is moveable or heritable. Nor indeed is it, we suggest, a real/personal issue. Rather, the point is that the 'vesting' confers no right in *private* law. The issue is a private/public law issue.

---

1 (1865) 4 M 23.
2 Confusion on the issue was perennial, however. T B Smith in his great work, *A Short Commentary on the Law of Scotland* (1962), expressed, at different places, the view that a bond and disposition in security does divest the granter and that it does not: see p 558 n and p 471.

The Edinburgh Corporation Order Confirmation Act 1967

The Edinburgh Corporation Order Confirmation Act 1967 s 191 provides:

> Subject to the provisions of this Order, all land acquired by or ceded to the Corporation for the purpose of constructing, widening or improving public streets shall vest in them without the necessity of any disposition or other conveyance of such land in their favour.

What does this mean? The Lord Ordinary said that the provision used 'vesting' in the sense of transferring ownership of the solum to the grantee roads authority, though she added that 'I do not accept that section 191 has any effect in respect of a subsisting road at the date of entry into force of the 1984 Act'.[1] Hence the provision was not relevant to the facts of this particular case. Her interpretation, which is based on looking at s 191 in the general context of the statute, may be right. But, if so, the law seems unsatisfactory, leading to ownership without registration. It may be added that the section applies only to property that the City Corporation has 'acquired'. There is arguably a circularity here. It becomes owner, but only after it has acquired the property.

Conclusion on the title issue

To recapitulate, the Lord Ordinary concluded (i) that the 1912 deed was a disposition, and (ii) that it included the solum of the wall, with the result that in 1912 the Trustees had been divested of that solum. That being the case, they could not, in 2018, dispone that solum to Leafrealm. The Edinburgh Corporation Order Confirmation Act 1967 was inapplicable to the title question, as was the Roads (Scotland) Act 1984.

The road-width issue

Given the decision on the title issue, the question of the width of the road, considered as a public right of way, made no difference. Leafrealm had lost anyway. Nevertheless this question was part of the focus of the case. In the event, it was held that the road, considered as a public right of way, did include the solum of the wall, so that even if Leafrealm had been successful on the title issue, such success would have been of very limited value to it.

This issue had to some extent been addressed by the Lord Ordinary (Lord Boyd) in the earlier, connected, case of *Trustees of the Grange Trust v City of Edinburgh Council*.[2] After considering earlier authorities,[3] Lord Boyd said that 'boundary walls or fences along the side of the road will normally define the limits of the right of passage and hence the limits of the road. On these authorities I would have been inclined to the view that the boundary wall does not form part of Comely Bank Road'.[4] But note the word 'normally'. While

---

1 Paragraph 28 of Appendix C.
2 [2017] CSOH 102, 2017 GWD 23-387 (*Conveyancing 2017* Case (19)).
3 Such as *County Council of Perth and Kinross v Magistrates of Crieff* 1933 SC 751 and *David Runciman & Sons v Scottish Borders Council* 2003 SLT 1405.
4 Paragraph 35.

Leafrealm pointed out that it would be odd if a public right of way could exist along a boundary wall, it was faced with the contrary authority of *Johnstone v Magistrates of Glasgow*.[1] After hearing evidence, the Lord Ordinary took the view that the wall had a practical function in relation to the road in that it had had a retaining function. Hence she held that it was part of the road, and accordingly that the same was true of its solum.[2] She also gave some weight to the fact that the inclusion of the wall in the statutory listing[3] had existed for many years without challenge.

The formal validity of the 2018 deed

As already mentioned, the disposition in favour of Leafrealm, purportedly of the solum of the former wall, had been submitted to the Keeper but had been neither accepted nor rejected. The reasons for the Keeper's hesitation are not known but may be surmised. In the first place, there was the question of whether the granters had title, and, as has been seen above, the court took the view that they lacked title. That in itself will presumably lead to the Keeper rejecting the application.[4] But the 2018 deed had another problem. Section 23(1)(c) of the Land Registration etc (Scotland) Act 2012, dealing with as-yet unregistered property,[5] says that a disposition of it must 'so describe the plot as to enable the Keeper to delineate its boundaries on the cadastral map'.

What did the 2018 deed say? It purported to dispone (our emphasis):

> ALL and WHOLE that strip of ground ..., shown delineated in red on the plan annexed and signed as relative hereto and situated generally along the north side of Raeburn Place/Comely Bank Road, Edinburgh, and bounded on the north by subjects disponed by Disposition (hereinafter called the '1979 Disposition') by [the Grange Trustees] ..., along which boundary it extends on the line of the north face of a wall now or formerly situated on the subjects hereby disponed (being the wall situated on the subjects hereby disponed at the time of the granting of the 1979 Disposition); on the east partly by ground pertaining to the Raeburn Hotel, Raeburn Place/Comely Bank Road, and partly by ground within the pavement of Raeburn Place/Comely Bank Road, Edinburgh (including that part of the pavement which comprises ground formerly pertaining to the said Hotel); *on the south by ground now situated within the pavement of Raeburn Place/Comely Bank Road, Edinburgh*; and on the west by North Park Terrace, Edinburgh ...

The Lord Ordinary held that the words describing the southern boundary failed to meet the requirements of s 25. We do not, however, know what the attached plan said.

---

1 (1885) 12 R 596. Lord Shand at 602 says: 'The walls which the first parties are required to erect are buttresses for that part of the embankment. They are part of the embankments, and properly speaking, as it appears to me, part of the road itself.'
2 Since the wall had disappeared in 2014, one wonders how much retaining function it really had, but this issue was not pursued in the case.
3 That is to say, s 1 of the Roads (Scotland) Act 1984.
4 As indeed the Keeper is bound to do under Land Registration etc (Scotland) Act 2012 ss 21 and 23(1)(b).
5 The solum was unregistered so this was a first registration application.

Litigation and pending applications for registration

The result of this decision will presumably be that the Keeper will reject Leafrealm's application for registration. But the case highlights a problem: what happens if there is, as here, a delay in the Keeper's decision whether to accept or reject an application? That of course can lead to many practical problems, with which all conveyancers are familiar. One of them, as here, is where for one reason or another it becomes important to know who owns the property in question. It might be thought that if Cressida dispones to Darius, Cressida will remain owner until Darius has been registered, so if that takes time, and during that time it is necessary to know who owns the property, the answer will be 'Cressida'. As applied to the present case, that would mean that Leafrealm could not be the owner, because there had been no registration in its favour.[1] But matters are not so simple. Following the Land Registration (Scotland) Act 1979, the Land Registration etc (Scotland) Act 2012 says that if an application to register a disposition is successful, the registration is deemed to take place when the application was received by the Keeper.[2] Thus when an application is received, the Land Register enters into a state of what might be called quantum indeterminacy, in the sense that while the register says that Cressida is still owner, a glance at the Application Record will show that that may turn out to be untrue. So if the application is made on 1 May and the Keeper decides on 1 July, it follows that the question 'who owns this property' if asked on 1 June cannot receive a definite answer. So long as registration applications are turned round reasonably promptly,[3] this is unlikely to matter much. But the longer the delay, the more likely it is that problems will emerge. In this particular case the problem could be got round because it was held that the 2018 disposition was invalid in any case. But in other cases the problems may be severe. The logic of land registration presupposes that accept/reject decisions will be made reasonably promptly.[4]

TENEMENT REPAIRS

Majority rule – except for shelter and support

What happens when owners in a tenement disagree about common repairs? Some want the repairs to be carried out; others are resolutely opposed. Which side is to prevail?

Normally, the answer is simply a matter of counting votes. Those in a majority will win. So if a majority of owners favours repairs, the repairs can go ahead

---

1 Though in the Cressida/Darius case we assume that Cressida began the story as owner, whereas in the actual case it eventually was held that the disponers (the Trustees) had no title.
2 Land Registration etc (Scotland) Act 2012 ss 36 and 37(1).
3 Which the Keeper is bound to do under s 35(3) of the 2012 Act. There was no such provision in the Land Registration (Scotland) Act 1979.
4 There is a considerable amount of discussion of the issues in various sections of part 12 of the Scottish Law Commission, *Report No 222 on Land Registration* (2010). On the current state of registration delays, see p 88 above.

and the dissenting minority must pay its share of the cost.[1] Conversely, if only a minority supports the repairs, nothing can be done and the building must be left to fester (as the minority would no doubt describe matters). We say that a 'majority' prevails because that is what the statutory Tenement Management Scheme says.[2] Of course, the titles can, and sometimes do, provide for a different – and usually lower – threshold for decisions. If so, the titles rule.[3] But, except where the titles otherwise provide, the default position is that decisions as to repair are taken by a majority.

The policy behind these rules rests on the view that tenement owners, being grown-ups, are presumptively sensible. The law therefore leaves them to reach their own decisions on what to do or not to do. But there is one case where the law is not prepared to be so indulgent. Where repairs are needed to ensure the preservation of either 'support' or 'shelter' within the building – which, typically, means repairs to the roof or external walls – *any* flat-owner can bring about the repair. To this end, two separate mechanisms are provided by the Tenements (Scotland) Act 2004.

One is to carry out the repairs for oneself and recover the costs from the other owners. This is open to any flat-owner who owns or co-owns the part of the building in question, but the distinction between owning and co-owning is important. As a matter of the general law, owners – that is to say, those who own 100% of a thing – are always free to maintain their property. No one else's permission is needed. But co-owners are more restricted in what they can do. Section 8(4) of the 2004 Act provides the rule: any co-owner can carry out repairs where the repairs are 'necessary' for support or shelter; repairs which are not 'necessary' in this sense cannot be carried out unilaterally, or at least not under s 8(4).

Once a repair is carried out, then – assuming that the repair really was needed for support or shelter – the cost can be recovered, under s 10 of the Act, as if the repair had proceeded by agreement on the part of the owners. So if the normal rule for the cost in question, whether under the titles or (if the titles are silent) under the Tenement Management Scheme, is that each flat-owner pays an equal share, then the go-it-alone flat-owner can recover an equal share from all of the other owners. This, admittedly, is not as good as it sounds. The normal reason for going it alone is that it has proved impossible to get agreement for the repairs. And if it was impossible to get agreement, it is unlikely that the dissenting owners will now rush to write the necessary cheque.

Going it alone is not, however, the only mechanism under the Act for repairs which concern support or shelter. By s 8(1) a person who does not own the part in question can require the person who does own it to carry out the repair – leaving that person with the task of recovering the cost in the manner just described. Similarly, a co-owner of the part can require the other co-owners to join with him in the repair.[4]

---

1 Tenement Management Scheme (in Tenements (Scotland) Act 2004 sch 1) rr 8.2 and 8.3.
2 This is the rule for 'scheme decisions': Tenement Management Scheme rr 2 and 3(1)(a).
3 Tenements (Scotland) Act 2004 s 4(4).
4 This also follows from s 8(1).

These provisions are, perhaps, less well known than they ought to be. But case law on them is now beginning to appear. In the last four or five years, there have been two cases involving the first of the two mechanisms (going it alone), in both of which the use of the mechanism was upheld in the particular circumstances which had arisen.[1] The first case on the second mechanism (getting others to do the repair) is still awaited.

The use of these mechanisms has arisen again in a new case, *Lacey v McConville*,[2] but this time unsuccessfully. The reasons for the failure are important, and provide helpful guidance for the future. In addition, the case raises the question of whether it is possible to use the two mechanisms in combination, thus creating a third, hybrid mechanism.

The facts

Lacey v McConville concerned a two-flat tenement in Christiemiller Place in Edinburgh.[3] The pursuer owned the upper flat and the defenders the lower. When the building was erected, in the 1930s, the brick of the external walls was faced with rendering (or harling). Although some repairs had been carried out over the years, the rendering was now in a bad state. In some places it had fallen off altogether; in other places it had become detached from the brickwork and was in danger of falling. Overall, the walls had become unsightly.

It was accepted that some repairs were needed, but whereas the pursuer wanted the rendering to be replaced in its entirety, at a cost of around £36,000, the defenders favoured the much cheaper option of patching and mending. The walls were the common property of both parties.

The dispute highlights a particular difficulty of two-flat tenements.[4] A majority of two is two, so that a majority means unanimity. Hence, unless both owners are in agreement, no repairs can normally be carried out.[5] In the present case, agreement proved impossible. The pursuer wanted the rendering redone; the defenders would sanction only limited repairs. The result was impasse. An evident source of friction was that some of the damage to the rendering had occurred as a result of work carried out by the pursuer in replacing the external staircase to her flat. Most of the damage, however, had nothing to do with the pursuer.

In order to break the impasse, and to do so in a way that ensured her own views prevailed, the pursuer resolved to go it alone. In this action she sought declarator that she was entitled to carry out the proposed repairs by herself. The legal basis of her action was a provision already mentioned, s 8(4) of the

---

1 *Humphreys v Crabbe* [2016] CSIH 82, 2017 SCLR 699, discussed in *Conveyancing 2016* pp 172–75; *Donaldson v Pleace*, 22 September 2017, Stirling Sheriff Court, discussed in *Conveyancing 2017* pp 127–31.

2 [2020] SC EDIN 35, 2020 SLT (Sh Ct) 237, 2020 Hous LR 108.

3 It was part of a four-in-a-block building, but the other two flats appear to have been treated as a tenement of their own.

4 Precisely the same difficulty had arisen in the two-flat tenement in *Humphreys v Crabbe* [2016] CSIH 82, 2017 SCLR 699.

5 Unless the titles say otherwise or unless the repairs are necessary for shelter or support, as the pursuer was to argue.

Tenements (Scotland) Act 2004. This applies to repairs of co-owned property, such as the walls in the present case, and allows any one co-owner, without the need for the agreement of the other or others, to 'do anything that is necessary' to ensure that the property in question provides support or shelter. The pursuer's argument was simple. Rendering made the walls watertight. Once the rendering began to fail, the walls became vulnerable to water penetration. Hence, to replace the rendering was to carry out a repair necessary to provide 'shelter'. Hence the pursuer, as a co-owner of the walls, was entitled to carry out the repairs on her own and recover half the cost from her neighbour.

The sheriff[1] was not persuaded. In his view, the pursuer's action failed for two distinct reasons. Both are of interest.

The first reason: rendering not providing shelter

In the first place, the pursuer failed because she failed to satisfy the court, on a balance of probabilities, that the rendering had the function of waterproofing the building. And if it did not waterproof the building, it could not be said to provide 'shelter' within s 8(4) of the Act. On this point, the evidence of the expert witnesses was not in agreement. According to the pursuer's expert, the rendering formed a rainwater jacket. According to the defenders' expert, it did no such thing. No doubt, where a wall was of solid brick construction, rendering did serve to protect the wall from water penetration. But, said the defenders' expert, in the present case there was a cavity between the external and internal walls, and it was the cavity, not the rendering, which protected against rain. Even if the outer wall was saturated, the cavity would ensure that the inner wall was dry. In the face of this contradictory evidence, the sheriff found himself unable to reach a clear view. It followed that the onus of proof on the pursuer had not been discharged.

Of course, even on the view taken by the defenders' expert, rendering made an incidental contribution to the dryness of the walls. But incidental, said the sheriff, was not enough.[2] If s 8 was read as including a merely incidental benefit, 'it would logically require to be extended to any external shelter, for example a coat of paint, or an overhanging decorative architectural feature'. The sheriff continued:

> In my view, the provision is not intended to encompass incidental benefit. If it did, it would operate to create duties in relation to parts of the building which were never designed to fulfil such a function. It would run contrary to the intentions set out in the Scottish Law Commission report which led to the Act, a truncated copy of which was produced by counsel, which refers throughout to 'essential' repairs.[3] It would

---

1 Sheriff N A Ross.
2 Paragraph 48.
3 No reference is given, but the relevant part of the Scottish Law Commission's *Report No 162 on the Law of the Tenement* (1998) can be found at paras 7.1–7.13. The only reference to 'essential' repairs comes at the end of para 7.5: 'We think that an owner who is unable to persuade a sufficient number of his neighbours to carry out a repair ought to have a second line of attack. If the repair is essential for shelter or support he should be able to insist, if necessary by litigation, that it be carried out.'

be difficult to regard repairs to an otherwise non-essential part of the building as essential repairs. Similarly, the duty in s 8(1) to 'ensure' shelter would be at odds with repairing a part which was never intended to provide shelter. In my view, an incidental and unintended (or at least not principally intended) benefit of shelter, as opposed to an intended purpose, is not sufficient to found any duty or trigger any obligation under s 8.

This is more than a narrow matter of statutory interpretation. The policy behind the legislation is that, except where disrepair affects structural stability or whether the building is wind and watertight, it is a matter for the owners to decide whether to carry out the repair. In the present case, the pursuer failed to satisfy the court that peeling rendering did more than affect the appearance of the building.

An easy way of sidestepping this first objection to the pursuer's case would have been to have relied on the common law rather than on s 8(4). For at common law a *pro indiviso* owner can carry out repairs without needing to worry about the function within the building of the part in need of repairs.[1] But this would have taken the pursuer only so far. In principle it would have allowed repairs, or at any rate some repairs,[2] to go ahead. But there would have been no right to recover the cost from the defenders. At common law there was indeed such a right, but it was removed, for tenements only, by s 16 of the 2004 Act.[3] There is nothing here, therefore, which is likely to have seemed attractive to the pursuer.

The second reason: repairs not 'necessary'

Even if the pursuer had succeeded on the first point – even if, in other words, the rendering was found to have played a significant role in providing shelter for the building – the pursuer would still have failed overall. This is because, in order for repairs to fall within s 8(4),[4] the repairs must be 'necessary' for the purposes of ensuring shelter. That necessity threshold, said the sheriff, had not been attained. No doubt it would be financially prudent, at least in the long run, to replace all of the rendering on the walls at one go. But such a far-reaching programme of work was hardly 'necessary'. Patching up the existing gaps in the rendering – the much cheaper option favoured by the defenders – would be perfectly sufficient to preserve shelter. The sheriff continued:[5]

> One owner cannot force another owner to be financially astute. It is clear from Mr Vince's evidence[6] that patching in the short term is considerably cheaper. It might be a false economy, but the test is one of necessity, not reasonableness. It is necessary to patch repair. It cannot be said to be necessary to replace. For a party for whom funds

---

1 See eg K G C Reid, *The Law of Property in Scotland* (1996) para 25. As such repairs must be 'necessary', this common law power might in any event have foundered on the second reason for failure, discussed below.
2 Provided they were 'necessary'.
3 The reasons are explained in Scottish Law Commission, *Report No 162 on the Law of the Tenement* (1998) para 10.30.
4 Tenements (Scotland) Act 2004 s 8(4).
5 Paragraph 53.
6 David Vince was the expert witness for the defenders.

are limited, it may not be financially possible to carry out any more than short term repairs. There may be other reasons for not wanting to carry out long term remedies. The law does not force a co-proprietor to do so.

The decision on this point is important not only for s 8(4) but for wherever the law imposes a rule allowing only 'necessary' repairs to be carried out. Although not surprising in itself, or controversial, it is nonetheless a welcome contribution to a topic on which existing authority is scant.[1]

Final comments

Two final comments may be made. The first concerns the remedy being sought by the pursuer. In addition to a declarator that she was entitled to replace the rendering on the walls, as mentioned above, she also sought, in the sheriff's words, 'to compel the defenders to pay a one-half share of complete replacement'.[2] We have not seen the pleadings, and so are uncertain whether the pursuer was seeking (i) payment up front, or (ii) payment only when the work had been carried out. The latter is plainly competent under s 10 of the Tenements (Scotland) Act 2004: it is simply the end result of the first of the two mechanisms for repair (ie going it alone) which was discussed above. The competency of the former, however, seems open to question. Its statutory basis is presumably s 8(1), which is also the statutory basis for the second mechanism (ie getting others to carry out the repairs) so that, overall, the remedies being sought may amount to a mixture of the two mechanisms. But s 8(1), in terms, imposes an obligation to carry out acts of maintenance, not to pay for the acts of maintenance carried out by someone else. It would take a generous interpretation to assist the pursuer.

The second comment concerns the potential safety hazard caused by falling rendering. It was accepted that the rendering was loose in places and also that, if it were to fall from a height, it would be 'hazardous' and pose 'a risk to health and safety'.[3] For that reason if for no other, the sheriff accepted that 'repair is urgently required'.[4] But, for the reasons already given, repair could not proceed under s 8 – the only basis pled by the pursuer. Hence the sheriff pronounced a decree of absolvitor. At the same time, however, he observed that, insofar as safety was threatened, 'there are likely to be other common law or title remedies open to the pursuer'.[5] It is hard, however, to identify any such remedies. There are none in the Tenements (Scotland) Act 2004 itself; even the right to carry out emergency repairs, attractive at first sight because of the reference in the relevant provision to repairs 'in the interests of health or safety', is only available when the emergency is so great that there is no time to consult the other owner or owners.[6] The common law is only slightly more helpful. Any co-owner can carry

---

1 As for example the common law rule, already mentioned, by which any *pro indiviso* owner can carry out necessary repairs.
2 Paragraph 1.
3 Paragraphs 34 and 35.
4 Paragraph 35.
5 Paragraph 36.
6 Tenement Management Scheme r 7.3.

out necessary repairs (which in the present case would mean patch repairs rather than new rendering), but the accompanying right to recover a share of the cost from the other co-owners was disapplied to tenements, as already mentioned, by s 16 of the 2004 Act. Fortunately, the issue did not arise on the facts of *Lacey v McConville*, because the defenders, although unwilling to pay for the walls to be re-rendered, accepted that some basic patching of the existing rendering was both desirable and necessary. So that relatively modest work at least could go ahead and be paid for by both parties. Not all neighbours in tenements, however, might be so accommodating, and it may be that the issue should be considered by the Scottish Law Commission as part of its forthcoming review of the law of the tenement.[1]

ARE PROPERTY MANAGERS ALWAYS 'PROPERTY FACTORS'?

The legislative background

Property factors are more usually objects of anger than of pity. Yet it is a tough job and, some would say, a thankless one as well. And adding to the difficulties of the work is a heavy burden of regulation in terms of the Property Factors (Scotland) Act 2011. The 2011 Act set up a Register of Property Factors[2] and required all property factors to register there.[3] Some 400 have now done so, and are collectively responsible for factoring some 650,000 properties.[4] Following registration, factors become subject to a Code of Conduct, prepared by the Scottish Government, which sets out mandatory rules on a wide range of matters including the provision of information to clients, transparent pricing, dispute resolution, and so on.[5] Disgruntled homeowners can refer their complaints to the First-tier Tribunal.[6] Failure to register is a criminal offence, punishable by a fine or even by imprisonment.[7] It is therefore important to be clear who is and who is not a property factor, and hence who is and who is not under an obligation to seek registration.

A lengthy definition of 'property factor' is given in s 2 of the Act. This makes an initial distinction between (i) local authorities and housing associations, and (ii) other persons and bodies who carry out property

---

1 As to which see *Conveyancing 2019* pp 101–02.
2 Available at http://sedsh119.sedsh.gov.uk/propertyfactorregister/.
3 Property Factors (Scotland) Act 2011 ss 3–7. For an overview of the Act, see *Conveyancing 2011* pp 109–16.
4 The latest available figures, for 2018/19, show a total of 648,477 properties being factored: see www.gov.scot/publications/foi-202000014788/. A list of property factors in Glasgow and Edinburgh is available at www.gov.scot/publications/foi-202000014599/.
5 PF(S)A 2011 s 14. See Property Factors (Code of Conduct) (Scotland) Order 2012, SSI 2012/217, and, for the Code of Conduct itself, www.scotland.gov.uk/Publications/2012/07/6791/0.
6 PF(S)A 2011 s 17. There is a steady stream of traffic to the First-tier Tribunal – far too many cases, and too fact-specific, to be routinely covered in this series. The Tribunal's decisions can be found at www.housingandpropertychamber.scot/property-factors/property-factors-decisions.
7 PF(S)A 2011 s 12.

management. The former, generally speaking, are always 'property factors' so long as they manage or maintain the common parts of residential developments. The latter, however, are only 'property factors' if they so manage 'in the course of that person's business'. So for example an ordinary flat-owner who organises common repairs in a tenement is not a 'property factor', does not have to register under the Act, and is not subject to the Code of Conduct. So far so satisfactory.

A difficulty has, however, arisen in respect of those who both manage property and also operate a business, but where the business which they operate is not the business of property managers. Are such persons 'property factors' under the Act on the basis that they manage property 'in the course of that person's business', even if the business is not about property management? Or, rather, should the statutory words, 'in the course of that person's business', be read as meaning 'in the course of that person's business *as property manager*', thus excluding those in business whose business is not that of property management?

This issue has become before the courts once before, in *Procurator Fiscal, Oban v Melfort Pier Holidays Ltd*,[1] an unreported criminal case decided in Oban Sheriff Court in 2017. In that case the defender managed a development of houses some of which it owned and rented out as holiday cottages and some of which were in the ownership of others. No management charge was made. The defender was admittedly in business, but the business was one of holiday lets not of property management. That, it was held, was sufficient to classify the defender as a 'property factor'. Hence the defender required to register under the Act (which it had not done). The sheriff offered a cogent defence of his decision:[2]

> Why then did Parliament include the expression 'in the course of its business'? In my view the answer lies in the mischief that it sought to remedy. The mischief arose from unscrupulous factors seeking to exact unnecessary and excessive charges and fees from homeowners, presumably in order to maximise their own profit. Business is generally an activity carried on with the aim of profit, regardless of whether that aim is in fact achieved. If the maintenance of land is conducted by a for-profit body such as a business, then, regardless of whether the profit comes from management fees, there is potential scope for conflict between the business and homeowners whose interest in the common land is of an entirely different nature. By including this expression, Parliament sought to ensure that 'self-factoring' amateurs, such as the advocate in senior counsel's example above, would not fall under the Act – he or she would not be acting 'in the course of their business', so no potential conflict would arise from any desire to make profit.

But there are arguments the other way, and the issue has now been revisited in a new case, in which the Inner House has come to the opposite conclusion.

---

1 13 September 2017, Oban Sheriff Court, unreported, discussed in *Conveyancing 2017* pp 220–23.
2 At p 14 of the sheriff's Note. The sheriff was Sheriff Patrick Hughes.

Proven Properties Scotland Ltd

The facts

The new case is *Proven Properties Scotland Ltd v Upper Tribunal for Scotland*.[1] The facts were close to those in *Procurator Fiscal, Oban v Melfort Pier Holidays Ltd*, just discussed. In 2007 Proven Properties (Scotland) Ltd erected a building in Helensburgh comprising 15 flats. Due to the recession, it proved impossible to sell more than a couple of the flats, and the remaining 13 were retained by Proven Properties and rented out. Initially, the block of flats was factored by B and B Estate Agents and Property Managers, but in 2011 Proven Properties assumed the factoring duties itself. It did not charge for its services. Nor, apparently, did it register as a property factor. In due course the owner of one of the two flats that had been sold came to be in dispute with Proven Properties about a leaking roof. Unable to reach agreement the homeowner applied to the First-tier Tribunal under s 17 of the Property Factors (Scotland) Act 2011 seeking a determination that Proven Properties had failed to carry out the property factor's duties and to comply with the Code of Conduct. In response, Proven Properties argued that it was not a 'property factor' within the 2011 Act, and hence was subject neither to the Act nor to the Code of Conduct.

At first instance, and again on appeal to the Upper Tribunal, this argument was rejected. Proven Properties, it was said, operated a business, namely as landlords in the block of flats. Hence it was a person managing the block of flats 'in the course of that person's business'. Hence it was a 'property factor' in the sense of s 2 of the 2011 Act. Both the First-tier Tribunal and the Upper Tribunal, therefore, followed the line taken by the sheriff in *Melfort Pier Holidays Ltd*, although there is no indication that they knew of the earlier decision. Proven Properties appealed again and this time found success. The Inner House held that Proven Properties was not, after all, a property factor within the Act. Accordingly, the decision of the Upper Tribunal fell to be quashed.

The lady with the piano

The basis of the Inner House decision was much as might be expected. It was too literal a reading of the words 'in the course of a person's business' in the definition of 'property factor' to say that *any* business would do.[2] The Act envisaged the situation where homeowners would manage the properties themselves without, apparently, becoming 'property factors'.[3] And that was all that was happening here. Proven Properties owned 13 of the 15 flats. There could be nothing more natural than to want to manage the flats by themselves. That did not make Proven Properties a 'property factor' within the Act, and so subject to the detailed regulation that the Act envisaged. To suggest otherwise, said Lord Menzies, would be 'quite untenable':[4]

---

1 [2020] CSIH 22, 2020 SC 455, 2020 SLT 566, 2020 Hous LR 32. The Extra Division comprised Lords Menzies, Drummond Young and Pentland.
2 Paragraph 27 per Lord Drummond Young.
3 PF(S)A 2011 s 9(2)(c).
4 Paragraph 15.

If a lady in the top flat gives piano lessons, she may consider it appropriate to clean and maintain the common stair, to encourage aspiring pupils to become clients. She does not require to register as a property factor before doing so. The first floor flat may be purchased as an office by a firm of solicitors or accountants. They may likewise decide that the common stairs need to be kept clean and well maintained, otherwise potential clients will not consult them. If a member of their staff cleans and maintains the stairs, they do not become property factors as a result, nor do they become subject to the penal consequences of failing to apply for inclusion in the register.

To Lord Menzies' piano teacher, solicitors and accountants, Lord Pentland added dentists and grocers. All might live in a block of flats. All might then assume responsibility for organising repairs. None could be regarded as a 'property factor'.

To this a possible objection is that a company which lets properties for a living is not the same as a piano teacher or dentist. The former owns the flats, admittedly, but there is no question of personal use. That might be a point of distinction. Another might be the fact that the business, while not one of managing properties, is at any rate one *concerning* properties. So, had the Inner House felt so inclined, it would have been possible to bring in Proven Properties as 'property factors' without also bringing in piano teachers. On policy grounds, as the sheriff pointed out in *Melfort Pier Holidays Ltd* in a passage already quoted, there was something to be said for that view.

What if payment?

Neither in *Proven Properties* nor in *Melfort Pier Holidays Ltd* did the manager charge for its services. Supposing that it had, would the result of *Proven Properties* have been different? There are passages in Lord Drummond Young's judgment which suggest that the answer may be 'yes'.[1] '[T]he purpose of the Act', said Lord Drummond Young, 'is to regulate those who carry on business as property factors *and are paid for so acting.*' He continued:

> A professional factor, *that is to say a factor who is paid by his clients,* may reasonably be the subject of detailed regulation; an obvious analogy exists with solicitors, accountants and financial intermediaries who are paid for their work. The position is otherwise, however, when a person who owns a flat or property within a tenement or housing development organises activities such as cleaning or maintenance of common parts or the upkeep of garden ground, *but does so without payment for the services so rendered,* only recovering sums paid to contractors and others for their work.

Payment matters because it means that the factoring is being done on a commercial basis. And factoring which is being done on a commercial basis ought, it might be thought, to be subject to regulation under the 2011 Act. It is true that a company conducting the business of a landlord, like Proven Properties, is different from a firm of professional property factors. But if the business of the former also includes, even if only incidentally, the business of property factors, then the case for regulation seems strong.

---

1 See para 25, from which the passages which follow are quoted (our emphases).

Practical implications

Following the decision in *Proven Properties* there are now certain categories of persons managing property who do not have to register as property factors under the 2011 Act – provided, at least, they do not charge for their services. One such category is the category represented in both *Proven Properties* and *Melfort Pier Holidays Ltd*, namely the landlord of multiple properties. Another is the developer of a residential housing estate who manages the development while in the course of selling off the individual houses.

The reaction of the Scottish Government

On the whole, the decision in *Proven Properties* seems to have been unwelcome to the Scottish Government. At any rate, in a closed consultation with stakeholders,[1] as part of revisions being made to the Code of Conduct,[2] the Scottish Government put forward a number of options for altering the statutory definition of 'property factor' in the light of the Inner House's decision. These include dropping the requirement that a person has to be acting 'in the course of that person's business', or bringing into the definition anyone who manages a development where the title deeds call for a property factor, or again providing a more detailed and targeted definition which would bring in certain categories of person and exclude certain others (such as owner-occupiers). At the time of writing, no firm proposals had yet emerged.

Contractual relations?

Finally, and briefly, a rather different point. Factors typically are appointed as a result of a decision taken by homeowners, often acting under provisions in a deed of conditions. But factors can also sometimes emerge out of nowhere and take on the work without the formal sanction of the owners. That appears to have been the case in *Proven Properties*, where Proven Properties took up management after the previous property factors, for reasons not explained in the decision, had ceased to act. It was also the position in another decision from 2020, *Zukowski v Charles White Ltd*.[3]

   Are factors in contractual relations with the owners of the property they factor? If so, is there a single contract between the factor on the one part and the numerous owners on the other, or is there rather a series of individual contracts between the factor and each owner? How is the contract formed, and what are its terms? The contractual side of factoring does not seem to have attracted attention. Yet it is of some importance, especially where the factor has simply taken it on itself to act on behalf of the owners. In the absence of a contract, a self-appointed factor has – presumably – no authority to act. That was the conclusion reached by the Upper Tribunal in *Zukowski v Charles White Ltd*, dismissing the idea that Charles White Ltd's position was justified on the basis of 'custom and practice'.

---

1 *Property Factor Code of Conduct Review and Policy Development on the Definition of a Property Factor* (28 September 2020).
2 As to which see *Conveyancing 2017* pp 91–92 and *Conveyancing 2018* p 110.
3 [2020] UT 26, 2020 GWD 30-386; this is Case (7) above.

It is relatively easy to see how a contract arises where the factor, in compliance with the Code of Practice,[1] issues to each homeowner a written statement of services, a statement which the homeowner may be taken to have accepted. But in the absence of a paper trail, any contract with the homeowners would rest, precariously, on implication from the facts and circumstances of acting on their behalf without apparent objection.[2]

PROPERTY TAXES IN SCOTLAND[3]

Overview

After previous years dominated by the prospect of Brexit, 2020 brought more of its reality, although the direct effect on property taxes in Scotland was minimal. Even in relation to value added tax, retained EU law will mean that little has changed; and in addition, continuing VAT rules directing services relating to land to take place where the land is located will mean that little will change in 2021.

But in Scotland the giant stool of external influences on tax has three formidable legs. In addition to Brexit, the changes ultimately deriving from Covid-19 are likely for the most part to be for the future, with tax increases almost inevitable, and the lure of land as a source for tax no doubt attractive. That certainly applies to the third external influence on the tax system, devolution and a renewed drive for independence. In the short term, Covid brought some very minor and currently time-limited reliefs, in an attempt to preserve the market in housing. In the longer term, all three legs (to which can be added of course simple UK and Scottish tax needs to make some inroads into unprecedented deficits and borrowing) seem certain to drive the need for higher taxes, perhaps with increased progressivity.

In the meantime, new tax changes in 2020 were relatively limited, although previous fundamentals such as devolved income tax continued their process of bedding-in. Scotland's primary devolved tax, land and buildings transaction tax, reached school age , while its unruly younger brother, additional dwelling supplement, continued its somewhat disruptive influence on conveyancing costs and process. After a significant flurry in 2019, the number of reported Scottish tax tribunal decisions declined, with relatively few new issues (but old ones clearly continued to rankle).

Developments towards a new process for Scottish tax legislation appeared to be put on hold to a significant extent. The Devolved Taxes Legislation Working Group[4] published an interim report in February 2020,[5] but (perhaps unsurprisingly) a final report promised for the summer of 2020 failed to appear.

---

1 Code of Practice s 1.
2 For contracts concluded by conduct in this way, see W W McBryde, *The Law of Contract in Scotland* (3rd edn, 2007) para 5–18.
3 This section is contributed by Alan Barr of the University of Edinburgh and Brodies LLP.
4 For the Group's terms of reference, see www.gov.scot/publications/devolved-taxes-legislation-working-group-terms-of-reference/.
5 See www.parliament.scot/parliamentarybusiness/CurrentCommittees/114453.aspx.

However, a new consultation was launched, as a prelude to the 2021 Scottish Budget, on the role of Scottish taxes in supporting the Covid-19 recovery and the fiscal framework more generally, due for review in 2021.[1]

The Covid crisis threw the Budget processes at both Westminster and Holyrood into disarray. The March 2020 UK Budget contained little by way of tax measures; and a promised or threatened Autumn Budget was then deferred until 3 March 2021. This means that, as with last year, the Scottish Budget (delivered on 28 January 2021) took place before its UK equivalent, and this sequential disarray creates significant uncertainties for all concerned (see below).[2] It is certainly possible that Scottish Budget proposals for 2021–22 will require to be revised in the light of the UK Budget.

There have been a large number of proposals and suggestions made by various bodies, the implementation of many of which would have significant effects on the UK and/or Scottish taxation of land. Perhaps the greatest effect would come from the introduction of a wealth tax, as formally proposed by the Wealth Tax Commission.[3] This essentially private body produced a detailed final report, *A Wealth Tax for the UK*, published on 9 December 2020.[4] Its conclusions and model set out will certainly attract attention, not least because a one-off wealth tax at 5% (albeit collected over five years) is estimated to raise some £260 *billion*. If this is a kite being flown, it is a gold-plated one.

The Office of Tax Simplification (OTS) has more official standing. At the request of the Chancellor, it has been looking at inheritance tax for some years. Some two years after the publication of its first report on IHT,[5] and a year after the publication of its second report on the tax,[6] the suggestions put forward continue to have resonance and, if there is to be significant reform of capital taxes, these reports provide much on which to draw. While little in these reports is directed specifically at land (with the exception of possible reform of agricultural property relief from inheritance tax), land is again an immoveable (and thus difficult to avoid) source for the tax.

Inheritance tax interacts with capital gains tax, notably because of the tax-free uplift for the latter which occurs on death. This may be considered less desirable where inheritance tax is not actually paid on a death. This issue was considered to some extent in the OTS's second IHT report. In July 2020, the Chancellor requested the OTS to review capital gains tax; and their first report on this tax, on policy design and principles, was published in November

1 Scottish Government, *Budget 2021–22: Supporting the COVID-19 Recovery: Scotland's Taxes and Fiscal Framework* (www.gov.scot/publications/budget-2021-22-supporting-covid-19-recovery-scotlands-taxes-fiscal-framework/pages/).

2 See *Scottish Budget: 2021–22* (www.gov.scot/publications/scottish-budget-2021-22/).

3 See www.ukwealth.tax/.

4 See https://static1.squarespace.com/static/5ef4d1da53822a571493ebd0/t/5fd2419675e8893321 cbed93/1607614883023/A-Wealth-Tax-For-The-UK.pdf.

5 Office of Tax Simplification, *Inheritance Tax Review – first report: Overview of the tax and dealing with administration* (2018: https://assets.publishing.service.gov.uk/government/uploads/system/uploads/attachment_data/file/758367/Final_Inheritance_Tax_Report_-_web_copy.pdf).

6 Office of Tax Simplification, *Inheritance Tax Review – second report: Simplifying the design of Inheritance Tax* (2019: https://assets.publishing.service.gov.uk/government/uploads/system/uploads/attachment_data/file/816520/Final_Inheritance_Tax_2_report_-_web_copy.pdf).

2020.[1] A second one is to follow, on key technical and administrative issues. Again, the impact on land is not exclusive to that asset, although it is among the assets most commonly affected by the tax (and at present has higher rates of tax for residential property).

It can be seen from all this that the stars may be aligning for a wholesale reform of capital taxes – and raising the tax burden on capital may well be considered less economically disruptive than income tax increases.

More direct proposals on taxation of Scottish land are found in a new paper from that prolific source, the Scottish Land Commission. *Land and property taxation in Scotland: Initial scoping of options for reform* was published in December 2020.[2] The report explores tax instruments relating to land, taking the view that tax policies and direct measures can contribute to certain key land reform policies, including more diverse land ownership, reducing the number of vacant and derelict sites, expanding agricultural tenancies and joint-venture farming, and expanding the supply of land for new housing. The report acknowledges that, under a partially devolved tax system, not all tax measures are available as economic instruments; and concludes by recommending further analysis of a range of possible tax changes. Specific examples include corporation tax super-deductions for development expenditure; business rate or council tax reductions for redevelopment activities; increased taxes on unproductive land; the removal or reduction of agricultural property relief for inheritance tax; adding agricultural land to the valuation roll for business rates; reforming council tax bands to make the structure more progressive; and (continuing a theme which has proved persistent and thought to be more comprehensively effective than other suggestions) implementing a land value tax on concentrated private estates.

Land reform has always been close to the present Scottish Government's heart; combining it with new necessities in taxation may prove a particularly attractive match. In the meantime, existing taxes continue to provide scope for development.

Land and buildings transaction tax

Covid reactions

In general, with some very limited exceptions noted below, there have been few reactions to the Covid crisis with direct relevance to LBTT. In particular, time limits for the most part were not extended (although see below); and penalties for failing to meet them will still be charged, although there was a temporary suspension of penalty and debt activity between March and December 2020. Revenue Scotland guidance includes the somewhat Delphic statement that: 'Revenue Scotland will take proportionate measures to alleviate the burden on taxpayers potentially facing penalties for late returns or payments.' There may be some consideration given to Covid in the general area of 'reasonable

---

1 Office of Tax Simplification, *Capital Gains Tax review – first report: Simplifying by design* (2020: https://assets.publishing.service.gov.uk/government/uploads/system/uploads/attachment_data/file/935073/Capital_Gains_Tax_stage_1_report_-_Nov_2020_-_web_copy.pdf).

2 www.landcommission.gov.scot/downloads/5fd0eef750f58_Alma%20Economics%20-%20Review%20of%20Land%20Tax%20Policy%20Final%20Report%20Dec%202020.pdf.

excuse', but for these purposes it is probably simply to be treated as a particular example of illness (of the taxpayer or those close to them), which can be a mitigating factor.[1]

Some slight operational changes were announced by Revenue Scotland on 1 December 2020, including on how to make contact with them; for the most part this confirmed that almost all submissions of returns and for other purposes will require to be online.[2] This includes for the first time claims for repayments of additional dwelling supplement.[3]

The January 2021 Budget brought no substantive changes in LBTT rules and rates (but see further below).

Temporary reduction in residential rates

With commendable speed, following the announcement of a temporary reduction in SDLT rates for England and Northern Ireland,[4] the Scottish Government's reaction to the Covid crisis included a similar (although more restricted) reduction in LBTT, in an attempt to keep the housing market active. For transactions settling between 15 July 2020 and 31 March 2021, the residential rates are as follows, with the increased nil rate band being raised to £250,000 reflected in the second figure of the first two lines of the table:

Cost	Rate
Up to £145,000/£250,000	Nil/Nil
£145,001–£250,000	2%/Nil
£250,001–£325,000	5%
£325,001–£750,000	10%
Over £750,000	12%

There were hopes that the Scottish Government would extend this LBTT holiday in the January 2021 Budget, but the Finance Secretary confirmed that the LBTT holiday would end as planned, so the residential nil rate band will come back to £145,000 from 1 April 2021, as in the table above. This means that LBTT first-time buyer relief becomes relevant again from the same date, as its effects were subsumed in the temporary rise in the general nil rate threshold.[5]

New lease rates

Unexpected changes to LBTT lease rates were announced in the Scottish Budget in February 2020 and have now been brought into effect.[6] For any lease with an

---

1 See www.revenue.scot/legislation/rstpa-legislation-guidance/dispute-resolution/rstp6009 for guidance on this.
2 See www.revenue.scot/news/covid-19.
3 See www.revenue.scot/news/covid-19/ads-repayment-claims.
4 See Stamp Duty Land Tax (Temporary Relief) Act 2020. It applies to transactions settling between 7 July 2020 and 30 June 2021 (as extended by the 2021 UK Budget).
5 *Scottish Budget: 2021–22* p 48.
6 By the Land and Buildings Transaction Tax (Tax Rates and Tax Bands) (Scotland) Amendment Order 2020, SSI 2020/24.

effective date on or after 7 February 2020 (subject to a very limited transitional provision), a new 2% LBTT band applies to the amount of any rental net present value (NPV) exceeding £2 million.[1] This represents a significant increase in the LBTT bill for commercial tenants compared to the old rates. It also means that leases of Scottish commercial property bear a higher tax cost than equivalent leases entered into in England and Northern Ireland, where the higher rate becomes chargeable at £5 million (so a potential difference of up to £40,000 on a single lease).

Additional dwelling supplement

Following the rise from 3% to 4% in 2019, no substantive changes were announced in 2020 to the highly lucrative (for the Scottish Government) additional dwelling supplement. In a very limited reaction to potential difficulties caused by Covid, it was recognised that those who buy a new main residence may have difficulty in disposing of their old one. The purchase in these circumstances is subject to ADS because the purchaser will own (at least) two dwellings on the date of settlement of their purchase; but the ADS can be reclaimed if the previous main residence is disposed of within 18 months of the purchase of the new one.[2] For purchase transactions settling between 24 September 2018 and 24 March 2020, that period is extended to 36 months.[3]

It should be noted that this legislation has already expired;[4] but for those who made a purchase of a new main residence before 25 March 2020, they have three years from the date of their purchase to dispose of their previous main residence and reclaim the tax. The clock is ticking faster, perhaps somewhat surprisingly, for those who have made more recent purchases. So, someone purchasing on 24 March 2020 has until 23 March 2023 to make the disposal and claim relief; someone purchasing on 25 March 2020 has only until 24 September 2021.

In the Scottish Budget in January 2021, there was a promise of a consultation to consider a range of ADS issues, such as extending the length of time within which a previous main residence must be sold for a repayment to be claimed, and various scenarios involving joint buyers. The intention is to consult on this early in the next Scottish Parliament.[5] It is to be hoped that the consultation covers the full range of issues that remain contentious in relation to the supplement, such as those which are regularly litigated.

ADS continues to form the subject of appeals to the Scottish First-tier Tax Tribunal, but these much reduced in number in 2020 as compared to 2019. Mention may be made of *Rosa Jane Yard v Revenue Scotland*,[6] which explored

---

1 2020/24 art 2.
2 Land and Buildings Transaction Tax (Scotland) Act 2013 sch 2A para 8.
3 Coronavirus (Scotland) (No 2) Act 2020 sch 4 part 5, para 6(3), inserting para 8B into sch 2A of the Land and Buildings Transaction Tax (Scotland) Act 2013 for a temporary period. See also guidance at www.revenue.scot/news/news/revenue-scotland-updates-guidance-reflect-coronavirus-scotland-no2-act-2020.
4 The change has 'expired' by virtue of the Coronavirus (Scotland) Acts (Early Expiry of Provisions) Regulations 2020, SSI 2020/249, regs 1, 3(b)(ii).
5 *Scottish Budget: 2021–22* p 48.
6 [2020] FTSTC 3.

what is, unfortunately for taxpayers, familiar ground. On 28 September 2018 Ms Yard purchased a new home in Perthshire (the 'Second Property'). At that time, she continued to own her previous home in Fort William (the 'First Property'), which she intended to sell – as was accepted by the Tribunal. But because she owned two properties at the date of her purchase, she paid ADS on the Second Property of £8,970. Ms Yard moved into the Second Property, but then (with some very unfortunate background events) her circumstances changed, and she had to move back to the First Property. She sold the Second Property within 18 months of its purchase and tried to reclaim ADS. This claim was refused. It is a requirement of the Land and Buildings Transaction Tax (Scotland) Act 2013 sch 2A para 8(1)(a) that the taxpayer disposes of a dwelling '... other than one which was or formed part of the subject-matter of the chargeable transaction'. Furthermore (for obvious and logical reasons) the Second Property could not have been the taxpayer's main residence at any time in the 18 months prior to its purchase, as required by para 8(1)(b). The appeal was dismissed, albeit with the 'considerable sympathy' of the Tribunal.[1]

Penalties

Penalties continue to be a significant source of revenue for the tax authority; and the rising number of three-year lease reviews provides a growing field in which penalties can flourish – often through apparent ignorance of the need to make such a return.[2] The first appeals (both unsuccessful) against penalties for this kind of failure were reported in 2019.[3] 2020 brought two further such appeals, with the same result.

The taxpayer was to some extent unfortunate in *Foodwood Ltd v Revenue Scotland*.[4] Its original LBTT return had given its address as that of its accountants. A Revenue Scotland reminder about the three-year return was sent to that address (with a small omission from the address). No return or reply was received; and the penalty notice was sent to that same address. Neither item of mail was returned. The appeal was on the basis that the taxpayer had informed various bodies (including HMRC and the local authority) of its proper address; and that it was up to Revenue Scotland to contact it at its proper address.

This was emphatically rejected by the First-tier Tax Tribunal. There was, it was emphasised, absolutely no requirement at all on Revenue Scotland to issue reminders about three-year returns, and therefore any problems with the address were a red herring. In any event, there was a warning from the Tribunal that:

---

1 Virtually the same circumstances had led to exactly the same result in *Chumas v Revenue Scotland* [2019] FTSTC 10; and the same result occurred again in *Macdonald v Revenue Scotland* [2020] FTSTC 4. In the latter case, the taxpayers were actively trying to sell *both* properties but only achieved the sale of the second property within the requisite period.
2 The requirement is to make a return within 30 days of the third anniversary of the effective date of a new lease (and on certain other events, such as assignation or termination): see Land and Buildings Transaction Tax (Scotland) Act 2013 sch 19 para 10.
3 See *Conveyancing 2019* pp 202–03.
4 [2020] FTSTC 1.

In a self-assessment regime it is the taxpayer's obligation to ensure that the relevant tax authority has up to date contact details. There is no doubt that it was the Appellant's responsibility to ensure that Revenue Scotland had the correct address at all times. They did not do so.

The question of what the accountants to whom the reminder had been sent had done with it was not discussed; but there was no reasonable excuse or special circumstance which prevented the penalty (of £100 – one shudders at the relative expense of the appeal) from being confirmed.

The same result was reached in relation to the penalty of £100 issued in *Shu Fang Yang v Revenue Scotland*.[1] Here the circumstances were that the subjects of lease (parking spaces) were an investment (not a successful one as matters transpired) by a non-resident who could not be expected to know, it was argued, of the need for the three-year return. This argument was rejected. While ignorance of the law could in limited circumstances amount to an excuse, this was not the case here and the location of the taxpayer made no difference. Despite being based abroad, it was reasonable to expect the taxpayer to have familiarised herself with relevant local legislation. Neither that, nor the commercial failure of her investment, provided a reasonable excuse or special circumstances.[2]

Scottish income tax

While income tax is not of specific relevance to the taxation of land, income from land is one of the categories of income of Scottish taxpayers which is affected by the differing rates (and thresholds) applied to Scottish taxpayers. For 2020–21, the following rates and thresholds were confirmed, which involved the upper two thresholds being frozen for the second year in succession.[3]

Bands	Band name	Rate
Over £12,500–£14,585*	Starter Rate	19%
Over £14,585–£25,158	Scottish Basic Rate	20%
Over £25,158–£43,430	Intermediate Rate	21%
Over £43,430–£150,000	Higher Rate	41%
Above £150,000†	Top Rate	46%

* Assumes individuals are in receipt of the standard UK personal allowance.
† Those earning more than £100,000 will see their personal allowance reduced by £1 for every £2 earned over £100,000.

For 2021–22, the Scottish Budget brought proposals for an inflationary rise in the first four rate bands for Scottish taxpayers, but a freeze of the top rate threshold. Those seeking neat, rounded figures for their tax bands will need to

---

1 [2020] FTSTC 2.
2 This was virtually the same situation analysed, with the same result, in *Kot v Revenue Scotland* [2019] FTSTC 1, to which approving reference was made in the present case.
3 See Scottish Rate Resolution, 4 March 2020: www.parliament.scot/parliamentarybusiness/ report.aspx?r=12555&i=113499.

look elsewhere; and we can count ourselves fortunate that the grunt work of tax calculation is, these days, almost always delegated to electronic brains. The proposed rates and thresholds for 2021–22 are as follows:[1]

Bands	Band name	Rate
Over £12,570–£14,667*	Starter Rate	19%
Over £14,667–£25,296	Scottish Basic Rate	20%
Over £25,296–£43,662	Intermediate Rate	21%
Over £43,662–£150,000	Higher Rate	41%
Above £150,000†	Top Rate	46%

* Assumes individuals are in receipt of the standard UK personal allowance.
† Those earning more than £100,000 will see their personal allowance reduced by £1 for every £2 earned over £100,000.

Some assumptions have been made in these proposals – notably that two announcements made by the UK Government in the UK Spending Review in November 2020 will be fulfilled. Those are to the effect that the personal allowance and the UK higher rate threshold will be uprated by CPI inflation (0.5%) for the tax year 2021–22. That would bring the figures for these to £12,570 and £50,270 respectively.

On the personal allowance itself, the Budget points out that it had been Scottish Government policy to implement an 'effective Personal Allowance' of £12,750 by the end of this parliamentary term. This has been at least deferred due to the unprecedented circumstances.[2] The reason for the slightly strange phrasing and punctuation around the personal allowance is that devolved income tax powers do not stretch to altering that (or other such) allowances. The policy aim would need to be achieved by the introduction of a very short nil rate band, a degree of complication from which we are spared, at least for the moment.

Other Scottish property taxes

Scottish landfill tax

Rates of Scottish landfill tax for 2020–21 were set by the Scottish Landfill Tax (Standard Rate and Lower Rate) (No 2) Order 2020[3] at £94.15 per tonne (standard rate) and £3.00 (lower rate). The credit rate for the Scottish Landfill Communities Fund (SLCF) was maintained at 5.6%. This increase ensures consistency with the planned changes to landfill tax rates in the rest of the UK.[4] The Scottish Government is continuing to explore the role that Scottish landfill tax can play in relation to reducing the amount of biodegradable municipal waste

1 *Scottish Budget: 2021–22* p 47, confirmed by Scottish Rate Resolution, 25 February 2021.
2 *Scottish Budget: 2021–22* p 47.
3 SSI 2020/105.
4 *Scottish Budget: 2020–21* pp 22–23.

(BMW) sent to landfill, in advance of an intended ban which is now delayed until 2025.[1]

The rates for 2021–22 were set out in the Scottish Budget in January 2021 at £96.70 (standard) and £3.00 (lower).[2]

Aggregates levy

There have again been no further developments in the actual devolution of aggregates levy. Devolution of the levy was on hold pending the results of a comprehensive review of the levy being undertaken by the UK Government, following the conclusion of long-standing litigation.[3] Separately, for Scotland, a detailed policy review was published in August 2020, with a range of options on the manner in which the devolved levy might be introduced.[4] The Scottish Government confirms that it will continue to work with the UK Government and stakeholders in anticipation of the eventual devolution of the levy.[5]

In the January 2021 Budget it was announced that, following the resolution of state aid issues, it will be the responsibility of the post-May 2021 Scottish Parliament to pass the necessary legislation to introduce the devolved aggregates levy. It was confirmed that previous hurdles in the shape of long-running litigation and concerns over state aid have been overcome or removed.[6]

Non-domestic (business) rates

Responsibility for non-domestic rates (NDR) is fully devolved to Scotland, and the regime continues to diverge from the position in the rest of the UK. A major revision of primary legislation was completed in 2020, with the passage of the Non-Domestic Rates (Scotland) Act 2020. Key provisions of the Act include:

- three-yearly valuations from 2022 to ensure that valuations are more closely aligned to current market values;
- a two-stage appeals system (proposal and appeal) to improve the administration and timeliness of the appeals system;
- greater information-gathering powers for assessors and a new civil penalty for non-provision of information in order to increase 'right first-time' valuations and improve ratepayers' trust in the rating system;
- the power to introduce general anti-avoidance regulation;
- removing charitable rates relief from mainstream independent schools; and
- reform of the rules on unoccupied properties.

---

1 See www.gov.scot/policies/taxes/landfill-tax/.
2 *Scottish Budget: 2021–22* p 50.
3 See UK Government, *Review of the Aggregates Levy: discussion paper* (2020: www.gov.uk/government/publications/review-of-the-aggregates-levy/review-of-the-aggregates-levy-discussion-paper).
4 See *Scottish Aggregates Levy: evidence review and policy options* (2020: www.gov.scot/publications/evidence-review-illustrative-policy-options-scottish-aggregates-levy/).
5 See www.gov.scot/policies/taxes/aggregates-levy/.
6 *Scottish Budget: 2021–22* p 55.

The amount of non-domestic rates paid is the rateable value of the property (ie its open market rental) multiplied by the 'poundage'. Rateable values are set at periodic revaluations; the last one for Scottish property was in 2017 (but see changes made by the 2020 Act, above). The non-domestic rates poundage for 2020–21 was set at 49.8p.[1] However, the Covid crisis brought a wide range of complete rates reliefs for a wide range of premises (retail, hospitality, leisure and aviation), as well as a more limited general relief of 1.6% for all non-domestic premises.[2]

A number of rating reforms have now been implemented in secondary legislation:

- an intermediate property rate for properties with a rateable value between £51,000 and £95,000, which will now only be charged an additional 1.3p on rates on top of the standard poundage;[3]
- properties with a rateable value above £95,000 will continue to be charged the higher property rate (formerly and confusingly called the large business supplement) of 2.6p plus the poundage;[4]
- the 100% relief for enterprise areas is extended to 31 March 2022;[5]
- an amendment to the reset period for empty property relief from six weeks to six months, reducing the possibility of avoidance;[6] and
- reforms of the relief for new and improved properties.[7]

The January 2021 Scottish Budget brought some significant continuations of reliefs introduced in the midst of the Covid crisis.[8] A key pandemic-driven headline was the extension of the 100% NDR relief for properties in the retail, hospitality, leisure and aviation sectors for at least the first three months of the financial year. This means that certain businesses will continue rates-free until the end of June 2021. This announcement will have been welcomed by many businesses that are still unable to trade – let alone pay NDR.

The more general 1.6% relief for all non-domestic premises will not extend beyond 31 March 2021. But, in a significant move, for all non-domestic properties still subject to rates, the NDR poundage has been reduced to 49p at all levels, a reduction of 0.8 pence from 49.8p. Such a reduction in the absence of a revaluation is nearly unprecedented.

That reduced poundage puts the Scottish Basic Property Rate just below England's equivalent, which was last set at 49.1p.

1 Non-Domestic Rate (Scotland) Order 2020, SSI 2020/37.
2 See the Non-Domestic Rates (Coronavirus Reliefs) (Scotland) Regulations 2020, SSI 2020/101, as extended by the Non-Domestic Rates (Coronavirus Reliefs) (Scotland) Amendment Regulations 2020, SSI 2020/230.
3 Non-Domestic Rates (Levying) (Scotland) Regulations 2020, SSI 2020/39.
4 SSI 2020/39.
5 Non-Domestic Rates (Enterprise Areas) (Scotland) Amendment Regulations 2020, SSI 2020/38.
6 Non-Domestic Rating (Unoccupied Property) (Scotland) Amendment Regulations 2020, SSI 2020/43.
7 Non-Domestic Rates (Relief for New and Improved Properties) (Scotland) Amendment Regulations 2020, SSI 2020/40.
8 *Scottish Budget: 2021–22* pp 51–54.

Further announcements in relation to NDR in the Scottish Budget included:

- more non-domestic properties will qualify for fresh start relief following an increase to the rateable value upper threshold from £65,000 to £95,000;
- 100% day nursery relief will be extended to at least 30 June 2023;
- continuation of the Small Business Bonus Scheme relief and transitional relief; and
- confirmation that self-catering properties will need to be let for 70 days or more to be classed as non-domestic from 2021–22.

UK taxes on land

Capital gains tax

From 6 April 2020, the final period of ownership qualifying for capital gains tax relief irrespective of occupation was reduced from eighteen to nine months, completing (one hopes) the rapid process of reduction from three years.[1]

The new rules requiring that a return is made of the disposal of UK land within 30 days of settlement were applied to residents disposing of (chargeable) residential property as well as to all other non-residents (generally those carrying on a trade, profession or vocation within the UK) from 6 April 2020.[2] Payment of tax on at least a provisional basis is also required within the same deadline.[3] The rules apply only where there is an actual CGT liability on the disposal.

Annual tax on enveloped properties

In relation to the annual tax on enveloped properties ('ATED'), there are increases by CPI inflation (1.7%) in the amounts chargeable for 2020–21.[4]

---

1 Taxation of Chargeable Gains Act 1992 s 223(1), as amended by Finance Act 2020 s 24(3)(a).
2 Finance Act 2019 s 14, sch 2 para 1.
3 FA 2019 sch 2 paras 6–8.
4 Annual Tax on Enveloped Dwellings (Indexation of Annual Chargeable Amounts) Order 2020, SI 2020/341.

❧ PART V ❧
TABLES

TABLES

CUMULATIVE TABLE OF DECISIONS ON VARIATION OR DISCHARGE OF TITLE CONDITIONS

This table lists all decisions since 1 January 2019 on opposed applications under the Title Conditions (Scotland) Act 2003 for variation or discharge of title conditions. Decisions on expenses are omitted. A table of decisions prior to that date can be found at the end of *Conveyancing 2018*. Note that the full opinions in Lands Tribunal cases are usually available at http://www.lands-tribunal-scotland.org.uk/.

Restriction on building

Name of case	Burden	Applicant's project in breach of burden	Application granted or refused
Toomey v Smith 2020 GWD 10-146	1995 disposition. No building without consent.	None.	Granted.
Christie v Carroll 2020 GWD 31-401	1882 disposition. No building. Servitude of recreational use.	Erection of a house.	Refused.

Servitudes

Name of case	Servitude	Applicant's project in breach of burden	Application granted or refused
Leehand Properties Ltd 2019 GWD 29-468	1994 feu disposition. Pedestrian right of way.	Building houses on site of the projected route.	Granted (unopposed).
Nicol v Crowley, 2019 GWD 40-646	1973 disposition. Pedestrian right of way.	Rerouting of path as part of garden redesign.	Refused (opposed).

Name of case	Servitude	Applicant's project in breach of burden	Application granted or refused
Mahoney v Cumming 2019 GWD 32-506	1907 feu charter. Pedestrian right of way.	Blocking of route to increase privacy.	Refused (opposed).
Savage v Thomson 2020 GWD 30-389	1961 disposition. Right of access and parking.	Building of a house, which would require the area covered by the servitude to be restricted.	Granted (opposed).
Pallot v Carter 2020 GWD 25-335	1988 disposition. Pedestrian right of way.	Building rear porch which would require minor re-routing of the access.	Supported in principle (opposed) but no final determination until planning consent for re-routing and reassurance as to building materials.

CUMULATIVE TABLE OF APPEALS

A table at the end of *Conveyancing 2008* listed all cases digested in *Conveyancing 1999* and later annual volumes in respect of which an appeal was subsequently heard, and gave the result of the appeal. A second table, at the end of *Conveyancing 2018*, covered the years from 2009 to 2018. This is a continuation of the tables, covering the years from 2019 onwards.

Anderson v Wilson

[2018] CSOH 5, 2018 GWD 4-62, 2018 Case (39) *affd* [2019] CSIH 4, 2019 SC 271, 2019 SLT 185, 2019 Case (44)

Ardnamurchan Estates Ltd v Macgregor

14 June 2019, Fort William Sheriff Court, 2019 Case (76) *rev* [2020] SAC Civ 2, 2020 SC (SAC) 1, 2020 SLT (Sh Ct) 49, 2020 SCLR 408, 2020 Case (65)

Commodity Solution Services Ltd v First Scottish Searching Services Ltd

[2018] SC DUNF 14, 2018 SLT (Sh Ct) 117, 2018 Case (53) *affd* [2019] SAC (Civ) 4, 2019 SC (SAC) 41, 2019 SLT (Sh Ct) 63, 2019 Case (51)

Johnston v Davidson

29 August 2019, Forfar Sheriff Court, 2019 Case (16) *affd* [2020] SAC (Civ) 22, 2021 GWD 1-12, 2020 Case (17)

O'Boyle's Tr v Brennan

[2018] CSOH 90, 2018 GWD 29-369, 2018 Case (83) *affd* [2020] CSIH 3, 2020 SC 217, 2020 SLT 152, 2020 SCLR 470, 2020 Case (69)

Ramoyle Developments Ltd v Scottish Borders Council

[2019] CSOH 1, 2019 SLT 284, 2019 Case (1) *affd* [2020] CSIH 9, 2020 SC 290, 2020 SLT 537, 2020 Case (1)

Ruddiman v Hawthorne

[2019] CSOH 65, 2019 GWD 29-463, 2019 Case (18) *affd* [2020] CSIH 46, 2021 SLT 111, 2020 Case (16)

Soofi v Dykes

[2019] CSOH 59, 2019 GWD 27-442, 2019 Case (74) *affd* [2020] CSIH 10, 2020 GWD 10-152, 2020 Case (59)

Other books published by the
EDINBURGH LEGAL EDUCATION TRUST

Studies in Scots Law (softback) £30.00 each

Ross Gilbert Anderson, *Assignation*, 2008; ISBN 9780955633201; 299 pp *

Andrew J M Steven, *Pledge and Lien*, 2008; ISBN 9780955633218; 303 pp *

Craig Anderson, *Possession of Corporeal Moveables*, 2015; ISBN 9780955633270; 195 pp *

Jill Robbie, *Private Water Rights*, 2015; ISBN 9780955633287; 227 pp *

Daniel J Carr, *Ideas of Equity*, 2017; ISBN 9780955633294; 217 pp *

Chathuni Jayathilaka, *Sale and the Implied Warranty of Soundness*, 2019;
ISBN 9781999611804; 197 pp *

Alasdair Peterson, *Prescriptive Servitudes*, 2020; ISBN 9781999611811; 197 pp

Alisdair D J MacPherson, *The Floating Charge*, 2020; ISBN 9781999611828; 263 pp

John MacLeod, *Fraud and Voidable Transfer*, 2020; ISBN 9781999611842; 255 pp

Old Studies in Scots Law (hardback facsimile reprints) £30.00 each

George Joseph Bell, *Principles of the Law of Scotland*, 4th edn, 1839
reprinted 2010 with an introduction by Kenneth Reid
ISBN 9780955633225; 910 pp

George Watson, *Bell's Dictionary and Digest of the Law of Scotland*, 7th edn, 1890
reprinted 2012 with an introduction by Ross Anderson
ISBN 9780955633232; 1134 pp

William Forbes, *The Institutes of the Law of Scotland*, 1722 and 1730
reprinted 2012 with an introduction by Hector MacQueen
ISBN 9780955633249; 912 pp

Lord Kames, *Principles of Equity*, 3rd edn, 1778
reprinted 2013 with an introduction by Daniel Carr
ISBN 9780955633256; 850 pp

John Erskine, *An Institute of the Law of Scotland*, 1st edn, 1773
reprinted 2014 with an introduction by Kenneth Reid
ISBN 9780955633263; 1025 pp

Copies of all of the books, priced at £30, can be obtained from:

AVIZANDUM LAW BOOKSHOP
56A Candlemaker Row, Edinburgh EH1 2QE
(t: 0131 220 3373; e: customerservice@avizandum.co.uk)
or order online at www.avizandum.co.uk;
or by emailing admin@edinburghlawseminars.co.uk

The volumes marked with an asterisk are available to download free of charge at
https://edinburghlawseminars.co.uk